# FUNDAMENTALS
## OF
# RHYTHM AND DANCE

# FUNDAMENTALS OF RHYTHM AND DANCE

*With an Analysis of The Rhythmic Approach
in Teaching Dance Skills*

BY

BETTY LYND THOMPSON, M.A.

*Assistant Professor of Physical Education
Oregon State College*

NEW YORK

A. S. BARNES AND COMPANY

INCORPORATED

1937

*Dedicated to*

THOSE YOUNG TEACHERS WHO GO OUT INTO
THE FIELD OF PHYSICAL EDUCATION TO IN-
STILL INTO THEIR MORE YOUTHFUL STUDENTS
A JOY IN ACTIVITY AND A PRIDE IN THE
POSSESSION OF A PERFECT, USEFUL BODY.

# CONTENTS

# LIST OF ILLUSTRATIONS

# CHARTS AND TABLES

# BIBLIOGRAPHY FOR SOURCE OF MATERIAL

# RECORDS FOR USE IN RHYTHM OR DANCING

# EXAMINATIONS

# PREFACE AND ACKNOWLEDGMENT

Perhaps in the field of dancing more than in any other activity the inexperienced teacher finds herself at a loss in presenting material to her students. It is hoped that this book will provide the teacher with a usable approach to rhythmic activity.

In writing this text an endeavor has been made to state the material clearly enough so that by conscientious study, a high school or college student might grasp the meaning without the help of an instructor. However, the work will undoubtedly be more interesting if it can be used in class work with an instructor and with the use of music.

The material herein is the result of the author's experience, and is written with the sincere desire of meeting the needs and answering the many questions of the young teacher.

The author wishes to acknowledge the assistance of the Oregon State staff in the preparation of the material on rhythm, which was originally compiled by that group as a part of the freshman course in Fundamentals of Physical Education for Women. The author has acted as chairman of the rhythm section of this course since its organization in 1927, and has been particularly assisted by Elsie Jacobsen, Natalie Reichart, Mildred Greenberg, Helen Jameson and Helen Burtis. The original material has been annually revised by a committee including the entire staff, all of whom teach the freshman course, and a brief syllabus has been prepared for the students. This syllabus has been sent out to various schools upon request, as course 112. Enlarging this outline in accordance with her own methods of teaching, the author prepared the material on Fundamentals of Rhythm.

The author's training in dancing was received principally with Margaret H'Doubler and Martha Graham, to both of whom the author is grateful for inspiration and help. For the time and interest given in reading and criticizing the manuscript the author expresses appreciation to Elsie Jacobsen, Margaret Jewell, Ruth Glassow, Marguerite Kellerman, Dr. Harry Scott, Elizabeth Bennett, Eva Seen and Laura McAllester. The author is indebted to many of her students and particularly to Margaret Jewell, Miriam Bleamaster, Emma Lou Schissler, Margaret Zimmerman, Phyllis Adams and Betty Frost for their cooperation in photographing the dance illustrations and to Mr. Edwin Yunker for his advice and help in their photography.

For the use, in Chapter One, of the illustrations from "Art in Everyday Life" by Goldstein, we wish to acknowledge the courtesy of the Macmillan Company. To that company as well as to the Yale Review and the Theatre Arts Monthly, we are grateful for the permission to use quotations for which they hold the copyright. Sources of all such quotations have been listed where used.

# INTRODUCTION

## WHY THE CHILD SHOULD DANCE

It would be interesting if we might assemble the pictures which come to each individual's mind as we ask the question, "Why Dance?" We may readily imagine that they are extremely varied, being colored by each one's experience and training. Many, perhaps, see a high school girl doing a more or less rhythmic fox-trot with the "boy-friend" from across the street. Some others see a tiny child dancing "Farmer in the Dell," while shrill, childish voices sing out the accompaniment. Others, perhaps, picture a stage with gorgeous curtains, lights, and costumes and see a small young lady dancing on her toes, with formal ballet steps. Still others, with a thrill of romantic reminiscence, see a child, lately grown to womanhood, dancing a very joyous waltz while trap drums clatter and saxophones sing out a modern syncopation, and young men in tuxedoes nonchalantly dip and sway with young ladies in long, slim evening dresses. Or does the moment's flash bring a picture of a modern miss, one hand holding a dish towel, the other holding her skirts above her knees, while nimble feet tap out interesting rhythms on the kitchen linoleum; or is it a jolly informal crowd of mothers, fathers, uncles, aunts, neighbors, and children of all ages dancing Virginia Reels and Square Dances in the community hall or the neighbor's new barn? Whatever the picture, it is vividly joyous; the dancer is all engrossed in her activity, happy with the joy of movement, although the expression on mother's face may be one of stern disapproval, jolly participation, unconcealed pride, or what not.

For ages, as far back as man can trace, people have danced, not as they work, laboring and tiring, but as they play, joyously, happily. Some one has said, "The smile is the dance of the face; the dance is the smile of the body."

The smile of the face is the natural response to happiness. It is spontaneous, sincere in every child. We want the child to know happiness and to smile. So also should we want our child to dance. How our child should dance and when she should dance are other questions,—but dancing for the pure joy of movement is a tendency which should not be crushed.

Let us consider the different forms of dancing. Which outlet to this smile of the body do we want to open up to the child? Her tendency and desire to dance is a thing we cannot curb without injury to her sensitive nature. We can, however, with thoughtful and sympathetic understanding, direct that tendency along lines which will develop in her a beautiful womanhood.

First of all, what is dancing? Is it standing on one's toes, is it bending over backward, is it tapping with one's feet, or is it pointing the toe and holding the arms just so? No! it is none of these. These are only external forms which dancing may take. True dance comes from within. It is the outward expression, through movement, of the emotion which the dancer feels. It may be joyous, sad, cynical; but to be truly dance, it must come from within the individual and must be colored by her individuality. The little child who skips gaily down the street is more truly dancing than many chorus girls in gorgeous stage shows; for in the case of the child, the skipping is an expression of the happiness which she feels within her, while in many cases the chorus girl merely goes through a routine of steps which someone else has planned and taught her.

Dancing has existed through the ages. Every race of people has indulged in some form of dance. It has been used in ancient times as a ritual to express certain religious feelings of worshippers. It has been used as a socializing means of recreation, as in the folk dances of foreign people and our own American country dances and our modern social dance. The Hawaiians tell long stories by the use of dance movements. The American negro uses the dance as an outlet for the expression of his highly rhythmic temperament.

From generation to generation the dance has changed with the degree of civilization and the taste and temperament of the people. Beginning with savage rhythm, it has advanced through the pastoral dances of shepherds and shepherdesses, the rituals of the ancient church, contrasting in their dignity with the cheaper forms used for attracting attention. Later it took on the artificial elegance of the court, and we had minuets and gavottes and other formal types, including the ballet which was elaborately planned and vigorously practiced. The rebellion against the formality of these last developed jazz which represents a swing of the pendulum in the other direction. Only in recent years have we begun to realize the true art which may be developed by the dance,—and today throughout the world there is a strong movement to bring dancing to its proper place as a sister art to music, sculpture, and drama.

The modern dance of today stresses creation and individuality. Instead of imitating the movement of someone else, the dancer is stimulated to express the thing which she feels, and to do so in as fine and in as sincere a manner as possible. How much she is helped by someone else depends upon her age, her personality, her physical skill and coordination.

A small child does not have to be urged to dance. All she needs is to be placed in the proper environment. Finding herself in a large open space, only the very inhibited, bashful child will fail to run and find joy in the ability to move without limitation. Invariably, when the instructor comes into our dance studio to greet a class of three- and four-year-olds, she finds them running up and down the room, squealing for the pure joy of unlimited movement. When the music starts the child begins to clap her hands or wave her arms in rhythm or to adapt the rhythm of her steps to the rhythm of the music. It takes only a suggestion, a song, a poem, or a picture to start the child telling simple stories through her movements. It is foolish to tell a child of this age to take three steps forward and point her toe, to bow just so, to bend this way or that. She must be asked to do things which are within her experience, such as acting out nursery rhymes, or pretending she is the wind chasing the leaves about; or that she is a flower waving in the breeze or growing tall; or perhaps a walking doll or a bouncing ball.

With the slightly older child comes the desire to test her accomplishment. She likes to learn definite dances which she can show off to others. It is important here to guard against an insincerity in expression. The child will dramatize and imitate, but she should not be made conscious of this imitation. She should be stimulated to try out certain movements. Where she fails she can be helped by the participation of the adult,—not with the suggestion, "Let me show you how," but, "Come, I'll dance with you." Simple folk dances, easy clogs, and athletic dances will appeal to the child of this age. She also enjoys dances which tell a story, such as "Old King Cole," "Queen of Hearts," and the like. The child of 6-12 years will want to do the things she sees older girls doing; so she will desire to do social dancing and ballet. She should be allowed to try these by herself, but she should not be given specialized training in them. She is too young to use social dancing, and ballet dancing does not have a place in the training of the child. The movements are stilted, and tend to over-develop certain sets of muscles, as those of the lower leg; usually because of toe dancing and foot positions, the arches of the feet are weakened, while the strenuous stretching and backward bending result in poor posture.

Parents frequently prefer ballet to other forms of dancing because the child is usually put into a public performance, and thus the parents' pride is inflated. But these parents are not looking ahead to the development of the child's personality. The public performance should be the last thing to be considered, and the child's character development should be first. In ballet training the public performance seems to get the main emphasis; the child goes through certain trained movements and enjoys it because her elders praise her, but her dancing usually does not come from within her, nor does it express anything.

With the girl of high school age we have an entirely new problem, and the form her dancing takes depends a great deal upon her development and her personality. The child who has been brought up in simple surroundings and who has kept her childlike sincerity will still enjoy simple group dances, folk dances, and clogs and may even be encouraged to create her own dances. If she has become a more or less sophisticated miss, she will probably insist upon some jazz and social dancing. These should not be frowned upon, for the forbidden fruit is always the most desired. If the high school child yearns to do social dancing she should be allowed to do so. She should be encouraged to dance at home with her brothers and father, as well as her friends. If she can take lessons where the class will be conducted on a genuine and educational basis she should be given the opportunity to learn to dance well. Under no circumstances should she be made to feel that she is wicked because she desires to dance;—she should be made to see the beauty in graceful, joyous dancing and the ugliness of the cheap, vulgar type which we sometimes see in public places. Opportunities should be made for her and her friends to spend occasional evenings dancing at home. The parents should be present, not in the capacity of ominous and to-be-feared chaperons, but as youthful companions who share the fun and exchange dances as happily as the young people. If this situation is present, the child will have no desire to sneak off to the public dance hall where the element of vulgarity is often allowed to enter.

For the girl of high school age and for the college woman, the highest and most valuable type of dance will be found in Creative Dancing. This form is taught in most large colleges and universities and in many high schools. It is developed along the lines of education and aims at developing personalities rather than dancers. It attempts to stimulate artistic efforts on the part of the individual. All of the movements are based on natural movements of the body, movements which we can normally do, but which are studied and practiced until they can be done with ease, perfect balance, and coordination. A beautiful body maintained in good posture is another aim, and through the study of the body in motion, the student begins to appreciate beauty of line in art. With this type of dancing, the music used is all of a high type, classical music of the world's greatest musicians being used almost entirely. Thus, while the girl dances she becomes acquainted with the work of real musicians, and she learns to appreciate and enjoy the finer type of music.

When the dancer has developed a certain skill in the control of her body, when she becomes able to sense the rhythm and the emotion of music, then she is encouraged to develop dances which will sincerely express her emotions. The easiest emotion to express is joy; later she will try some of the harder ones, and finally her dancing will be a true expression of her personality and character. Her attempts to create original dances will make her less self-conscious, but instead more conscious of self,—there is a difference. It is the difference between embarrassment and poise. Besides this she will be stimulated to try to create something original along other lines of art as in poetry, music, or drawing. We frequently find bits of real art coming from students as a result of their work in dancing.

Dancing should be to everyone a joyous activity as well as a stimulating process of development and a constant source of inspiration. Frequently it is disliked because it has been so presented that the student is made self-conscious, or is confused as to its aims or the ultimate result. If dancing is taught, not as an imitated activity, but in such a way that the student gains a clear understanding of the use of her body in expressing emotion, in following rhythmic patterns, and in a sincere interpretation of music; if she is made to realize the value of dancing as an art; if she finds herself able to appreciate the work of the world's greatest artists, not only in the field of dancing, but in music, sculpture, painting, architecture, literature, and drama, she will have been given one of the finest experiences which could come into her life. It is our privilege as dance instructors to so plan our work that it may meet the needs of our students and be to them a true inspiration.

Rhythm is a common element in all forms of art. It is an important element in all physical skills. It can be approached in a way which will be neither embarrassing nor confusing to the child of any age or to the adult. For these reasons it has been found that dancing taught from a rhythmic approach is most universally enjoyed and of greatest value to beginners. This book is planned with the idea of opening up to the dance instructor a means of acquainting her students with rhythm, its value in life, and its relation to dancing.

# FUNDAMENTALS OF RHYTHM

# CHAPTER I

In discussing rhythm in a large group we will find many definitions, some vague, others concrete, some concise, others very elaborate. Everyone will be familiar with rhythm in sound, especially in music and poetry, all will agree that there is rhythm in dancing; but in its broader sense, many will fail to realize how universal rhythm is.

Someone has aptly defined rhythm as the "ordered movement which runs through all beauty." One who defined it in those terms would see rhythm not only in music and poetry, but also in prose; not only in dancing, but in all pleasurable movements of the body, in swimming and sports and even in the movements concerned with everyday life. He would be quick to sense the rhythmic make-up of the body, not only in its external form, but in its organic movements as well, in the inspiration and expiration of our breathing, in the rhythmic flow of blood moved by a succession of impulses given by the rhythmic beating of the heart. He would see beyond the individual and find rhythm in his environment, in the design of his clothes, in the arrangement of the furniture in his house, in the architecture of the

Few persons passing the Women's Building on the Oregon State Campus fail to admire the lines of its structure. It is a pleasing example of rhythm in architecture developed through a progression of sizes, a repetition of units and continuous flowing lines. In both external and interior design, the architect has achieved great beauty with no sacrifice of utility, thus making the building doubly admirable.

3

buildings in which he worked,* in the winding of rivers, and in the sweeping lines of the mountains and valleys of the country in which he lived. Throughout the entire universe, in the movement of the tides, in the alternation of day and night, in the months and seasons, in the turning of the earth about its axis and in its revolution about the sun; in fact, wherever there are repetition, symmetry of form or ideas, a methodical grouping of parts in a whole, one may find rhythm.

Psychologists tell us that we can learn as many groups of units as we can learn single units; therefore, by grouping units in a satisfying manner we find we can learn many more than when we learn them as single units, ungrouped. This is the thing the child does when he chants "Thirty days hath September, April, June and November." We do much the same thing in learning telephone numbers; we group the numbers in twos and threes, as,

1 9—2 5—L or

Grace land—2 3—6 5

The grouping of large figures makes the whole easier to grasp, as $65,781,431 or numbers on a license plate—633-421. This grouping is a manifestation of a tendency to organize. It is an indication of the satisfaction resulting from rhythm. We may say then that *rhythm aids learning.*

Rhythm does more than aid learning. After a thing is learned rhythm may assist in our obtaining the *best results through a minimum waste of energy.* Someone following a familiar design in knitting, crocheting, or lace-making will make few mistakes if she continues in a smooth rhythm, and she may think of other things as she works. However, if she is interrupted she may lose the rhythm, make a mistake, and have to concentrate her attention upon reestablishing the rhythmic swing of the activity.

*Rhythm may save physical energy* as well as mental energy. A vivid example may be seen in any swimming pool. The person who has not yet mastered the rhythm of the stroke will expend much energy and become exhausted before he has gone but a few feet, while the swimmer who has incorporated the rhythm of the stroke in his movements will relax during a part of the stroke and use his energy only at the time when it will result in the most progress. Thus he not only saves energy, but swims a long distance without exhaustion. The author found this true in learning the crawl. Although an experienced diver and swimmer with good endurance on the sidestroke, she had been unable to swim more than 75 feet using the crawl stroke until one day a fellow swimmer brought clearly to her attention the lack of rhythm in her stroke. That one suggestion so improved her crawl stroke that she swam, that day, eighteen lengths of a 75-foot pool, although never before had she gone over one length with ease.

---

* See illustrations of rhythm in lace, furniture and architecture, pages 3, 6, 11, 16 and 17. For illustrations of rhythm in art, dress design, interior decorating, advertising and other fields—see Chapter on Rhythm in "Art in Everyday Life," by Goldstein.

In most forms of manual labor, as well as in the operating of machinery, one will find that the rhythm of the activity saves both mental and physical energy and results in the greatest accomplishment both in amount and quality.   The rhythm makes it possible for us to anticipate the complete act and adjust our effort so as to meet the most strategic point, and to relax and rest between moments of effort. "Especially is this true of handling tools, any instrument from a tack hammer to a battleship," is a similar statement made by a leading educator.   He continues, "You must form an accurate image in your mind of the time, length and sequence of the motions of which special skills consist. You must know before you start just how it ought to feel, the rate at which the momentum should accumulate, and just where the stress should come." *

Learning is made easier, effort is lightened, and accomplishment is increased by rhythm.   But rhythm does more—it enriches life.   "All work and no play makes Jack a dull boy" is a common expression.   We are all familiar with the type of student known as a "book-worm" who makes an "A" average, but makes not a friend; who can tell you the derivation of any algebraic formula, but doesn't know a waltz from a two-step, a baseball diamond from a hockey field; who never could be caught skipping or running for the pure joy of the activity. We all know the person who is in a rut, who limits his life to one narrow channel because he has not learned the relative values of the many phases of life.   His conversation is upon one subject only and he refuses to waste his time or money on anything which will not directly further his one aim in life.   How many friends does he have, how much pleasure does he find in life, and how much pleasure does he create for others?

But on the other hand we have the individual of broad knowledge and experience who can chat on any subject from world politics down to building a camp fire on a rainy day, who is eagerly welcomed into any circle, who finds life not a bore, but a constant source of interest and pleasure.   His life is rich with beauty and he brings a fullness into the lives of those about him.

"But," you are saying, "how does this relate to rhythm?   What has rhythm to do with an enriching of life and personality?"   You may answer your own question by another.   "How do the friends whom I find most interesting, most worthwhile, spend their leisure time?"   The majority of answers will be, in sports and dancing, with music, art or drama; and probing to the foundation of each of these we find a common element—Rhythm.

The most common form through which rhythm may be either expressed or perceived is sound.   We would speak of this as auditory rhythm for which we may use the examples of the ticking of a clock, the sound of the beating of the heart, speech, or music.

Likewise, we may have visual rhythms, that is, those which we see; for example, the swing of the pendulum of a clock, the movements of the arm of an orchestra

---

* Joseph Lee—"Play in Education."   The Macmillan Co., N. Y., Publishers.   The quotation is used with the permission of the publishers.

leader, or the rhythmic form in design or architecture,* or the graceful lines of furniture.

Rhythm may be perceived through a tactile sensation; that is, through the sense of touch. If the fingers are placed over the artery in the wrist, one may feel

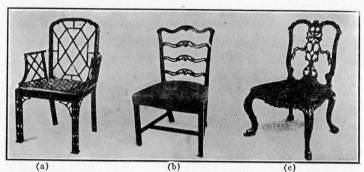

(a)            (b)            (c)

An example of good and poor rhythm in furniture. "Three Chippendale chairs showing: (a) a lack of rhythm; (b) beautiful rhythmic lines and spaces; (c) excessive movement, resulting in loss of dignity and restraint."—From "Art in Everyday Life" by Goldstein. Used with permission of The Macmillan Company, Publishers.

the rhythmic throbbing of the pulse, or one may place the fingers over the heart and feel its rhythmic beat.

Still another medium for the perception of rhythm is the kinesthetic sense, sometimes spoken of as "muscle sense," which refers to our ability to sense, even though our eyes are closed, the position of our bodies, or to be conscious of any movement which our body or any part of it makes, either as we make the movement or later in recalling it. If one is walking with his eyes closed, his kinesthetic sense may tell him whether he is taking long steps or short ones; if he is swinging his arm, his kinesthetic sense, without aid from his eyes, can tell him whether the arm is moving forward or backward. It is also possible to remember a kinesthetic feeling, as when the golf player who has just returned from a game can recall the "feel" of a series of movements which he used in driving his ball over the fairway.

Some psychologists go further to state the belief that under the proper conditions, rhythm could also be perceived through the senses of smell and taste. However, for our purposes the auditory, visual, and kinesthetic senses are sufficient for perceiving rhythm, and all three, the kinesthetic sense, especially, are valuable in our final objective of developing skill in dancing and sports through a rhythmic approach to those activities.

We speak of our senses of sight, taste, and smell, of hearing, and feeling, and of our kinesthetic sense. Is there another sense, that of rhythm? There would perhaps be as much argument in response to such a question as to the query, "is a table a table; or is it merely a mass of atoms which we think of as a table, after the sensation which results from seeing it is transmitted to the brain?"

* See footnote, page 4.

Such a discussion is beyond our field, interesting but impractical for our present purposes. We may or may not be safe in speaking of it as a "Sense of rhythm." We can at least approximate the truth when we say that within each individual, along with his other potentialities, there is a certain quality, possessed in varying degrees by different individuals, which allows him to respond to rhythmic stimuli, and which appears in the form of a pleasurable reaction to such stimuli.

Practically as soon as a child can move he is capable of rhythmic movements. Psychologists even claim to have seen evidence of a response to a rhythmic stimulus in babies only a few weeks old. We see rhythmic movement in the waving of tiny arms, the kicking of small feet, in the crying, feeding, and baby chatter. This same phenomenon of rhythm is tied up with his love of rocking, his enjoyment of nursery rhymes, his fascination in listening to the ticking of a clock, watching the swing of its pendulum, or seeing "the wheels go 'round."

In the games of early childhood rhythm plays a large part. We find it in swings and teeter-boards, in rope-jumping and the bouncing of balls, which are many times improved by the sing-song verses which accompany them. We find it in circle games like "Ring Around the Rosy," "Drop the Handkerchief," "Farmer in the Dell," where verses have been handed down from one generation to the next, but never grow old. Even in the non-rhythmic games we find that the preliminary counting-off rhymes hold an important place.

Someone has said that there are persons who are as unable to sense the presence of rhythm as the person who is color blind is unconscious of the presence of certain colors. However, due to the conspicuous presence of rhythm in the activities of childhood, it seems safe to surmise that a person, though he may possess it in a smaller degree than someone else, is not totally without the ability to perceive rhythm. Rather would it seem probable that he had lost a large degree of the ability through certain inhibitions which he has built up in response to his environment.

Here again we might encounter grounds for argument, and many experiments have been performed in an endeavor to answer such a question. The results have been variable. Perhaps the thing which is not there to start with cannot be produced, but this belief has discouraged many who are merely held in the confines of conventions and inhibitions, or who are handicapped by a lack of vocabulary or means of expression.

One of our foremost psychologists has said that "it is hardly possible to do a physical act without rhythm." Did you ever stop to think, as you walk along, that if it were not for your rhythmic sense you would have to be thinking of each step you take, instead of being able to trust your legs with that activity? You start the activity voluntarily and then you allow the rhythmic swing of it to carry you along. You will call it habit, but rhythm is a large part of habit. In learning a new skill, we hesitate or stumble until we get the "swing of it," but once the swing has been acquired it carries us along while we think of other things. Compare the concentration which a small girl has to place on her first sewing with the ease with which Grandmother's needle flies through its duties.

In many articles on the subject of sport skills, we find rhythm emphasized, as in the Golfer's Magazine,* we find an article on "Faith in Rhythm" which includes these words, "The governing power of the golf swing must come from and be left to rhythm. You must be able to banish all fears and put your whole faith in rhythm."

It is not only in the big movements that we need rhythm, but in the small ones as well. The person who writes rhythmically writes better and with less fatigue. Rhythm in speaking is an absolute necessity, not only in avoiding stuttering, but in speaking beautifully, and in many schools for the deaf, rhythmic activity is used in speech training. Dr. Currier † refers to this as "waking the deaf child up" and claims that such training in rhythm is necessary to convey to the deaf child the real meaning of sound and spoken language.

The importance of rhythmic training for the musician is undeniable when we find great teachers expressing such views as "A pianist's greatest asset is his rhythm" or "Rhythm is the element which gives meaning to music," and we find musicians gathering from all parts of the world to study a system of rhythm training through body movements.‡

In the field of dramatics rhythm is also valuable. The two passages quoted below bring out the fact that it plays a big part, not only in the speech, but in the movements of the dramatist.

> Shakespeare excelled in his acute sense of the emotional value of rhythm in the speech of his characters. The young dramatist must look deeper than the superficial value of mere words in handling dialect or even characters; oaths, slang, catchwords, are of but slight importance. Even as he must learn to go behind words to the ideas of his characters, so to understand that his characters become real in his handling, he must go behind the mere words of his people to their cadences and their rhythms till what he brings back reveals the very spirit of their speech. Such rhythmic dialogue means great truth in characterization phrased with a beauty too subtle to have been used heretofore except by the masters of drama.¶

> "Perfection in dramatic art can only be attained through a proper understanding and practice of rhythm" was one of Sarah Bernhardt's favorite sayings. She often added that her success was directly due to the fact that she realized this years before other great actors and actres-

---

* The Golfer's Magazine, January 1929.
† Dr. Currier of Rhode Island School for Deaf.
‡ Dalcroze Eurhythmics.
¶ Rhythm in Recent Dramatic Dialogue—G. P. Baker, Yale Review, S' 1929. The quotation is used with the permission of the Yale University Press, copyright owners.

ses of the Paris stage.—Actors in general know too little about rhythm. One reason why there are so many failures among them is that they do not understand that their bodies should be as plastic and responsive as their voices.—Before dedicating one's body to the service of art, it is necessary to perfect its mechanism, and rhythm is the key to this perfection. The actor who has a finely tuned, rhythmic body will have a perfect instrument for the expression of his art.*

In view of the important place which rhythm holds in the many activities around which our life is built, every effort should be made to develop the ability to perceive rhythm and to incorporate rhythm in our movements. In physical education classes especially, we are interested in rhythm because it is a large factor, not only in the art of dancing, but in all movement, and because it aids learning and adds pleasure and efficiency to movement. Since it is a means of securing the greatest effect with a minimum waste of energy, each of us should develop her abilities to perceive rhythm through sight and sound, and to express that rhythm in movement. Through this means we may acquire and perfect those physical skills which make us capable of a fuller enjoyment of life.

The attempts which have been made to measure objectively the possibility of developing rhythmic ability indicate that the human body is the best instrument for the study of rhythm; that large movements of legs, arms and trunk train one in rhythmic ability much more definitely than singing or clapping. A combination of all of these methods linked with an intelligent and interested attitude should prove to be a pleasant and profitable experience.

* Rhythmic Practice—Elsa Findley—Theatre Arts Monthly, S, 1927. This quotation used with permission of the Theatre Arts Monthly, copyright owners.

# CHAPTER II

## A VOCABULARY OF RHYTHM

In discussing any specialized subject, one uses many terms which have a special meaning. Misunderstandings often arise because the reader or the listener places a different interpretation upon the words used. For this reason we will define the meaning we give to those terms most frequently used and which must be understood in reading this text.

A *unit* might be defined as one of the parts into which a larger whole has been divided. For example, if one has a pie which is cut in five pieces, each piece is a unit. In this case all the units which make up the whole are alike. However, if the pie had been cut into a half and three sixths, the parts would not be equal in size but would still be units of the whole.

In rhythm, the unit depends upon the medium in which the rhythm is expressed. If we are speaking of auditory rhythms, we may use as an example the ticking of a clock. In that case the unit is each sound, or each "tick." If we use the beating of the heart, the unit is each impulse of the heart. If the example is a series of sounds on a drum, the unit is each sound made as the stick hits the drum head. In speech, the unit is the sound of the voice in syllables. In music, the unit is the musical tone. In visual rhythms, it is each movement of the eye until its movement is interrupted, for example, in looking at a dotted line, as the one below, the breaks in the line interrupt the movement of the eye.

Each portion of the line is a unit of that visual rhythm. In looking at scallops on lace, the eye travels along the curve of the scallop, but is interrupted when a new scallop begins.

Each scallop then is a unit of this visual rhythm. In examining a finer piece of lace, as in the example on the opposite page, the eye follows along the line of the design which stands out clearly upon the background. In watching the director of an orchestra, we see his arm following a definite rhythm, each unit of which is each movement of his arm in a new direction.

The word *tempo* refers to the rate of speed with which a series of units occurs. For example, the tempo is fast in the ticking of a small clock or watch, while in the large grandfather clock the tempo is slow. In the sound of foot-

steps, the tempo is fast in running, and slow in walking.  We may have a change
of tempo within a series of units.  If the tempo or rate of speed increases we
call it acceleration; if it decreases we call it retardation or deceleration.  We
may have a change in our rate of speed in speaking, as when one becomes excited
and talks much faster than usual.  The tempo of the heart beat is moderately slow
except when accelerated in certain types of illness or immediately after a person
has been very active or excited.  Likewise in musical sounds we recognize changes
in tempo or rate of speed.  For measuring tempo, one may use a metronome,
an instrument which ticks as an upright arm swings from side to side.  The tempo

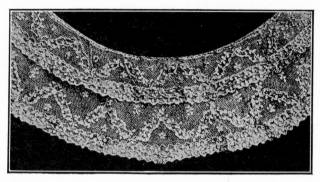

RHYTHM IN LACE

"Three types of rhythmic movement are seen here.  There is
rhythm through the continuous line in the center of the
bottom border, repetition in the row of dots above this line
while the wavelike lines in the open space above show
rhythm through progression."  This illustration and its accompanying quotation is from Art in Everyday Life, by
Goldstein and is used with permission of The Macmillan
Company, Publishers.

of the metronome may be changed by moving a small weight toward or away from
the free end of the lever, thus shortening or lengthening the length of the pendulum.  Since a metronome is calibrated to indicate the number of sounds per minute, it may be used in testing the regularity of a rhythm, or in estimating the
tempo of a series of sounds, or in accurately measuring the relative values of several units.

*Stress* is the result of placing an emphasis upon a certain unit, thereby attracting the attention to that unit.  Stress may be accomplished by several methods, as by a change in intensity, by an increase in temporal value, by a change in
quality.  Let us try each method.

First—by a change in intensity.

Using the voice as the medium of expression and a syllable as the unit, count
1, 2, 3, 4, 1, 2, 3, 4.  Emphasize the syllable "one" by saying it with more force,
1, 2, 3, 4, 1, 2, 3, 4, 1, 2, 3, 4.  You will be conscious of a stress on the syllable
"one."

Second—by an increase in temporal value.

Using the same units count again but increase the length of the syllable "one" by omitting the syllable "two." 1   3 4 1   3 4 1   3 4. Again you will feel a stress on "one."

Third—by a difference in quality.

Repeat the syllables, g c c g c c g c c. The difference in the quality of the two letters will make one conscious of a stress on the letter "g."

Stressed and unstressed values are called respectively, strong and weak. Each is a comparative term for we may have a strong value which is stronger than another strong, as also we may have a weak value which is weaker than another. As, for example, in the intensity of the following lines:

The second value is weak in comparison to the first, but strong in comparison to the third. In the illustrations given above under stress, the syllable "one" would be the strong value while the numbers 2, 3 and 4 would be weak values. Likewise the letter "g" would be strong, the letter "c" weak.

Representing the strong values by a heavy line, the weak values by a light line, the above illustrations could be represented graphically, as follows:

1 2 3 4 1 2 3 4
1  3 4 1  3 4
g c c g c c

All regulated rhythm is built upon a standard of time and stress, called an *underlying beat*. It consists of a series of units or beats which are regularly repeated like the ticking of a clock. An underlying beat serves a function much the same as the yardstick. It measures off rhythm. One might measure dress goods either by the yard using an inch as the unit of measure, or by the meter using a centimeter as the unit. Likewise we may use various units in underlying beats. But for one measure the units must all be equal in length just as the yardstick is built upon inches of equal length, and the meter is built of equal units, the centimeters. Never is either measure built of a combination of inches and centimeters.

An underlying beat is not always heard or seen, but it should be felt, in order to keep rhythm regulated. In the above example where we omitted the count "two" in order to add stress to count "one," we did not actually say the count "two" aloud, but nevertheless we were conscious of its presence. The 1 2 3 4 1 2 3 4 was the underlying beat of the rhythm 1  3 4 1  3 4.

If in rhythm a stress is so placed that it interrupts the regularity of a rhythm we have a condition called *syncopation*. In unsyncopated rhythm, we find that the stress of the rhythm occurs simultaneously with the stress of the underlying beat. That is, we may say, the stress of the rhythm synchronizes with the stress of the underlying beat. This is true in our last example.

```
| 1    3 4 | 1    3 4 |  — Rhythm
| 1 2 3 4  | 1 2 3 4  |  — Underlying beat
```

There is a stress on the "one" of 1    3 4 as well as on the "one" of 1 2 3 4. However, if you count 1 2 3 4 1 2 3 4 and suddenly leave out count "one," the stress which it should have received will be placed on count "two" instead. This result is one form of syncopation.

$$1\ 2\ 3\ 4\ 1\ 2\ 3\ 4 \qquad \underbrace{2\ 3\ 4 \qquad 2\ 3\ 4}_{\text{syncopation}}$$

Meanwhile, the underlying beat should continue in its regularity, giving a feeling of a stress on "one," but an actual stress on "two."

```
|   2 3 4  |   2 3 4  |  — Syncopation
| 1 2 3 4  | 1 2 3 4  |  — Underlying beat
```

In the following discussion of rhythm and rhythmic pattern the terms *long* and *short* refer to the temporal length of units; that is, the duration of time between the beginning of one unit to the beginning of the next. Take, for instance, beats on a drum. The length of each unit of the rhythm heard is the length of time which elapses from the time a drumstick hits the drum until it strikes again. Let us try out the same thing. Clap your hands five times. You have five units of sound. The length of each is equal to the amount of time between claps. Now clap again five times, pause a second or two, and then repeat. After pausing again, repeat once more. You will have a rhythm similar to this line:

$$1\ 2\ 3\ 4\ 5 \qquad 1\ 2\ 3\ 4\ 5 \qquad 1\ 2\ 3\ 4\ 5$$

In terms of longs and shorts you would be clapping four *shorts* and one *long* and repeating the same.

Notice that it is not the duration of the sound alone which determines the length of the unit, for all five sounds may be equal in length. The term *long* or *short* refers to the length of time of the sound plus the silence between sounds; that is, the length of time which elapses from the beginning of one sound to the beginning of the next.

Let us try another demonstration. Clap twice and pause, then repeat several times, clapping always at the same rate of speed, and with pauses of equal length after each second unit. You are now clapping longs and shorts, similar to the following:

$$1\ 2 \qquad 1\ 2 \qquad 1\ 2 \qquad 1\ 2 \qquad 1\ 2$$

In terms of *longs* and *shorts*, we have one *short* and one *long* repeated. If we let the letter *s* represent a *short* and the letter *l* a *long*, the rhythm which you just clapped would be.

s l s l s l s l s l

It should not be necessary in representing a rhythm in terms of *longs* and *shorts*, to leave a longer space after the *l* than after the *s*, for the letter alone should indicate the relative length of the unit. If we are representing the rhythm by lines, the relative lengths of the lines should represent the relative length of the units, as:

▬  ▬▬  ▬  ▬▬  ▬  ▬▬

However, if using the letters *s* and *l* spacing is not important.

s l s l s l s l represents the same rhythm as<br>sl   sl   sl   sl   or   s l   s l   s l   s l

Using the same letters we could represent our other rhythm:

1 2 3 4 5   1 2 3 4 5   as    s s s s l    s s s s l

It must be remembered that the terms long and short are comparative words; therefore they cannot be used to express the absolute length of a unit, but only the relative length. For instance, in clapping s l s l s l, one person might pause a longer time than someone else; nevertheless, in each case the second unit is longer than the first, though one person's *long* may be not so long as the other person's. Since the two longs are clapped by two different people who are clapping individual rhythms we do not need to worry about the relative length of the two longs. Each is clapping s l s l s l though in absolute length one girl's clapping might compare to the other one's as these two lines.

▬  ▬▬  ▬  ▬▬  ▬  ▬▬  ▬  ▬▬<br>▬  ▬▬▬  ▬  ▬▬▬  ▬  ▬▬

However, there are cases in which the comparative length of two longs is important. This is true when they occur within the same rhythm, as in the one represented by the following line. Here the middle unit is longer than the third, but not as long as the first.

▬▬▬  ▬▬  ▬

In a case of this sort let us represent the relative length of the units by the letters L l s, a capital *L* representing the longest value, a small *s* representing the shortest, while the small *l* represents an intermediate value, one which is longer than an *s* but shorter than an *L*. A capital *S* could be used in the same manner representing a value longer than an *s* but shorter than an *L*.

Clap the following rhythms, keeping in mind the relative length of the longs and shorts:

(a)  l  s  l  s  L    l  s  l  s  L
(b)  s  s  l  s  s  l  s  s  l  l  L
(c)  s  s  s  L  s  s  s  L  s  s  s  L  L  L
(d)  s  s  s  l  s  l  s  L      s  s  s  l  s  l  s  L

The term *even* is used to refer to a rhythm in which all units within that rhythm are of equal length, as is true in the ticking of a clock, or the swing of its pendulum. In such a case the rhythm might be written as any one of the following:

L  L  L  L  L  L  L  L
l  l  l  l  l  l  l  l
S  S  S  S  S  S  S  S
s  s  s  s  s  s  s  s

If, however, the relative length of the units within the rhythm vary, then that rhythm is called *uneven*. Those rhythms given in explaining the terms "long" and "short" are uneven rhythms.

s  l  s  l  s  l
s  s  s  l      s  s  s  l
l  s  l  s  L      l  s  l  s  L
s  s  l  s  s  l  s  s  l  l  L
s  s  s  L  s  s  s  L  s  s  s  L  L  L
s  s  s  l  s  l  s  L      s  s  s  l  s  l  s  L

A *pattern* is a grouping of units into one whole which is appreciable by attention; that is, it must not be so large that we cannot grasp its entirety. To illustrate we might use the week. To the adult the week may appear as a pattern, a grouping of days; however, to the small child the week is not a pattern because he cannot appreciate it. His span of attention extends over only one day, or possibly two.

We might take another example from Architecture. To the person trained in sensing the rhythmic relationship of the parts of a large building, the structure may appear as one complete rhythmic pattern, while to the untrained person, rhythm may seem present only in the design over the doors, or the borders on the walls. (See examples, pages 3, 16 and 17.)

A grouping of rhythmic units is called a *rhythmic pattern*. If one listens to the ticking of a clock and hears the same sound, tick, tick, tick, tick, indefinitely, we have no grouping, only a constantly recurring even unit. But if one hears, though it may be only a subconscious feeling, tick tock, tick tock, tick tock, we have a grouping of units or a pattern. The two units "tick tock" form the pattern which is repeated over and over. This is the simplest pattern we can have because it is made up of only two equal units. One unit cannot form a grouping.

Since stress tends to produce a grouping, a rhythmic pattern may be accomplished in the same ways by which we get stress, namely, by an increase in the in-

RHYTHM IN DESIGN

In borders based on classical design, one is conscious of the
presence of rhythm.

tensity of one unit, by a temporal change, or by a difference in quality. Then in producing stress in these ways we also produce patterns or groupings.

In 1 2 3 4 1 2 3 4 the pattern is 1 2 3 4 or s s s s
In 1̄    3 4 1̄    3 4 the pattern is 1̄    3 4 or L̄   s s
In g c c g c c        the pattern is    g c c or    s̲ s s

We may also define a rhythmic pattern as a group of units which is repeated. The pattern is considered as that sequence of units which occurs before the same arrangement of units is repeated. Using an arrangement of short lines we may demonstrate a pattern as follows:

pattern

The first five units form a pattern because they are immediately repeated in the same relation to each other. The above pattern might be written as

l s s L s

This brings us to a discussion of *simple* and *complex patterns*. A simple pattern is one in which we feel only a single group of units, as in

1 2 3 4
1̄    3 4
L̲   s s
g c c

When we feel more than one group of units, that is, a pattern built of a combination of several simple patterns, we have a complex pattern. For example, in the pattern

l s s L s _____ __ __ _____ __

we have two simple patterns l s s and L s.

The term *part pattern* refers to the number of units which are combined to form a pattern. We speak of two-part patterns, three-part patterns, four-part patterns, etc.; in fact we may have as large patterns as we can group units and still

RHYTHM IN ARCHITECTURE

In many of our public buildings, excellent rhythm is seen, both in the structural design as well as in the decorative lines.

keep the group within the span of attention.   When the pattern is immediately repeated, we count only the number of units used before the same pattern is repeated.   The following patterns then could be referred to as follows:

two-part
$$\begin{cases} \text{tick, tock, tick, tock, etc.} \\ \text{l s l s l s etc.} \\ \text{s l s l s l etc.} \end{cases}$$

three-part
$$\begin{cases} \text{g c c g c c g c c} \\ \text{l s s l s s l s s etc.} \\ \text{1 \quad 3 4 \quad 1 \quad 3 4 \quad 1 \quad 3 4} \end{cases}$$

four-part $\begin{cases} \text{1 2 3 4 1 2 3 4 1 2 3 4} \end{cases}$

five-part $\begin{cases} \text{l s s L s l s s L s etc.} \end{cases}$

six-part $\begin{cases} \text{l s s s s l l s s s s l l s s s s l} \end{cases}$

The terms *step pattern* and *foot pattern* are used interchangeably to refer to what one's feet might do in following or constructing a rhythmic pattern. For instance, if someone clapped the rhythmic pattern of 1 2 3 4   1 2 3 4 at a moderate rate of speed and evenly, another person might follow that rhythmic pattern by walking with a stamp on count "one".   The step pattern would then be:

stamp, step, step, step, stamp, step, step, step.

Another person however might follow the pattern by hopping, always on one foot, with a higher hop on count "one" to represent the stress.   Her foot pattern then would be:

Hop, hop, hop, hop, Hop, hop, hop, hop.

For any one rhythmic pattern there may be many foot patterns which may be used in reproducing the rhythmic pattern by an activity of the legs and feet; for example, for the rhythmic pattern   l s L   we might have the following step patterns.

| l | s | L |
|------|-------|------|
| step | close | step |
| step | hop | step |
| hop | hop | step |
| step | step | jump |

For certain skills we might use such expressions as *arm pattern*, or *trunk pattern*, to indicate the rhythmic relationship of the units within movements of those parts of the body.  An example of the arm pattern might be the

<u>L</u>  <u>L</u>  <u>L</u>

used by the orchestra leader in indicating the underlying beat of waltz music.  For other examples see pages 49, 50, 51.

The term *floor pattern* * is used to designate the imaginary design followed by the feet.  To help visualize the floor pattern one might imagine herself running in fresh snow, attempting to mark out a definite design with her footsteps.  For example, if a person skips in a circle, the floor pattern is a circle; if she then runs from one corner of the room to the diagonally opposite, she cuts her circle by a diagonal line.  She may, then, run backward toward the center, skip in a smaller circle and exit on the diagonal.  Her floor pattern would be one circle within another, both cut by a diagonal line.  Suggestions for simple floor patterns may be gained from letters of the alphabet, geometric designs, scallops and design of lace.

* See pages 126 and 161.

# CHAPTER III

In every rhythmic pattern we must have two or more units which are grouped as a whole. If the unit is a sound, we must have at least two sounds before we can be conscious of rhythm. If these sounds occur in an even succession, always with the same intensity, much as the dripping of water from a leaky faucet, the effect would be one of monotony. Repetition alone cannot make a rhythmic pattern. We must have a grouping, and the simplest form of grouping is by stress. This addition of stress is the thing we do consciously or unconsciously to relieve the monotony of water dripping, a clock ticking, or, as we ride on a train, the sound of the turning of the wheels on the rails. We often hear the wheels actually sounding the rhythm of a familiar song.

It is important to recognize that the addition of stress does not change the time value of the unit. In listening to a rhythm made up of units equal in length but unequal in stress, there is a tendency to feel that the strong beat takes more time than the weak. One must guard against this tendency and judge the time value of the units without being influenced by the stress. In order to check on one's accuracy in judging even and uneven rhythms, a metronome or the pendulum of a clock may be used, for these are always even. Have someone clap in unison with the metronome, then stop the metronome while your partner continues to clap. Ask your partner to stress every other beat without changing the rate of speed. Does her rhythm still sound even to you? It should if she has kept the rate steady. If you think she is not clapping in an even rhythm, start the metronome again, and test her accuracy as well as your own judgment.

Now let us experiment with stress and with uneven rhythms. Set your metronome at a moderate rate of speed, that is, a comfortable rate, one which you might use in a brisk walk. If you do not have a metronome count out loud, keeping your count even. Clap in unison with the metronome or your counting. Now every third count leave out a clap. You will have a rhythm which may be represented as follows:

$$\frac{1\ 2}{s\ 1}\ \frac{4\ 5}{s\ 1}\ \frac{7\ 8}{s\ 1}$$

Continue clapping and try to determine whether both units are equal in intensity or if a stress falls on one of each two. Undoubtedly you will feel a stress on the longer of each two units, for as was said in discussing stress under the vocabulary an increase in the temporal length of a unit adds stress to that unit.

20

Try the same thing walking, taking more time for the step on the right foot than for that on the left. Which foot seems to step with more force, the right or the left? As in the clapping, you will undoubtedly find that the unit taking the longer time gets the emphasis.

To test the truth of this statement clap a rhythmic pattern made up of a short and a long, repeated

<u>s l   s l   s l   s l</u>

and attempt to place the stress upon the short unit. It will not be easy at first, but by concentrating upon it you may be able to do it. Does it feel natural? Let your attention drift to something else and see if you continue to stress the short. Try it out on a partner. After she has established a stress on the short, divert her attention and see if she unconsciously changes the stress to the long. The natural tendency is to stress the longer of two units.

The placing of stress affects the mood resulting from rhythm. When a nurse speaks to a patient for whom she is caring, or when a mother sings to a baby which is about to drop off to sleep, she speaks in a soft tone, but when an officer gives a signal to his company, he puts force behind his voice. It is not a difference in voices or ability to use them, for you can find little girls who give as emphatic commands as boys, and you will find fathers who sing as effective lullabies as mothers. The difference is due to the result desired. The officer wants his company to respond with a snap, heightened interest, and concentrated attention. The nurse wishes to avoid such an effect. The response to intensity is easily apparent.

Try it with a partner or with a group of small children; tell them to skip lazily as you clap a moderate but soft rhythm. As they continue, gradually put more force behind your clapping. You will notice a change in the energy with which they skip, for they will be stimulated to skip with more vigor, probably lifting the body higher from the floor. Try the same thing, using a gallop as the activity; when you clap lightly the gallop will be done more like a slide, with the feet close to the ground. As you add intensity to the clapping, the galloping "horses" will lift their feet higher and show a decided change in interest and vigor.

To further prove that the placing of stress affects the mood resulting from rhythm, clap a steady, even succession of units with a stress on the first of every six.

<u>1</u> 2 3 4 5 6 <u>1</u> 2 3 4 5 6 <u>1</u> 2 3 4 5 6, etc.

The effect is not stimulating but rather solemn. If you begin accenting every other unit as

<u>1</u> 2 <u>1</u> 2 <u>1</u> 2 <u>1</u> 2 <u>1</u> 2, etc.

you will find that the effect is quite stimulating and almost vivacious.

Clap the following rhythmic pattern and notice that as the accents become closer together you have a feeling of acceleration and excitement, although the beats are quite even:

Take the same pattern walking, accenting with a stamp. As the stamps come in a closer succession you will get the same feeling of acceleration. The same thing may be done jumping, taking a higher jump on the accent.

Work out the same pattern with a group of girls in a circle, sliding sideward and changing direction on each accent. It will be eight slides to the right, eight to the left, four right, four left, two right, two left, and the last three will be in place. It is fun to do this singing or humming the Soldiers' Chorus, which starts, "Glory and Love to the Men of Old."

Besides acceleration, the placing of accent may give us a feeling of syncopation. Tap with your toe an even rhythmic pattern with an accent on the first of every four beats. Then begin clapping in unison with the noise made by your foot. Suddenly leave out count "one" and "three" in your clapping, although the foot continues as before. You will have syncopation. It will be

Syncopation

Hands 1 2 3 4 1 2 3 4   2   4   2   4

Feet   1 2 3 4 1 2 3 4 1 2 3 4 1 2 3 4

In syncopation we must have two rhythms. The syncopated, or irregularly stressed rhythm, plus a simultaneous regularly stressed rhythm or underlying beat. The underlying beat need not be heard, but its presence must be felt. If we clap the above pattern for the hands, though the feet do not take the underlying beat, we will be conscious of it, because the hands started with the regular beat. So, when the syncopation interrupts the regular beat, we, having a tendency to continue it, are still conscious of its regularity.

If, however, we continue the syncopated pattern for a while, it will tend to become regular, or eventually monotonous. The occasional syncopated pattern is interesting and stimulating, but the continued one becomes monotonous, and may even be irritating.

Clap the following patterns and notice the places where syncopation is introduced:

Hands 1 & 2 &   & 4 & 1 &   & 3 & 4 &

Feet   1 & 2 & 3 & 4 & 1 & 2 & 3 & 4 &

Hands 1 &   & 3   4 &   & 2   3 &   &

Feet   1 & 2 & 3 & 4 & 1 & 2 & 3 & 4 &

Hands 1 & 2 &   & 4 & 1 & 2   3 & 4

Feet   1 & 2 & 3 & 4 & 1 &   & 3   4 &

A change in the rate of speed or tempo will also affect the mood resulting from rhythm. Anyone who has listened to a drummer, or to a tap dancer, knows that the rhythm has an effect on the mood of the individual listening, this mood varying with the rhythm heard. A fast uneven rhythm is stimulating and usually makes one feel joyous or energetic, while a slow steady rhythm is more quieting. Contrast, for example, the rhythmic patterns and rate of speed in hymns, chants, and processionals used in religious services with the merry swing of folk dance music, or the stimulating rhythms of jazz. Clap the rhythms from "Turkey in the Straw" or "Captain Jinks," then compare them with the rhythms of "My Country 'Tis of Thee" or "Swanee River." The former will make one feel spritely and happy; the latter will soothe.

The composer and the poet are conscious of the fact that the ear demands different rhythms for the expression of different emotions. For ecstasy and joy, a quick eager rising movement is needed, while sadness and meditation are slow and emphatic. Compare the following passages from familiar verse, the power and animation of the first with the softness and smoother melody of the second:

> 1. "Awake, Sir King, the gates unspar!
>    Rise up and ride both fast and far,
>    The sea flows over bolt and bar."

> 2. "In Flanders fields the poppies grow
>    Between the crosses, row on row,
>    That mark our place; while in the sky
>    The larks, still bravely singing, fly
>    Unheard amid the guns below."
>                    —JOHN McCRAE.

Compare similarly these two:

> 1. "Oh, young Lochinvar is come out of the West,—
>    Through all the wide Border his steed is the best!
>    And, save his good broadsword, he weapon had none,
>    He rode all unarmed, and he rode all alone."
>                    —SIR WALTER SCOTT.

> 2. "Three fishers went sailing out into the West
>    Out into the West as the sun went down;
>    Each thought of the woman who loved him the best
>    And children stood watching them out of the town;

> For men must work, and women must weep;
> And there's little to earn, and many to keep,
> Though the harbor bar be moaning."
>                                       —CHARLES KINGSLEY.

The rate of speed or tempo is an important element in producing the desired mood. Neither acceleration nor retardation can effect the rhythmic pattern, but they may greatly effect the mood which results from hearing the rhythm. To test this statement clap a slow even rhythm, such as ▬ ▬ ▬ ▬ ▬ ▬ ▬ ▬ ▬ ▬ It is not stimulating, but quieting. Without changing the evenness, change the rate of speed to a very fast one; the rhythm will become stimulating and you will feel hurried. You have changed the mood resulting without having changed the pattern itself. It is still a series of equal units, grouped into threes by stress. This may be effectively tested by use of a metronome,* or by comparing the pendulum of a Grandfather clock with the pendulum of a tiny one. It's like the story of the engine pulling a heavy load up a hill. It seems to be saying very slowly,

**"I    THINK    I    CAN,   I    THINK    I    CAN."**

Soon it reaches the top and starts down the other side. Its song has changed to,

"I THOUGHT I COULD, I THOUGHT I COULD, I THOUGHT I COULD."

The wheels are turning in the same rhythm but the mood has changed.

Take the rhythmic pattern of this bit taken from a familiar Funeral March:

L    l    s    L    l    s    l    s    l    s    L

Clapped slowly or walked out, it is bound to result in heaviness and depression, but the same pattern clapped or executed at a faster rate of speed brings a resultant mood which is brisk and gay. There is a folk dance tune which has the same rhythmic pattern in a faster tempo which, when played, never fails to lift one on her toes or to start heads tossing gaily.

Rhythm, it has been said, is composed of a series of temporal units, grouped by stress. In all regulated rhythms these units are based upon an underlying beat.

* See Tempo, page 10.

The first step in determining the pattern of the underlying beat is to decide at what rate of speed the beat occurs.  It was explained in the vocabulary that the underlying beat occurs as regularly as the ticking of a clock; that is, it is always even, but the tempo may vary without disturbing the regularity of the underlying beat.  Perhaps the best way for determining it is by trial and error.  If you are listening to a rhythm in sound (as in poetry or music or in beats on a drum), clap, tap your toe, or count very regularly at a moderate rate of speed which seems neither hurried nor dragging.  If your count seems to occur simultaneously with the majority of the units in the rhythmic pattern you have probably happened upon the recurring beat.  If the result is not satisfying, increase or decrease your tempo until the majority of units do occur at the same time as your count.  This will be much the same effect as when you succeed in getting in step with someone with whom you are walking.

When you think you have determined the evenly recurring unit, you must begin to listen for accents.  Since all rhythmic patterns are grouped by a stress which occurs at regular intervals, you should be able to hear that certain units seem to have more emphasis than others, and that the number of underlying beats between the stressed units is always the same.  In the underlying beat, there is a stress which occurs (except in syncopation) at the same time as the stress of the rhythmic pattern for which you are trying to determine the underlying beat. When the recurring unit as well as the stress of the underlying beat has been de- termined, the rhythmic pattern of the underlying beat is determined by counting the number of beats which are grouped together by accent.  You will find that you have a two-part, three-part, four-part, or six-part even pattern as an underlying beat.  (It is quite possible to have five, seven, nine or various other part patterns in the underlying beat but since two, three, four and six part are the most common, we shall disregard the others in this text.)

Take for example, the Soldiers' Chorus which we used before.  Analyzing its underlying beat, we might count it thus:

| Glor | | | y | and | love to the | men | of | old | |
|------|---|---|---|-----|-------------|-----|----|-----|---|
| 1 | 2 | 3 | 4 | | 1 | 2 | 3 | 4 | |

| Our | | | sons | will | copy their | virtues | bold | | |
|-----|---|---|------|------|------------|---------|------|---|---|
| 1 | 2 | 3 | 4 | | 1 | 2 | 3 | 4 | |

In this case we have a four-part even pattern as an underlying beat.  However, someone else might hear the accents occurring every two counts, thus analyzing it as a two-part underlying beat.

| Glor | | y | and | love to the | men | of | old | |
|------|---|---|-----|-------------|-----|----|-----|---|
| 1 | 2 | 1 | 2 | 1 | 2 | 1 | 2 | |

| Our | | sons | will! | copy their | virtues | bold | |
|---|---|---|---|---|---|---|---|
| 1 | 2 | 1 | 2 | 1 | 2 | 1 | 2 |

It is not always possible, nor is it necessary, in order to understand the material in this text, to be always able to discriminate between a "two-part" and a "four-part" underlying beat because the "four-part" is merely a "two-part" doubled.

two-part ▬ ▬

four-part ▬ ▬ ▬ ▬

In the four-part underlying beat, there is a secondary accent on count three which is not as strong as the primary accent on count one.

A four-part underlying beat could be represented as follows:

$$\underline{1} \quad 2 \quad \underline{3} \quad 4$$

Two groups of a two-part underlying beat would sound almost the same as one group of a four-part, except that the accents are both primary ones.

$$\underline{1} \quad 2 \quad \underline{1} \quad 2$$

Now let us analyze "America."

| 1 | 2 | 3 | 1 | 2 | | 3 |
|---|---|---|---|---|---|---|
| My | count | ry | 'Tis | | of | thee |
| Sweet | land | of | Lib | | er | ty |
| Of | thee | I | Sing | | | |

We find we have a three-part rhythm as an underlying beat.

It is easily possible and necessary to discriminate a three-part from either a two- or four-part because the accents in a three-part do not occur simultaneously with a two- or four-part even though the tempo is the same.

Two groups of two-part     1  2  1  2
"     "     " three-part 1  2  3  1  2  3
"     "     " four-part  1  2  3  4  1  2  3  4

On the other hand, the six-part may be confused with any of the others. The six-part is made of two groups of threes with a secondary accent on the first of the second group, namely on count 4.

$$\underline{1} \quad 2 \quad 3 \quad \underline{4} \quad 5 \quad 6$$

If it is not possible to distinguish between the primary and secondary accent, the six-part will sound like two groups of threes, just as the four-part may sound like two groups of twos. The tempo of a six-part underlying beat is usually more rapid than that of a two-, three-, or four-part, and this knowledge may aid in discriminating between a three and six.

Occasionally in a rapid six-part underlying beat one hears only the accents, and then it sounds like a two-part pattern, as for example: "Captain Jinks" might sound as if based upon either a fast six-part pattern, a slow two-part, or a fast three-part pattern.

| Oh | I'm | Cap | | tain | Jinks | of | the Horse | | Mar | ines | | |
|---|---|---|---|---|---|---|---|---|---|---|---|---|
| 5 | 6 | 1 | 2 | 3 | 4 | 5 | 6 | 1 | 2 | 3 | 4 | 5 | 6 |
| | | 1 | | | 2 | | | 1 | | | 2 | | |
| 2 | 3 | 1 | 2 | 3 | 1 | 2 | 3 | 1 | 2 | 3 | 1 | 2 | 3 |

For the time being, until we have had more practice in determining the rhythmic pattern of the underlying beat, let us attempt to discriminate only between two- and three-part patterns. The four-part patterns may be considered as two-part, while six-part can be called a fast three-part or a slow two-part.

Let us take the rhythm

L l s L l s l s l s L

Using the trial and error method of determining the tempo of the recurring units we will find that the units of the underlying beat occur at the same time as each long in the rhythmic pattern given. Then if we were counting the units of the underlying beat we would count it as follows:

L l s L l s l s l s L
1 2 & 3 4 & 5 & 6 & 7 (8)

The shorts come in between beats. For instance we might count 1 2 and 3 4 and 5 and 6 and 7. The numbers come in regular succession and the "ands" in between take less time than the numbers which they follow. The stresses are felt on 1 3 5 and 7 or on 1 and 5. We know that the pattern of the underlying beat is a two-part or four-part. It cannot be a slow three-part. If it were clapped as with a three-part underlying beat it would sound like this:

| 1 2 & 3 | 1 & 2 & 3 & | 1

instead of like this:

| 1 2 & 3 4 & | 1 & 2 & 3 |

Let us take as another example, the song "School Days." One can clap the rhythm of the first four words as slow beats with a stress on each word "School."

School Days School Days

But, at the words "Those were golden rule days" we find our rhythm uneven. Since the underlying beat must always be even we come to the conclusion that part of the words come between units of the underlying beat, as

| School Days | School Days | Those were Gold en | Rule days |
|---|---|---|---|
| 1   2 | 1   2 | 1   &   2   & | 1   2 |

or that there are more beats in the underlying rhythm than there are syllables of words. When we come to the words "Reading and Writing and" we find that our last conclusion was true. Here the underlying beat is definitely grouped into threes.

| Read ing and | writ ing and |
|---|---|
| 1   2   3 | 1   2   3 |

However, before we can say that the underlying beat of School Days is a three-part pattern, we must try it out on the part for which we previously found a two-part. If it fits that part, also, we are safe in calling the underlying beat of School Days a fast three-part rhythmic pattern.

As we analyze it we find the three-part underlying beat synchronizes with the rhythm of the words.

| Rhythm of Words | School | Days | School | Days |
|---|---|---|---|---|
| **Underlying Beat** | 1   2   3 | 1   2   3 | 1   2   3 | 1   2   3 |
| | Those   were | Gold   en | Rule | Days |
| | 1   2   3 | 1   2   3 | 1   2   3 | 1   2   3 |
| | Read ing and | Writ ing and | Rith   me | tic |
| | 1   2   3 | 1   2   3 | 1   2   3 | 1   2   3 |
| | Taught to the | Tune of a | Hick   'ry | stick |
| | 1   2   3 | 1   2   3 | 1   2   3 | 1   2   3 |

Try the same analysis with other familiar songs or nursery rhymes, as "Hi Diddle Diddle" or "Jack and Jill."

In order to make your body more sensitive to the underlying beat, walk or run in time to the rhythm of the underlying beat while you clap the rhythm of the words.

A large number of patterns may have the same underlying even beat; so in order to train one's self in the ability to determine the rhythmic pattern of the underlying beat, one should practice building rhythmic patterns based on a certain underlying beat.

Interesting patterns may be built by combining the units of the underlying beat. Let us start with a three-part underlying pattern s s s. We may think of it as strong weak weak or in terms of temporal value as short short short. We call the units shorts because we wish to combine them into longs. The following patterns are possible:   L   s   by combining first and second units;   s   L by combining second and third units.

Let us take a four-part pattern and combine units.

Let us try another method, taking for example a two-part underlying beat. We may think of it as strong weak or in terms of temporal value as   L   L   .

Upon this underlying beat we may build a number of rhythms by dividing either unit as follows:

—the result of splitting the second long into 2 equal parts.

—the long is split into 3 equal parts.

—the second long is divided into two unequal portions.

—the first unit is split.

We call this deriving a rhythmic pattern by splitting the beat. With a three-part underlying beat we can derive even a greater number of patterns, as:

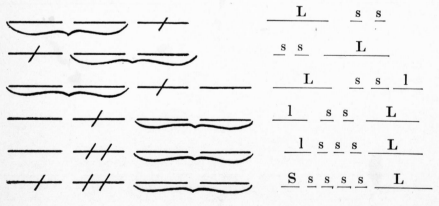

L   L   S S

L   L   l   s

L   L   s   s   s

L   S S   L

L   l   s   L

L   s   s   s   L

L   S   S   S   S

L   l   s   l   s

L   s   s   s   s   s

L   S   S   s   s

L   l   s   s   s   s

S   S   L   L

l   s   L   L

s   s   s   L   L

l   s   s   s   L

and so on until all possible combinations are exhausted. A still larger number could be built from a four-part underlying rhythmic pattern.

By a combination of both methods (combining and splitting), we get still more interesting patterns:

L   s   s

s   s   L

L   s   s   l

l   s   s   L

l   s   s   s   L

S   s   s   s   s   L

We could carry our pattern building still farther by combining simple patterns into complex ones.  For example, put the last two patterns together and we have l s s s L S s s s s L.

Complex
pattern

Underlying
beat

Note.—Since the accent of the rhythmic pattern should (except in syncopation) synchronize with the accent of the underlying beat, and since we naturally tend to put the accent on the longer of two units, you will find a beat split into a long and a short more often than into a short and a long.  For instance, if one wants the pattern long—short—long, based on a two-part underlying rhythm, it will be most naturally accomplished by splitting beat one rather than beat two. It will be

l    s  L                        L    s  l
                    rather than

This general rule may make it easier in analyzing the relative values of the units in a rhythmic pattern.

# CHAPTER IV

## FAMILIAR FORMS OF RHYTHMIC PATTERNS

In what forms are we most accustomed to experiencing rhythm and rhythmic patterns? Music, poetry, and dancing would in the majority of cases be the answer to the question, because each is so definitely dependent on rhythm, because the rhythm of each is so apparent that we find it easy to isolate, and because we have been taught to speak of these in terms of rhythm.

Approaching learning from the angle of one's experience has been found one of the greatest aids in the understanding of new material. A certain amount of the knowledge and skill learned in one situation carries over into a similar situation and speeds the learning process. The child who has been accustomed to seeing printed words in connection with his playthings, even though no attempt has been made to teach him to read those words, will find his lessons easier. Having learned to recognize certain words and phrases in connection with the material to which they refer will make his reading lesson more easily understood. Watch a class in swimming or a group at folk dancing. The person who has learned to swim one stroke will master another stroke more quickly, while the dancer will find in the new dance certain skills which were learned with a former folk dance, and the new dance pattern becomes easier.

The ultimate objective of material in "Rhythm" is to help one to become more sensitive to rhythms and rhythmic patterns, capable of reproducing them through sound and movement, and by so doing to make the learning of skills easier and the execution of them more efficient. Every girl has had some experience in the field of music, poetry, or dancing. She need not have had years of practice at the piano; she need not be a poet or a professional dancer. If her knowledge of music is only from singing at home, school, church or camp, her knowledge of poetry, only in nursery rhymes, limericks and jingles, her dancing nothing more than a happy skip in a circle, singing "A Tisket, A Tasket, a green and yellow basket," a start in rhythm training has been made. There has been planted a seed which may grow into a fine garden, or may be crowded out by weeds. Instead of limiting herself by such fears as "I have no sense of rhythm," "No ear for music," "I'm too awkward to learn to dance," she may go back into her experience and seek out those things which will carry over into a study of rhythm and rhythmic patterns. By comparing the similarities of the rhythm in music, verse and movement, she will attain not only the object of her study, but will find that as a by-product she has formulated a clearer understanding of that with which she is already familiar.

Let us start with music and continue to poetry, finding what is there that will make the understanding of rhythm more clear. First of all we must agree on certain terms which will be used in our discussion.

What are some of the common terms used in expressing the rhythm of music?

Since music is based on regulated rhythm, it has always an *underlying beat*, a beat being, as previously defined, a division of time occurring in even succession as regularly as the ticking of a clock, although the speed may vary. Hold your watch to your ear and you will hear an even beat which occurs regularly, but in a fast succession of units. Listen to the ticking of a large clock, and you will find the same regularity but at a much slower rate of speed, or if a large clock is not available, hold two fingers on the pulse in your wrist and listen to the regularity of your heart beats. Reproduce it by clapping. You may change the speed of your heart beat by taking some vigorous activity as running about the room or in place for several minutes, but the regularity will be there although the speed will be changed.

In an underlying rhythm we have the beats grouped into intervals by stress or accent. In music these groupings are called *measures*. For example, in the songs "School Days," "My Wild Irish Rose," "America," the underlying rhythm is equal units with an accent every three beats.

| My | Count | ry | 'Tis | | of Thee | Sweet | Land | of | | Lib | | er ty |
|----|-------|-----|------|---|---------|-------|------|----|---|-----|---|-------|
| l | l | l | L | s | l | l | l | l | | L | s | l |

Each group of three equal beats ▬ ▬ ▬ is called a measure.

In the song "America the Beautiful," however, we have the underlying beat grouped by accent into fours.

| Words | | Oh | Beaut- | i- | ful | for | spac- | ious | skies | and |
|-------|---|----|--------|-----|-----|-----|-------|------|-------|-----|
| Rhythm of words | l | | L | s | l | l | L | s | l | l |
| Underlying beat | | | | | | | | | | |

| Words | | wav- | ing | fields | of | grain |
|-------|---|------|-----|--------|-----|-------|
| Rhythm of words | | l | l | l | l | L |
| Underlying beat | | | | | | |

Each group of four beats ▬ ▬ ▬ ▬ is called a measure.

In the song "The Farmer in the Dell," we have the underlying beat grouped by accent into twos. Therefore, two beats equal one measure.

The Farm er in the Dell    The    Farm er in the Dell

Exactly as is true in all regulated rhythm the four-part measure in music has on the third beat a secondary accent; and, therefore, may sound like two measures of a two-part underlying rhythm instead of one measure of a four-part.

The difference between two measures of a two-part underlying rhythm and the measure of a four-part might be represented as follows:

Two measures of 2-part  ▬ — ▬ —  or *Strong*, weak, *Strong*, weak
One measure of 4-part  ▬ — — —  or *Strong*, weak, *Weak*, weak

Clap the two-part rhythm giving equal stress to each accent. Now clap the four-part rhythm giving less stress to the secondary accent than to the primary accent.

While it is sometimes difficult to distinguish between a two- and a four-beat measure, one should always be able to differentiate either of these from a three-beat measure, for the accent of the latter can not synchronize with the accents of the two others.

Two measures of 2 beats each    1  2  1  2

"        "        " 3 "        "      1  2  3  1  2  3

"        "        " 4 "        "      1  2  3  4  1  2  3  4

(This is exactly the same as was explained under the discussion of characteristics of rhythm.)

Music is based on a division of time called *notes*. A note shows how long a tone, which is the unit in musical rhythm, is to be sustained. The time value of notes is mathematically derived, there being whole, half, quarter, eighth, sixteenth, even thirty-second notes, a whole note being equal to:

two half notes

four quarter notes

eight eighth notes

sixteen sixteenth notes

or thirty-two thirty-seconds

A quarter note is sustained for approximately the length of time in the interval between heart beats, or ordinary walking steps. The other notes take relatively longer or shorter according to their value. For instance, half notes would come in succession about the speed of a very slow march (funeral march), while whole notes would be twice that slow, for example, a slow hesitation march, such as occasionally is used at weddings.

Eighth notes on the other hand would resemble a more moderate run, while sixteenths would be similar to the steps of a very fast run. One could scarcely run as fast as thirty-second notes, but in whirling, the feet sometimes move as rapidly as thirty-second notes.

Try walking and clapping quarter notes, continue clapping quarter notes but walk half notes, later whole notes. Try running eighths and sixteenths. Join hands with a partner and whirl, moving the feet as fast as thirty-second notes. See if you can locate the various kinds of notes on a sheet of music. You will also find dotted notes. A note followed by a dot has its length increased by one-half its value. For example, a quarter note ordinarily equals two eighth notes; then a dotted quarter will equal three eighths. How much will a dotted half equal? How much would a dotted eighth equal?

Occasionally in place of notes one will find symbols indicating a rest. These symbols indicate silence for a certain time; for example, silence for the amount of time equal to a quarter note is represented by this symbol $\gtrsim$ while a rest equal to an eighth note is written as $\gamma$ , and a sixteenth note rest is $\gamma$ . Half and whole note rests are written as a small bar ▬ , a half rest being placed above the second line of the staff, while the whole rest is placed below the second line

as,                   Half-rest        Whole-rest.

Just as in rhythmic patterns in sound, the silence is included as a part of the unit, so in music the rest is included with the preceding note in determining the long and short units of the rhythmic patterns.

*Time* of music is determined by the number of beats occurring in each measure. For example, the accent may occur every two beats; if each beat has the value of a quarter note, the music is said to be written in 2/4 time. The symbol for the time of the music (the *time signature*) is written at the beginning of the composition, the symbol being one number over another, the upper number indicating the number of beats to a measure, and the lower number indicating the value of each beat. The most common times of music are 2/4, 3/4, 4/4, 6/8.

4/4 indicates four beats to a measure, each beat having the same value as a quarter note. A measure of music written in 4/4 time therefore contains two quarter notes or their equivalent.

2/4 indicates two beats to a measure, each beat having the value of a quarter note.  A measure of 2/4 contains two quarter notes or their equivalent.

3/4 indicates three beats to a measure, each beat having the value of a quarter note.  A measure of 3/4 time contains three quarter notes or their equivalent.

6/8 indicates six beats to a measure, each beat having the time value of an eighth note.  A measure of 6/8 time contains six eighth notes or their equivalent.

*Tempo* expresses the mood and rate of speed of a musical composition, and is usually signified at the beginning of the music.  Some examples of tempo are:

Adagio—Italian for slow; to be played slowly.

Allegro—Italian for cheerful; played quickly with animation.

The tempo in which the music is to be played may also be indicated at the beginning of the music by a metronome reading which indicates the adjustment of the metronome and so the number of beats per minute.  (See also Tempo, page 10.)  For example, a metronome reading of 72 indicates that the beats occur at a rate of 72 per minute.

*Phrases* are groupings of measures.  The number of measures in a phrase is usually a multiple of two, that is, two, four, or eight.  A phrase is a complete feeling.  Some speak of the first half of a phrase as being like a question, with the last half, the answer; or, the last half as being the echo of the first half.  Illustrating this with a simple composition, we have

SCHOOL DAYS

| School | Days | School | Days | Those were | golden | rule | days |

Measure                        Measure

Half Phrase                     Half Phrase

Whole Phrase

In this material we will refer to either a half phrase or a whole phrase merely as a phrase.

Beyond the phrases we have a still larger grouping, that of the whole composition.  Taking our analogy from the discussion on rhythm we may say the measure is like a simple rhythmic pattern, the phrase is a complex rhythmic pattern, while the composition is a series of complex patterns combined in such a way as to give the effect of a complete whole.

We may in music as in all regulated rhythm have rhythms derived from an underlying beat.  Let us study some examples of derived rhythms taken from well-known songs.  Take, for example, the waltz "My Wild Irish Rose."  The underlying rhythm is one made up of equal units with a stress the first of every three beats; that is, the underlying beat is an even three-part pattern, strong, weak, weak, strong, weak, weak, etc., which may be represented as

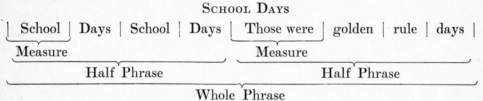

However, in the melody we have an uneven rhythmic pattern s L l s L, etc. In singing the word "Wild," we hold it for three units of the underlying rhythm, the syllable "I" of Irish is held for two units, while the word "Rose" is held five. The rhythm of the song may be synchronized with the underlying beat and represented as follows:

| Words | My | Wild | I | rish Rose | The |
|---|---|---|---|---|---|
| Rhythm of words | s | L | l         s | L | s |
| Underly-ing beat | — | ▬ — — | ▬ — — | ▬ — — | ▬ — — |

| | Sweet est | flow'r that | grows, | You |
|---|---|---|---|---|
| | l         s | l         s | L | s |
| | ▬ — — | ▬ — — | ▬ — — | ▬ — — |

Let us analyze in similar fashion, "Let Me Call You Sweetheart" and "America the Beautiful." See page 38. In each of these the rhythmic pattern of each phrase is exactly the same throughout the song.

Let us compare some of the rhythmic characteristics of these last two songs. Each has an underlying beat which is constant throughout. In each, rhythmic patterns have been formed by combining beats. In "Let Me Call You Sweetheart" two beats have been combined to form a short "l," and three beats to form a long "L," while the final "L" uses six beats. In "America the Beautiful," a long has also been formed by splitting and combining. In measures I and II, beat two has been split and part of it combined with beat one to form a long, while the other portion forms the short. The simple patterns of the measures have been combined to form a complex pattern or phrase. The accents in the complex pattern synchronize with the accents in the underlying beat. In measure III of the waltz an interesting effect has been gained by increasing the length of beat two, so that it tends to be accented, resulting in a tendency to sound syncopated. Notice that in "America the Beautiful" the rhythmic pattern of the phrase begins not on the accent of measure I but on the beat preceding it, which later becomes the last beat of measure IV.

This is also a splendid place to see the use of dotted notes, both in an uneven pattern which results from a splitting and combining within two beats, and also in a combining of an odd number of notes. Since all other types of notes have been derived from a whole note by successively dividing by two, three equal notes combined cannot be expressed as one note but must be expressed as a dotted note. For this reason a whole measure in 3/4 time cannot be written as a whole note, since it is only equal to three quarter notes or a dotted half note.

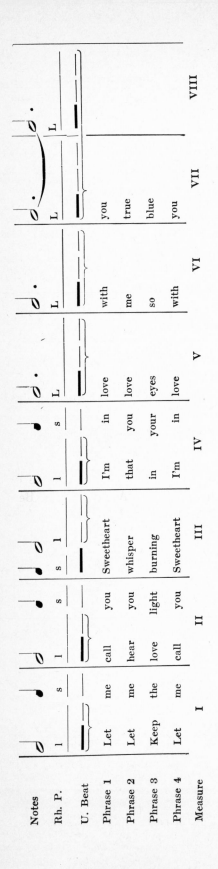

Using an example from 4/4 time we might take "America the Beautiful." In this song the rhythmic pattern of the words in each group of four measures is the same.

**First example (Let Me Call You Sweetheart):**

| | | | | | | | | | | |
|---|---|---|---|---|---|---|---|---|---|---|
| **Notes** | | | | | | | | | | |
| **Rh. P.** | l | s | l | s | s | l | l | s | L | L | L |
| **U. Beat** | | | | | | | | | | | |
| **Phrase 1** | Let | me | call | you | Sweetheart | | I'm | in | love | with | you |
| **Phrase 2** | Let | me | hear | you | whisper | | that | you | love | me | true |
| **Phrase 3** | Keep | the | love | light | burning | | in | your | eyes | so | blue |
| **Phrase 4** | Let | me | call | you | Sweetheart | | I'm | in | love | with | you |
| **Measure** | I | II | | III | | IV | | V | VI | VII | VIII |

**Second example (America the Beautiful):**

| | | | | | | | | | | | | | | | | |
|---|---|---|---|---|---|---|---|---|---|---|---|---|---|---|---|---|
| **Notes** | | | | | | | | | | | | | | | | |
| **Rh. P.** | l | L | s | l | l | L | s | l | l | L | l | l | l | s | L | s |
| **U. Beat** | | | | | | | | | | | | | | | | |
| **Phrase 1** | Oh | beau- | ti- | ful | for | spac- | ious | skies | and | wav- | ing | fields | of | grain, | | For |
| **Phrase 2** | | pur- | ple | moun- | tain | maj- | es- | ties | a- | bove | the | fruit- | ed | plain, | | A- |
| **Phrase 3** | | mer- | i- | ca, | A- | mer- | i- | ca, | God | shed | his | grace | on | thee, | | And |
| **Phrase 4** | | crown | thy | good | with | broth- | er- | hood | from | sea | to | shin- | ing | sea. | | |
| **Measure** | | I | | | | II | | | | III | | | | IV | | |

In music there are many terms such as measure, phrase, time and tempo which we use in connection with dancing; therefore, in discussing music terminology we took up each of these rather fully. In verse, on the other hand, there is a certain amount of terminology such as the words scansion, foot, stanza, which we will rarely use in connection with this text; therefore, it does not seem wise to spend much time on those words. Let us review them hastily, however, so that they may be linked up in our minds with the terminology which we are using. *Scansion* is the term used in connection with analyzing the rhythmic pattern of verse. It is much the same as "keeping time" in music, or analyzing the underlying beat of rhythm and rhythmic movement.

The groupings of the underlying beat, which in music we refer to as the measures, and in general rhythmic terms as the rhythmic pattern of the underlying beat, is in verse called the *foot*. Instead of speaking of part patterns, or time signatures, verse terms them as the iambic foot, trochaic foot, etc. Since a memorizing of such terms will not aid us in our present study let us speak of the underlying beat in verse in terms of two- and three-part groupings.

In music the unit is the *note*, in verse it is the *syllable*. In verse as in prose we have phrases, groups of words, as "at the door," "into the room," but the term phrase as it is used in music is in poetry the thing which is called the *line*. A group of syllables form a simple rhythmic pattern, the *foot*, while a group of *feet* form a complex pattern, the *line*. These are in turn grouped together into stanzas or a composition.

Let us find some derived rhythms in familiar verse. In the nursery rhyme "Little Miss Muffet," the underlying rhythm is built of equal units with a stress every three beats, while the rhythmic pattern of the words is as follows:

| Lit- tle Miss | Muf- fet | sat on a | tuf- fet |
|---|---|---|---|
| s s s | l s | s s s | l s |

| Eat- ing her | curds and | whey | A- |
|---|---|---|---|
| s s s | l s | L | s |

| long came a | spi- der and | sat down be- | side her and |
|---|---|---|---|
| s s s | s s s | s s s | s s s |

| frightened Miss | Muf- fet a- | way |
|---|---|---|
| s    s    s | s    s    s | L |

In analyzing nursery rhymes there is a danger of disagreement, because, as they have been handed down from generation to generation, several versions have resulted. Recalling "Tom, Tom the Piper's Son" from childhood days, it seems to go like this:

| Tom | Tom    the | pip-    er's | son |
|---|---|---|---|
| L | L        s | l        l | L |

| Stole    a | pig    and    a- | way    he | ran        The |
|---|---|---|---|
| l        l | l      s      s | l        l | L          s |

| pig    got | loose    and | stole    a | goose    and |
|---|---|---|---|
| l        l | l        l | l        l | l        l |

| Tom    was | put    in    the | cal-    a- | boose |
|---|---|---|---|
| l        l | l      s      s | l        l | L |

Here, as in the previous rhythms, we find we have an even underlying beat, the accent of which synchronizes with the stress of the rhythm of the words, and which is split or combined in order to form rhythmic patterns. We have complex patterns built of simple ones and combined in such a way as to form a complete whole.

Some of us may have a knowledge of music which will aid us in rhythmic analysis, others may be helped by their love of poetry—but movement should be a form of rhythmic expression common to all. If we have walked, run, or skipped, we have experienced rhythmic activity.

The rhythmic sensation which one has from listening to singing or to the reading of poetry, or from watching someone dance, is entirely different from the sensation of rhythm which one has when he himself sings, reads, or dances. It is readily apparent to those who have tried both that the actual participation in an activity brings the most stimulation and makes a more lasting impression.

Since one of our objectives in developing our "Sense of Rhythm" is the improvement of our physical skills, both in dancing and sports, we will attain our end most quickly through activity.

We cannot experience the sensation of flying by standing on the ground and looking up into the sky at many planes; by sitting at the edge of a tank and watching even the world's greatest divers, we cannot know the joy of a lift from a springboard and a clean cut dive into cool, clear water; we cannot know the feel of a perfect drive in golf by reading an article by Bobby Jones. No more can we sense the rhythmic pattern in movement by reading its analysis. We must first experience the sensation ourselves. Later, by watching others, by talking with them, or by reading description of their experiences, we can enrich our own.

The rest of the material in this text will mean little if we try to absorb it from an armchair. The consciousness of rhythm demands the co-operation of all the conscious muscles of the body, not eyes and ears alone, but legs and arms and body.

Let us begin with the most simple activities, such elementary forms of locomotion as walking, running, skipping, sliding, galloping, leaping, jumping, hopping.

*Walking* may be described as a series of steps, a step being a transference of weight from one foot to another. If one tries this, thinking intently about the fact that a step is a transference of weight from one foot to the other, the result may be a very jerky unnatural walk. It is apparent that walking at its best is more than this, and it is rhythm which makes walking a joyous, pleasurable activity. As has been said before, rhythm will make it automatic so that it goes on without conscious effort; therefore, at the saving of energy.

Let us feel the beat of our pulse; then reproduce that beat through walking. Or, as we walk let us sing some familiar song that has a good marching rhythm, for example: "There's a Long, Long, Trail," "America the Beautiful." The rhythm of the music will carry us along.

If we stop to analyze the rhythm of walking we will find it an even succession of units, coming at a moderate rate of speed. It may be represented by the following line:

———————  ———————  ———————  ———————  ———————

or in terms of relative time values by

L  L  L  L  L  L  L

or in terms of music by quarter notes

Let us all walk but gradually hurry our steps until it is hard to really walk. What activity would be easier? *Running*, of course. If you were ever in a walking race you know that it is hard to walk fast without changing to a run, which is very similar. Running is really only a fast walk, our heels seldom touch the ground, but we transfer the weight from one foot to the other just as in the walk. Even the rhythm is the same, a series of equal units. The only difference is one of tempo, just as in the ticking of a small clock as compared to a large one.

Let us try developing a run, not by increasing the speed of a walk, but by synchronizing the walk and the run. Set a metronome or have a partner clap, or clap yourself, at the same rate of speed at which you like to walk. Now begin to run, taking two steps to each unit of the rhythm for walking. Run, taking three steps to each unit of the walk. When you run in this manner the rhythm of the walks tends to accent one unit of the run, so that your steps feel grouped in twos or threes. You can do this grouping yourself, by taking a heavier step at the same time you hear the metronome or your partner clapping the walk. Rest and clap for your partner while she runs. Try running while your partner walks, taking every second (or every third) running step just as she takes each step of the walk. The rhythm of the run might be represented

as a line        — — — — — — — —        or in terms of

time values, as      s   s   s   s   s   s   s   s      or

by notes, as      ♪ ♪ ♪ ♪ ♪ ♪ ♪ ♪

Try running as you sing "London Bridge is Falling Down."

Next let us *skip*. A good tune for skipping is "The Farmer in the Dell," or "Hunting We Will Go." Why do we choose those songs? Because of the rhythm which is gay and uneven like the rhythm of the skip which is L s L s L s Ls or — — — — — — — —.        Represented by notes the skip may be

♩ ♪ ♩ ♪ ♩ ♪        or it may be        ♪. ♪ ♪. ♪ ♪. ♪

Now that we have the rhythm let us decide what our feet do. Is the skip like the walk or the run? We have already seen that its rhythm is not, for it is uneven, while the walk and run are even. Is there a transference of weight from one foot to the other? There is on the "long," but on the short unit of the rhythm, the weight stays over the same foot. We merely hop. So the skip is made up of a step and a hop, alternating, in a rhythm of

| L | s | L | s | L | s |
|---|---|---|---|---|---|
| step | hop | step | hop | step | hop |

skip        skip        skip

Next let us clap the rhythm of a *gallop*. It is similar to the rhythm of a skip, being made up of a long and a short alternating, L s L s L s L s, etc. Gallop in that rhythm. You may find yourself skipping because the rhythm is the same as a skip rhythm.

What is the essential difference between a skip and a gallop? You may say, "We do not hop." That is true. You will notice that in the gallop one foot stays in the lead but we have a constant transference of weight from one foot to the other. In that respect it is like the run, but the second foot never seems to quite catch up with the first; at least it never passes the first.

Gallop as you sing "Captain Jinks." You can also gallop to the songs used for skipping, since the rhythm of a skip is like a gallop, or you can skip to "Captain Jinks." Try all of them. Try skipping awhile then change to a gallop. Do this with a partner doing the same activity as your partner. Later, do the opposite activity. What other songs can you find which make good accompaniment for skipping or galloping?

How does *sliding* compare with galloping or skipping? It is like galloping in that the second foot never passes the first. Usually we think of sliding as done sideward and with the feet always close to the floor. In rhythm, sliding is the same as skipping or galloping, being L s L s L s, etc.

Try a series of *leaps* and decide whether leaping is like running or skipping in rhythm and in transference of weight. It is not at all like skipping, but very similar to running except that it may be slower, and an effort is made to get up into the air as you leap from one foot to the other.

How do *hopping* and *jumping* differ from leaping? In the *hop* the weight is not transferred from one foot to the other, but stays on the same foot; that is, hopping is a succession of springs from one foot to the same foot. *Jumping* differs from hopping in that the spring is from one or both feet, but the landing is on both feet. As far as the rhythm of hopping or jumping is concerned it is variable. Usually it is even, but it may be uneven. Also, the speed may be slow or fast. Try jumping rope and notice the rhythm. Using a rope, hop on one foot and notice your rhythm.

An analysis of these elementary forms of locomotion is summarized in the following table:

| Activity | Part Pattern | Rhythmic Pattern in Terms of Longs and Shorts and Unevenness | Description of Activity | Speed of Execution |
|---|---|---|---|---|
| Walking | 1 | L./L./L./L./ Even | A series of steps, a step being a transference of weight from one foot to the other | Moderate |
| Hopping | 1 | L./L./ Even | Springing from one foot to the same foot. | Any rate |
| Jumping | 1 | L./L./ Even | Springing from either or both feet and landing on both. | Any rate |
| Leaping | 1 | L./L./L./L./ Even | A series of steps with height and momentum. | Slow |
| Running | 1 | S./S./S./S./ Even | A series of steps with rapid transference of weight. | Moderate or fast |
| Skipping | 2 | L.S./L.S./ Uneven | A step and a hop completed on one foot, then repeated on other. | Moderate |
| Slide | 2 | L.S./L.S./ Uneven | Two steps, one foot is brought up to the other foot and the weight is transferred to it. | Moderate |
| Gallop | 2 | L.S./L.S./ Uneven | Resembles a slide, but differs in execution in that when the transference of weight occurs from rear foot to forward foot, there is a decided knee action. | Fast |

Note: In counting the number of parts to an activity, each activity is considered complete when the same foot pattern is repeated either on the same foot or the opposite foot. The step hop when done evenly is not a true skip; therefore, we will refer to it merely as a step hop. Running, walking, leaping, jumping, and hopping can be done unevenly, but usually are done in even rhythm. A slide done slowly is referred to as a step and close. The term "close" indicates bringing one foot to the other, changing weight.

For Folk Dances and music which may be used in teaching these activities, see chart, page 180.

# CHAPTER V

## THE RHYTHMIC APPROACH IN THE LEARNING AND PERFECTING OF SKILL

Now that a vocabulary of rhythmic terms and the characteristics of rhythm have been discussed, the next step is to find how much these can help one in learning new skills and in perfecting old ones. Let us start with dancing and continue to sports.

At the word dance some of you will settle back in your chair with the old familiar wail, "I'm too awkward to dance. I should have started when I was little." But you have already denied your own statement, when you demonstrated that you could walk, run, skip, and gallop in rhythm. In dancing as in all locomotion there are only a limited number of ways in which you can move using your feet as a support. You can step, hop, or jump. Anything else you do is merely a variation of one of those, a combination of two or three, or a difference in execution or direction. You need not be a Pavlowa or a Ruth St. Denis to enjoy dancing any more than you need to be a Kreisler to enjoy playing the violin, a Caruso to enjoy singing, or a Wordsworth, Shelley, or Keats to enjoy poetry.

It is not the purpose in this chapter to give a course in dancing, even of an elementary type. We only intend to take certain elements which you will find present in Folk Dancing, Clogging, and Interpretative Dancing, and study them through an analysis of their rhythms. The Dance patterns included here are very simple combinations of the elementary forms of locomotion which may be put together into more complex patterns and so be an endless source of enjoyment.

The *Schottische* is a dance pattern which used to be popular with our Fathers and Mothers and their parents when all gathered together for social dancing. It is very frequently used in folk dancing and clogging and in some forms of interpretative dancing. Almost everything about a schottische is in terms of the number four. For example, schottische music is written in 4/4 time, which, as we said above, has an underlying even rhythm of four beats with an accent on the first of every four. Clap such a rhythm, keeping it slow, for 4/4 means that each beat gets the time value of a quarter note or an ordinary walking step. The rhythmic pattern of the schottische is exactly the same as the four beats in a measure of 4/4 music; namely, L L L L.

The step pattern is made up of four parts: a step, close, step, hop. Beginning with the left foot, it is done as follows:

1. Step to the left,
2. Bring the right foot up to the left, transferring the weight,
3. Step left again,
4. Hop left swinging the right leg across in front.

The same thing is then repeated to the right. See Fig. 41, page 194.

One often has a tendency to shorten the last count because a hop does not take long, but if you remember that the schottische is an even rhythm you will be able to do the hop slowly and give to the schottische the slow smoothness which is its characteristic.

When you feel you have the rhythm and co-ordination of the schottische well learned, find some music, either on the victrola or take a song which you can sing which has a definite 4/4 time and try the schottische to music. Remember that the first step in the schottische is done on count "one" of the measure; that is, on the accented beat. All music does not begin with count "one"; some pieces have a note or two before the first accented beat; so before beginning to dance the schottische to music, listen and determine which is the first accent, then start so that the first step of the schottische comes on the accented beat, the first beat of the measure. Take, for example, the song used before to illustrate 4/4 time, "Long, Long Trail." The words of the song begin, "There's a long, long trail awinding." The first accent is on the word "long," not on "there's." Then in dancing the schottische to that music, you do not begin on *There's* but wait and begin on the first *long*.

| There's a | long | long | trail | a | wind | ing | in to the |
| | Step | close | step | hop | Step | close | step | hop |
| | | Schottische | | | | Schottische | |

If you are using a victrola you may find that there is an introduction, then a pause, before the music gets under way. It is better to wait until after the introduction and start the schottische on the first accent after the pause. Some records which have a good schottische rhythm are "Glow-worm," "Dance of the Frowsy Heads."

Perhaps you would like to work out a dance using the schottische. The "Barn Dance for Four," * is fun to do and quite easy. As the name indicates it is planned for four people. The interesting part of the dance is the formations made by the four people. All the feet need to do is two schottisches and four "step hops" and repeat over and over. (A "step hop," as was said before, is done evenly, L L. If done unevenly, L s, the step hop becomes a skip.) If you try two schottisches and four step hops, you will find that the four step hops take exactly the same amount of music (two measures of 4/4) as did the two

* Dancing on the Green—Social Games and Group Dances, by Elson & Trilling—J. B. Lippincott, Publisher.

CHART ANALYZING SIMPLE DANCE PATTERNS

| Name of activity | No. of parts in pattern | Rhythmic pattern in terms of longs and shorts and even or unevenness | Description of activity (step pattern) | Mood | Time of music | Foot pattern according to notes and count of music |
|---|---|---|---|---|---|---|
| Waltz | 3 | L L L  Even | Step-step-close | Slow Smooth | 3 4 | 1 2 3 — Step step close |
| Two-step | 3 | S s L / l s L  Uneven | Step-close-step | Lively | 2 4 | 1 & 2 — Step close step |
| Schottische | 4 | L L L L  Even | Step-close-step-hop | Stately | 4 4 | 1 2 3 4 — Step close step hop |
| Polka | 4 | s l l L  Uneven | Hop-step-close-step | Lively | 2 4 | a 1 & 2 — Hop step close step |
| Mazurka | 3 | L L l  Even | Step-cut-hop | Vigorous | 3 4 | 1 2 3 — Step cut hop |
| Polish Mazurka | 3 | L L L  Even | Leap-stamp-step | Vigorous Heavy | 3 4 | 1 2 3 — Leap stamp step |

schottisches. Before learning the "Barn Dance for Four," do two schottisches and four step hops over until you can dance it without concentrating on it. In other words, it will become automatic, and just as in walking, your feet will be able to dance that pattern without any conscious effort on your part. Your concentration may now be centered upon the group formations and changes.

The "Barn Dance for Three" and "Skating Dance," from the same book are also interesting to use in connection with practicing the schottische. Later similar dances may be created using the schottische as a part of the step pattern.

Other dance skills which may be learned by studying their rhythms are the polka, the waltz, the two-step, and the mazurka. On page 47, in outline form, is an analysis of these patterns. Study this chart and try to work out these patterns. Then turn to Chapter XVI for a more detailed analysis and to Chapter XV * for a list of dances in which these skills are contained.

It is comparatively easy to sense the rhythm of the dance patterns described above. One should be able to feel the rhythmic pattern in the movement of the feet and legs as well as to hear the rhythmic pattern of the music used for dance accompaniment.

The analysis of rhythm in sport skills is more difficult. The athlete is not limited by the regulating influence of music and therefore we see more variety in the rhythmic patterns of sport skills than in dance patterns. Also one finds difficulty in isolating parts of a skill from the whole movement. For example, in pitching baseball, the foot pattern depends a great deal upon the arm and body movement and to consider the foot pattern separately might tend to weaken the skill. There are, however, many skills which possess a rhythmic pattern which may be clearly analyzed, and by attempting to analyze the rhythm of a sport skill, one may not only aid herself in more quickly learning a new skill, but by following the rhythm of an expert one may be able to improve a skill which has already been acquired.

The *crawl* stroke in swimming is one upon which most experts agree. Therefore in the crawl one may find a rhythmic pattern which is used almost universally. It is necessary here, as in all sport skills, to designate the part of the body which is to be watched in analyzing the rhythmic pattern. Take, for example, the leg movement. Most swimmers use a six count leg movement with a stronger kick on the first of every three. Then the rhythmic pattern carried by the legs in swimming the crawl may be analyzed much as the underlying beat of a waltz.

$$\text{s} \quad \text{s} \quad \text{s} \quad \text{s} \quad \text{s}$$

During these six leg movements, each arm completes two circles; on the first three counts the left arm pulls downward as the right arm lifts out of the water and reaches forward, and on the second three counts the right arm pulls downward as the left arm lifts out of water and reaches forward. Since the

* See page 180.

stronger part of each arm circle is the downward pull, we have the sensation of following an even rhythm L L with the arms while the feet simultaneously carry the six counts *s s s s s s*. We might then analyze the crawl as two rhythms synchronized.

| Arms | L | | L | |
|------|---|---|---|---|
| Legs | *s* *s* | *s* | *s* *s* | *s* |

The writer has found it successful to swim the crawl stroke to waltz music, with the legs following the underlying beat as the arms pull on the accent.

In learning to breathe with the crawl stroke the rhythm is important. For example, if the left arm is pulling on counts one, two, three, it is recovering on counts four, five and six. The breath may be exhaled into the water on counts one, two and three. As the left arm lifts to recover, the head may be turned to the side so that a breath may be taken through the mouth on counts four, five and six.

The complete rhythm as analyzed above would be:

| Arms | L<br>(Left) | L<br>(Right) | L<br>(Left) | L<br>(Right) |
|------|-------------|--------------|-------------|--------------|
| Legs | *s* *s* *s*<br>R L R | *s* *s* *s*<br>L R L | *s* *s* *s*<br>R L R | *s* *s* *s*<br>L R L |
| Breathing | Exhale | Inhale | Exhale | Inhale |
| Underlying Beat | 1 2 3 | 4 5 6 | 1 2 3 | 4 5 6 |

The *back crawl* may be analyzed in the same rhythm.

The *elementary back stroke* has been taught to beginners with success by analyzing it as an even four-count pattern as follows. The initial position is that of floating on the back, arms resting down at sides.

| Arms | Bend | Stretch<br>sideward | Pull to sides | Rest |
|------|------|---------------------|---------------|------|
| Legs | Rest | Spread | Close | Rest |
| Breathing | Inhale | Exhale | s l o w l y | |
| Underlying Beat | 1 | 2 | 3 | 4 |

To beginning swimmers the author analyzes the *side stroke* as follows: The initial position is floating on right side with the legs together, left arm at side and right arm extended above head.

| Right arm | Pull down | Bend | Stretch ahead | Rest |
|---|---|---|---|---|
| Left arm | Rest at side | Bend | Pull to side | Rest |
| Right leg | Rest | Reach back | Pull together | |
| Left leg | Rest | Reach ahead | | Rest |
| Breathing | Inhale | Exhale | s  l  o  w  l  y | |
| Underlying Beat | 1 | 2 | 3 | 4 |

In *bowling* and *tossing* we may find several rhythmic patterns, those of the feet, arms and hand. In the *toss*, as in pitching horseshoes or tossing rings or bean bags, we frequently see the following rhythms. The right arm swings back and forward in an even pendulum swing. As the arm swings backward the knees bend and then extend so that the body is lifted on the toes. As the arm swings forward the body falls forward and the left foot takes a step ahead on completion of the swing. The rhythm in this form of tossing is:

| | | | |
|---|---|---|---|
| Arm | L<br>Swing back | | L<br>Swing forward |
| Leg | 1<br>Bend knees. | s<br>Rise on toes. | L<br>Step forward on left. |

In one of the common forms of *bowling*, the step pattern is three steps in uneven rhythm, l s L; the arm pattern is an even pendulum swing, L L, and if one watches closely, the rhythm of the hand may be seen as s L L. These rhythmic patterns synchronize as follows:

| Foot pattern | | l | | s L | | |
|---|---|---|---|---|---|---|
| Arm pattern | | L | | L | | |
| Hand pattern | s | L | | L | | |
| Underlying beat | 6 | 1 | 2 | 3 | 4 | 5 | 6 |

The first short of the hand pattern is a slight lift upward which the bowler makes preparatory to the backward swing. As the right arm and hand swing backward carrying the ball the bowler takes a long step forward left, followed by a short step right. The final step forward left is taken as the right arm swings forward releasing the ball close to the floor.

Frequently we see a *scissor high jump* done in the following rhythm, l s l s L. The first three units represent the approach to the jumping standard. The last two units represent the landing. If the approach is taken in a diagonal line from the right end of the bar, the foot pattern begins on the left foot and is three steps in uneven rhythm. As the bar is reached on the third step the right leg swings over the bar, the left is lifted and the landing on the opposite side of the bar is made on the right and left foot in quick succession. It may be counted to an underlying beat of six.

| | l | s | l | s | L | |
|---|---|---|---|---|---|---|
| Feet | Left | Rt | Left | Rt | Left | |
| | | approach | | landing | | |
| Underlying beat | 1 | 2 3 | 4 5 | 6 | 1 | |

Many other skills may be similarly analyzed. By such an analysis, including a study of the relative time values of the various movements with particular attention to the proper placing of the stress, one may have more consistent success, rather than an occasional success among many failures.

By watching an expert in a skill which one wishes to learn, one may be able to catch the rhythm in which he moves. By trying the same rhythm one may be able to do the skill well, not the first time perhaps, but surely sooner than by a more or less blind trial and error.

We all know that education today is based on the objective of developing better citizens, people who contribute something to life. The people who are more sought after are those with a real aim in life and with a personality which will carry them to success. Personality is the big thing we strive for. Everyone desires it. We are eager to develop that side of our lives. We cannot do it, either mentally or physically, without rhythm, for as Rugg * has said, "Life and Character are best conceived as a harmony of rhythms. If physical education is to aid development of character it must obey, first, the laws within these rhythms themselves, and, secondly, the laws of the relations between these rhythms. The feeling of possessing power and poise, the feeling of the ability to control and direct our power is a known requisite for continued efficiency and success."

* Co-author of "The Child Centered School." Quotation used with permission of author.

# CHAPTER VI

## SUGGESTED LESSON PLANS AND TESTS FOR A COURSE IN RHYTHM

The following lesson plans are given as a suggestion of a term's work in rhythm. It is not expected that the teacher follow this plan, but that she use it merely as a guide for planning her own lessons. The methods and material used will vary with each group of students depending upon their ages, their previous training, their interests, the time available, and the ultimate aims and objectives of each particular course.

### LESSON I

Equipment—None.
Objective—To introduce subject and induce interest of student.
Content—Informal discussion (with student participating) of
    (a) Universality of Rhythm.
    (b) Sense of Rhythm.
Assignment—Ask students to bring to class a list of things which possess
    rhythm.

### LESSON II

Equipment—Blackboard and chalk.
    Illustrations of rhythm in design, as example—Chapter on Rhythm—*Art in Everyday Life*—Goldstein.
Objective—To further emphasize universality of rhythm and to encourage observation of its presence.
Content—(a) From student contributions compile list of things which possess
    rhythm. Classify these according to visual, auditory, and kinesthetic
    rhythms, or design, sound, movement.
    (b) Discuss rhythm in design bringing out fact that rhythm results from the movement of the eye. Use example as broken line or scallop.

    (c) Show illustrations of rhythm in design using examples from architecture, painting, lace, dress, arrangement of furniture, etc.
Assignment—Ask students to bring in picture or object possessing good
    rhythm, with explanation of why it is good.

## Lesson III

Equipment—Blackboard and Chalk
> Tom-tom (drum or tambourine may be used)
> Metronome

Objective—To introduce auditory rhythms.
> To introduce characteristics of rhythm, discussing
>> Unit
>> Stress

Content—(a) Accept assignments of previous lesson and discuss examples if not too many.  Otherwise pick out best and show to class.

(b) Explain unit in auditory rhythm.

(c) Demonstrate same through
  1. Clapping
  2. Beating on drum
  3. Listening to metronome
  4. Listening to watches
  5. Stamping feet.

(d) Explain stress.

(e) Demonstrate stress through
  1. Clapping
  2. Beating on drum
  3. Clapping with metronome
  4. Stamping feet.

(f) Using various speeds, but an even beat, group units into twos, threes, fours, fives, sixes and eights by stress, using any of above media.

(g) Diagram rhythms on board and ask class to duplicate through clapping or stamping.
(In using dotted line, emphasize that length of line indicates relative length of time assigned to that unit, for example

$$ 1 \quad\quad 2 \quad 3 \quad\quad 4 $$

would indicate four beats or claps, the first and third being held twice as long as the second and fourth.
If it is desired to stress units 1 and 3, indicate by a heavier line, as

When using a scalloped line to indicate rhythmic units, let length of scallop indicate time value, while height represents stress; namely,

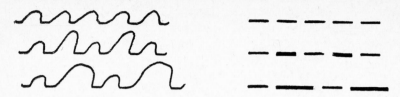

(h) Have students diagram rhythms on board or paper and clap for class.

## Lesson IV

Equipment—Same as Lesson III.
Objective—To introduce rhythm in movement.
Content—(a) Review parts of previous lesson.
    (b) Ask class to take rhythms with feet, either walking or running, each step representing one unit with stress obtained through stamping.
        (1) Walk grouping steps in twos by stressing always with same foot. Group steps in threes, fours, sixes, and eights.
        (2) Same running. Use accompaniment on tom-tom to keep steps regular.
    (c) Take rhythms which have been written on board, first clapping, then in running or walking.
    (d) Ask different members of class to beat rhythms on tom-toms; then let class clap these and reproduce through running and walking.

## Lesson V

Equipment—Same as before.
Objective—To aid students in analyzing rhythm by use of verse.
Content—(a) Beat rhythms and ask class to reproduce them through running and walking. (Step patterns.)
    (b) Suggest familiar nursery rhyme. Ask class to clap the rhythm of the words. Then reproduce this rhythm through running and walking.
    (c) Let class suggest rhymes. Repeat (b).
    (d) Divide class in groups of 5 to 8 and ask each group to work out foot pattern for any nursery rhyme which they choose. After several minutes' practice, let each group perform for rest of class. They may chant the rhyme, and one member of group may beat it on tom-tom.
Assignment—Students may be asked to prepare step pattern for poetry and bring it to class.

## Lesson VI

Objective—To aid student in analyzing rhythm and phrasing by use of song.

Content—(a) Follow Lesson V using familiar songs. Ask class to clap and respond to the rhythm of the words with an appropriate step pattern, and later to respond to phrasing by a change of direction or a change of activity.

(b) Teach formations from Folk Dancing, such as "Grand Right and Left" or "Arming," in order to give the class practice in responding to phrasing. If music is available, teach the Virginia Reel, or similar dance, paying attention to phrasing.

## Lesson VII

Objective—To give class practice in analyzing rhythms.

Content—(a) Explain relative time values of units, and use of terms long and short.

(b) Beat simple rhythms and have class reproduce in terms of longs and shorts. Let each one test her own accuracy by writing on board or paper. Correct each immediately and repeat until class has had good practice.

(c) Ask each student to make up a rhythm, giving it first in terms of longs and shorts, then reproducing it through clapping. Let class judge accuracy.

## Lesson VIII

Objective—To give class practice in analyzing rhythms.

Content—Explain use of capital L, small l, capital S, small s, for indicating relative values of units; then proceed as in Lesson VII using more difficult patterns.

## Lesson IX

Objective—To aid class in analyzing the elementary forms of locomotion in terms of rhythmic pattern.

Content—(a) Explain such terms as pattern, step-pattern, rhythmic pattern, even and uneven rhythm.

(b) Define and have class demonstrate ability to step, hop, jump, close.

(c) Ask class to walk in a class rhythm—then to clap rhythm of walk. Discuss and agree on rhythmic pattern and step pattern of walking.

(d) Same as (c) with running, leaping, sliding, galloping, skipping.

## LESSON X

Equipment—Metronome and tom-tom.
Objective—To help student recognize the underlying beat.
Content—(a) Explain underlying beat, comparing it to the regularity of a clock ticking, heart beating.  Let each student listen to her watch or feel her pulse; then reproduce the rhythm.
    (b) Beat uneven rhythms on tom-tom while class claps an even beat.
    (c) Let class clap uneven rhythms while metronome carries underlying beat.
    (d) Have class clap and produce uneven rhythms by leaving out certain counts in an even rhythm.  Have one part of class continue the even beat while the rest clap the uneven.
    (e) Group students in twos.  Let one walk, while the other skips, slides or gallops.  The one walking is the underlying beat.

## LESSON XI

Objective—Same as Lesson X.
Content—(a) Explain grouping of underlying beat through stress.  Let class clap underlying beats, grouped in twos, then in threes, later fours, and sixes.
    (b) Let them walk and run in these rhythms stamping the accent.
    (c) Let them clap these underlying beats as instructor or student beats uneven rhythms.
    (d) Let one run in three-part underlying beat while partner skips, slides or gallops.
    (e) Using nursery rhymes, clap the underlying beat.  Let one group clap the underlying beat while other claps rhythm of the words as all chant the rhyme.
    (f) Same as (e) using familiar songs.
    (g) Let students work out step patterns of rhymes or songs, partner carrying underlying beat with a walk or run while other carries rhythmic pattern of words with steps, hops, and jumps.

## LESSON XII

Equipment—Number of song books or pieces of music.  They need not be the same.
Objective—To familiarize student with music terminology.
Content—(a) Explain the note, kinds of notes, rests, measures, time signature and tempo, asking class to identify each on sheet of music.
    (b) Comparing usual length of a quarter note to the length in time of a walking step, have class walk quarter notes, half and

whole notes and run eighth, sixteenth, and thirty-second notes.
(The last will be difficult to do except by whirling.)

(c) Write combinations of notes on board, asking class to clap the
rhythmic pattern and to produce appropriate step patterns.

(d) Practice clapping underlying beat as occurring in measures.

(e) Teach method which many musical directors use in beating underlying beat of music—

Example—2/4—right arm swings down on beat one, and across
body on beat two, thus

**Lt   2   1   Rt**

4/4—right arms swings down on 1, across body on
2, out to side on 3 and up on 4, thus

3/4—right arm swings down on 1, out to side on
2, up on 3, thus

(f) Practice this method of beating the underlying beat while
singing familiar song.

(g) Let one group sing while others try to determine time signature.

### LESSONS XIII AND XIV

Equipment—Victrola or Piano

Music—Good 4/4 rhythm as "Dancing on the Green"
"Dance of the Buttercups."

(If unable to have music let class sing some song in 4/4 time as "There's
a Long, Long Trail.")

Objective—To teach the schottische.

Content—(a) Have class clap a four-part even rhythm slowly.

(b) Clap same in time with music.

(c) Explain that the schottische is a four-part pattern—step pattern is step, close, step, hop—rhythmic pattern is LLLL.

Let each one try to develop the schottische.

Choose those who are doing it correctly, and let them teach others.  Let all practice with count, with tom-tom beat, and with music.

(d) Teach step hop in similar way, bringing out that four step hops equal time value of two schottisches.

(e) Help students work out dance using schottische.  Good dances for this purpose are—

"Dancing on the Green" for 4 people.

"Barn Dance for Three" for 3 people.

"Skating Dance" for 2 people.

(All may be found in Social Games and Group Dances, by Elsom and Trilling.)

(f) Explain how schottische corresponds in rhythm to the underlying beat in 4/4 music.

## Lessons XV and XVI

Equipment—Same as Lesson XIII.

Objective—To teach the polka.

Content—(a) With students in circle, all skip in unison—change to a gallop or slide.

(b) Gallop with right foot in lead, change to left in lead on signal.

(c) Let signal come more and more frequently until the class is changing on every other gallop.

(d) Let class analyze their foot pattern and rhythmic pattern. They are step–close–step–hop and long–short–long–short ( l   s   l   s )

(e) Practice same starting with a hop.  Beat on tom-tom; later use music such as "The Hatter."

(f) When class can do "hop-step-close-step" in rhythm s l s l, ( s   l   s   l   ) explain that this is almost a polka.

Analyze polka as "hop-step-close-step" in rhythm s l l L ( s   l   l   L   )

Let class clap rhythm; then from that develop a true polka.

(g) Practice Polka at different speeds, slowly, for accuracy and fast for gaiety.

(h) Teach or develop dances which use the polka.  (As—Swedish Clap Dance, see folk dancing.)*

(i) Explain how a two-part underlying beat is split to form the rhythmic pattern of the polka.

* See page 180.

## Lesson XVII

Equipment—Music.

   2/4 music similar to that used for polka.

Objective—To teach the two-step.

Content—Let class develop the two-step from the polka by leaving out the
   hop.

Polka               Hop   step   cl   step   Hop   step   cl   step

Two-step                      Step   cl   step        Step   cl   step

## Lesson XVIII

Equipment—Waltz music—slow and regular as "Dreamy Melody," "Let Me
   Call You Sweetheart."

Objective—To teach the waltz.

Content—(a)  Play or sing a waltz and clap the underlying beat.

   (b)  Sitting or standing, sway with each measure.

   (c)  Walk with the music or to a tom-tom, accenting count one by
       bending knee.

   (d)  Teach waltz, standing in back right hand corner of an imagi-
       nary square or one drawn on floor.
           Emphasize forward or back step on count "one," always a
           step sideward on count "two" and a close on count "three."
       (Remind class that on a *close* the weight is shifted.  Many
           students make the mistake of bringing one foot up to other
           without shifting weight.)

   (e)  After each individual has mastered the fundamental waltz step,
       try in partners, one stepping forward right on count "one,"
       other stepping back left.

   (f)  Teach waltzing with a turn or balance and other combinations.

## Lesson XIX

Equipment—Music for mazurka.

   "Polish Dance"—Scharwenka.

   "Polka Mazurka."

   (Records must be played slowly.)

Objective—To aid student in recognizing mazurka music.

Content—(a)  Beat or clap 3/4 time.

   (b)  Explain to class, stress produced through length of temporal
       value of unit.  Clap uneven rhythms, noting that the stress
       falls on the longer unit.

(c) Explain producing stress by lengthening unit or shortening preceding unit—

    (1) Produce stress on count "two" of 3/4 beat, by leaving out count "three."

$$1 \quad 2 \quad 3 \quad 1 \quad 2 \quad\quad 1 \quad\quad 2$$

    (2) Produce stress on count "two" of 3/4 beat by splitting count "one."

$$1 \quad 2 \quad 3 \quad 1 \text{ \& } 2 \quad 3 \quad 1 \text{ \& } 2 \quad 3$$

(d) Have one group clap a 3/4 underlying beat while others clap each of above rhythms.

(e) Compare this to mazurka in music.

    Accompaniment carries an even three-part pattern. Melody carries an uneven pattern with stress on count "two."

(f) Clap the following rhythm:

$$S \quad L \quad\quad S \quad\quad L \quad s \quad s \quad l \quad l \quad s \quad s \quad l \quad\quad l$$

and then play first part of Scharwenka's Polish dance. Let class identify above rhythm in music.

(g) Play other mazurkas; then alternate with waltzes or other music, and let class try to recognize mazurka music.

### Lesson XX

Equipment—Mazurka music—slow.

Objective—To teach the mazurka foot pattern.

Content—(a) Work on fundamental mazurka step—"step, cut, hop"—in rhythm L L L. Let class adapt step pattern to music.

    (b) Use same, changing direction, with three stamps in place.

    (c) Work out simple dance using mazurka step.

### Lesson XXI

Equipment—Tom-tom.

    Number of records in different time.

Objective—To review work of past lessons.

Content—(a) Play records and have class name time signature, clap underlying beat, clap rhythm of melody, or name appropriate step-pattern.

    (b) Play in succession various records appropriate for dance patterns and let class do those which fit the music.

    (c) Review the dances taught in class.

## Lesson XXII

Final examination on material in course.   (See suggestions for testing.)

SUGGESTIONS FOR TESTING ABILITY TO SENSE RHYTHM IN MOVEMENT AND SOUND, AND VISUAL PATTERN

A.  Practical examination on skill.*
1.  Execute the following series of movements in the rhythm designated:
    a. Leap, leap, run, run, run, leap, leap, jump.  l l s s s l l L
    b. Skip,skip,run,run,run,step.  l s l s s s s L
    c. Step,step,skip,step,skip,skip,step,step.  L L l s L l s l s L L
    d. Hop,step,step,hop,step,step,hop,step,hop,step,hop,step.
       s L l s L l s l s l s L
    e. Hop,step,hop,hop,step,hop,hop,step,hop,step,hop,step.
       s L l s L l s l s l s L
2.  Build other step patterns to the following rhythms:
    a. L L l s L
    b. l s l s L L
    c. s s s s s s l s L
    d. L L l s L l s l s L L
    e. l s L l s L l s s s s L L
3.  Execute the following combinations to 4 measures of music which is written in 4/4 time:
    a. 2 schottisches, 2 step hops and 1 schottische.
    b. 1 schottische, 4 steps and 4 polkas.
    c. 1 schottische, 2 two-steps, 1 schottische and 2 polkas.
    d. 1 schottische, 2 polkas, 1 schottische and 2 polkas.
    e. Combine a, b, c, and d, and do all in succession, and repeat, using 32 measures of music.
4.  Do the following to 4 measures of waltz music:
    a. Four waltz steps in place (in a square).
    b.   "      "      "   forward.
    c.   "      "      "   backward.
    d.   "      "      "   turning.
    e. Combine a, b, c, and d, and do all in succession and repeat, using 32 measures of music.
5.  Using 4 measures of mazurka music do
    a. 3 mazurkas and 3 stamps (to right).
    b. 3 mazurkas and 3 stamps (to left).
    c. Step, leap, step, and repeat three times (four times in all).

* Should be revised according to age and amount of training, or to accommodate size of class.

d. Step, leap, step; step, leap, step; six running steps (to one measure); step, jump.

e. Combine a, b, c, d, and do all in succession, to 16 measures of music.

B. Suggestions for written examinations to test knowledge of terminology and ability to sense rhythm.*

I. Fundamentals of Rhythm—Mid-semester Examination

Name _____

Instructor _____

Section _____

1. Three pieces of music will be played. For each, underscore the activity which would best fit the music, and in the second column indicate by a circle around correct answer, whether you feel an accent every 2, 3, or 4 beats.

|  Activity | Accent |
|-----------|--------|
| a. Walk, Run, Skip | 2, 3, 4 |
| b. Walk, Run, Skip | 2, 3, 4 |
| c. Walk, Run, Skip | 2, 3, 4 |

2. Three records will be played. For each one state the number of phrases which were played and the number of strong accents within each phrase.

a. _____ phrases        _____ accents within phrases.

b. _____ phrases        _____ accents within phrases.

c. _____ phrases        _____ accents within phrases.

3. Five records will be played. After each record, circle the number 2 if you hear a strong accent every two beats; the 3 if there is an accent every three beats; the 4 if the accent comes every four beats. After each, indicate by a circle around the proper word, whether the beats were slow or fast.

a. 2 3 4        slow, fast

b. 2 3 4        slow, fast

c. 2 3 4        slow, fast

d. 2 3 4        slow, fast

e. 2 3 4        slow, fast

4. Five records will be played—indicate whether it is a waltz, two-step or fox-trot by encircling the proper word.

* These written exams should be revised and shortened, according to age of student and amount of training. The mid-semester examination may be used early in the term to test the student's previous knowledge for the purpose of estimating accomplishment during the term's work, or it may be used as a means of classifying students.

    a. Waltz, Two-step, Fox-trot.
    b. Waltz, Two-step, Fox-trot.
    c. Waltz, Two-step, Fox-trot.
    d. Waltz, Two-step, Fox-trot.
    e. Waltz, Two-step, Fox-trot.

5. Five rhythms will be beat on the tom-tom. Indicate whether that rhythm corresponds to the rhythm of the sound of your feet in walking, running, skipping, galloping or sliding. Circle the correct answer. (Each beat represents each time one of your feet touches the floor.)

    a. Walking, running, skipping, galloping, sliding.
    b. Walking, running, skipping, galloping, sliding.
    c. Walking, running, skipping, galloping, sliding.
    d. Walking, running, skipping, galloping, sliding.
    e. Walking, running, skipping, galloping, sliding.

6. Is the rhythm of each of the following rhythmic patterns even or uneven—that is, do the beats come in an even succession of equal intervals, or are some of the intervals longer than others? Circle the correct answer.

    a. Even, uneven.
    b. Even, uneven.
    c. Even, uneven.
    d. Even, uneven.
    e. Even, uneven.

7. A beat will be carried on the tom-tom with an accent (strong beat) at regular intervals. Does this beat occur within every two, three, four, five or six beats? Circle the correct answer.

    a. 1, 2, 3, 4, 5, 6
    b. 1, 2, 3, 4, 5, 6
    c. 1, 2, 3, 4, 5, 6
    d. 1, 2, 3, 4, 5, 6
    e. 1, 2, 3, 4, 5, 6

8. Six rhythms will be beaten on the tom-tom. Write down each rhythm in dots and dashes—using a dash (—) for a beat which has a long time interval, and a dot (-) for a beat which is short. As an example, the correct answer to the first is given.

    a. —— - —— - —— - ————
    b.
    c.
    d.
    e.
    f.

II.  Fundamentals of Rhythm—Final Examination

Name _____

Instructor _____

Section _____

A.  Check at left of each column all of the correct parts of sentences.

1.  The methods of locomotion of uneven rhythm are:
a.  skipping
b.  sliding
c.  galloping
d.  waltz
e.  two-step
f.  schottische

2.  In the waltz the feet come together on the
a.  first count of the measure
b.  second count of the measure
c.  third count of the measure
d.  fourth count of the measure

3.  The schottische is
a.  faster than the polka
b.  slower than the polka

4.  The schottische is a
a.  two-part pattern
b.  three-part pattern
c.  four-part pattern

5.  The rhythm of the schottische is
a.  long, long, long
b.  long, long, long, long
c.  long, short, long, short

6.  The number of measures in a phrase is most often a multiple of
a.  two
b.  three
c.  five

7.  In doing a series of skips, if the first skip is started on the right foot, the second skip will start on the
a.  right foot
b.  left    "

8.  The true two-step is done in
a.  even rhythm
b.  uneven rhythm

9.  The rhythm of a skip is
a.  even
b.  uneven

10.  Waltz music is written in
a.  4/4 time
b.  3/4 time
c.  2/4 time
d.  6/8 time

11.  The waltz is a
a.  two-part pattern
b.  three-part pattern
c.  four-part pattern

12.  The polka is a
a.  two-part pattern
b.  three-part pattern
c.  four-part pattern

13.  3/4 time indicates that there are
a.  three beats in a measure
b.  four beats in a measure
c.  six beats in a measure
d.  eight beats in a measure

14. In listening to music one judges time by listening for
    a. accents
    b. melody
    c. phrasing

15. A rhythm made up of all short equal values is
    a. always even
    b. always uneven
    c. varies

16. The tempo of leaping is
    a. slower than running
    b. faster than running
    c. the same as running

17. A complete waltz pattern is taken to
    a. one measure of waltz time
    b. two measures of waltz time
    c. three measures of waltz time

18. A waltz is
    a. smoother than a mazurka
    b. faster than a mazurka
    c. more vigorous than a mazurka

19. The following is done to 3/4 time
    a. schottische
    b. mazurka
    c. polka

20. In listening to music one may sense
    a. only one rhythm
    b. only two rhythms
    c. several rhythms

21. A change in direction may be used to indicate
    a. the accent of the measure
    b. the underlying beat
    c. the end of a phrase

B. 1. Place at the right of the name of the activity the number of the rhythm and the letter indicating the correct step pattern.

| | Rhythm | Step Pattern |
|---|---|---|
| Skipping | _____ | _____ |
| Sliding | _____ | _____ |
| Waltz | _____ | _____ |
| Mazurka | _____ | _____ |
| Polka | _____ | _____ |
| Schottische | _____ | _____ |
| Two-step | _____ | _____ |

| Rhythm | | Step Pattern | |
|---|---|---|---|
| 1. | s l l L | a. | Step close step hop |
| 2. | L s | b. | Step close step |
| 3. | L L L | c. | Step step close |
| 4. | s L s L | d. | Step hop hop |
| 5. | L L L L | e. | Step step hop |
| 6. | L L | f. | Step hop |
| 7. | S s L | g. | Hop step close step |
| 8. | L s L s | h. | Step close hop |
| 9. | l s L | i. | Hop step step |
| 10. | S S S | j. | Step close |

(NOTE: A step is a transference of weight from one foot to another. The step being taken ahead, or the moving foot may come up to other—that is termed "close" or "together." The moving foot may slide along the floor or be lifted off.)

2.  Listen to the following music and write the activity which it suggests

    1.                                    6.
    2.                                    7.
    3.                                    8.
    4.                                    9.
    5.                                    10.

3.  Listen to the following music and tell whether it is a slow or a fast 2/4, 4/4, 3/4, 6/8.

    slow, fast   2/4 4/4 3/4 6/8              slow, fast   2/4 4/4 3/4 6/8
    1._____  _____        6._____  _____
    2._____  _____        7_____  _____
    3._____  _____        8._____  _____
    4._____  _____        9._____  _____
    5._____  _____        10._____  _____

4.  Listen to the following music and tell how many accents occur in each phrase.

    _____ accents in a phrase.

5.  Listen to the following music and tell how many phrases occur in the amount played.

    _____ phrases were played

6.  Write name of activity done by demonstrator.

    1                 3                 5
    2                 4                 6

7.  Write in terms of longs and shorts the rhythms of these step patterns.

    1                 3                 5
    2                 4                 6

8.  Write in terms of longs and shorts the rhythms heard.

    1                 3                 5
    2                 4                 6

9.  Write in terms of longs and shorts the rhythm of the following demonstrated sport techniques.  Indicate the accent by an oblique line above the part on which the accent falls.

    1           3           5           7           9
    2           4           6           8           10

The following Victor records have been used in teaching rhythmic activities. (For others, see page 180—also Victor Educational Catalogue, sections on Rhythms for Children, and Folk Dancing.)

Schottische
19907—Schottische
20992—Cshebogar
35922—Glow-worm
20416—The Secret

Waltz—slow
19907—The Ripple
19910—Varsovienne
20162—Brahms Waltz

Waltz Run
20151—Norwegian Mt. March
21938—Skaters, Waltz
6617—Valse de Fleurs

Mazurka
19776—Odessa-Polka Mazurka
20203—Polish Dance
31M—Kuiawaik

Changes in Tempo
20432—Carrousel

Polka
19909—Heel toe polka
19909—Seaside polka
20432—Kinderpolka
20450—Klappdans

Slides, skips and gallops
20151—Pop Goes the Weasel
20736—Camp of Gypsies
20736—Skipping
22162—Wild Horseman
20444—Black Nag
20432—Carrousel

Walking
20802—Country Gardens
35805—Stars and Stripes
35804—Soldiers' Chorus

Phrasing
20151—Pop Goes the Weasel
20151—Norwegian Mt. March
20447—Virginia Reels

For additional reading on Rhythm see the following:

Play in Education (Chap. 21, Rhythm and Life)—Joseph Lee.

Psychology of Musical Talent (Chapter V. Sense of Rhythm)—C. E. Seashore.

The Child Centered School (Chapter on Rhythm)—Rugg and Shumaker.

Creative Activities in Physical Education—Olive Horrigan.

Art in Everyday Life (Chapter on Rhythm)—Goldstein.

Eurhythmics, Art, and Education—Dalcroze.

The Importance of Being Rhythmic—Pennington.

For other material, Rhythm in Nature, Rhythm in Speech, Rhythm in Music, Psychology of Rhythm, etc., see the Readers' Guide, Encyclopædia Britannica, or the card index of any Library.

# CREATIVE DANCE

*Courtesy of The Ball Studios, Corvallis, Oregon*

# CHAPTER VII

## CREATIVE DANCE, ITS AIMS AND OBJECTIVES

Modern creative dance is the most valuable form of dancing because of its physiological and psychological effect on the participant. Since it stresses the use of natural body movements for the expression of emotion, it results in a fine responsive body, full of strength and vitality. Since emphasis is placed upon the creation of dances by the participant it stimulates originality. Used with music of great artists and with reference to art form in general, creative dance will develop in the student an appreciation of those finer, more idealistic things in life which tend in this busy rush and whirl to be crowded out of our environment. Creative dance may be so presented as to be truly educational and to be effective in producing finer women, with an intelligent, capable attitude toward life.

The method of presentation and the aims of the work will vary slightly with each instructor depending upon her personality, her training, and the group with whom she is working. The objectives in general, however, will be similar to those stated below.

### OBJECTIVES OF COURSE IN CREATIVE DANCE

To aid the student in acquiring the following:
1. Attitudes
    a. An appreciation of the human body as an instrument for the expression of beauty and emotion.
    b. An appreciation of good music, developed by the use of music from the works of great composers.
    c. An appreciation of the value of rhythm and its place in music and dancing.
    d. An appreciation of the value of artistic effort in everyday life.
    e. Group consciousness and constructive self-consciousness.
2. Knowledge of
    a. The structure and use of the body in motion
        (1) Movements of the trunk; flexion, extension, rotation, circumduction.
        (2) Movement of the legs
            (a) Independent of the rest of the body, as in walking, running, leaping, hopping, skipping, galloping, sliding.
            (b) Resulting from movements in other parts of the body.

(3) Movements of the arms, control coming from shoulder or trunk, resulting in strong natural movements of the arms without artificiality.

b. Tempo, pitch, mood, and rhythmic form of music through its analysis for use in the dance.

c. Common laws of art in terms of line, balance, symmetry, rhythm, tone and color.

d. Use of creative dancing in a public performance developed as a result of class work, and in which all students are given opportunity of participation.

e. Brief history of the dance with

    (1) An appreciation of the difference in various forms of the dance, especially between ballet and modern creative dance.*

    (2) A knowledge of outstanding leaders in the field of dancing, as Isadora Duncan, Ruth St. Denis, Margaret H'Doubler, Martha Graham, Mary Wigman, Harald Kreutzberg, and others.

3. Skill

a. Control of the body in rhythmic execution of all forms of locomotion and simple dance combinations, as polka, mazurka, schottische, waltz.

b. Ability to move by localization of movement in certain parts of the body with a controlled relaxation of the rest of the body.

    Examples: Turn with shoulder lead
                Turn with leg lead
                Lifts of body initiated by hip movement
                Controlled falls

c. Ability to respond to

    (1) Certain emotions stimulated through music.
    Examples: Walking—expressing heroism, joy, depression, dignity.
                Running—expressing joy, competition, fear.

    (2) Changes in tempo and pitch.

d. Ability to execute dance studies of both a lyrical and dramatic type, progressing from simple patterns for group work to more difficult studies subject to individual interpretation and execution.

e. Ability to create and present before the class a simple, original dance composition which shows good choice in music, with appropriate interpretation of mood through well-controlled movement.

* Elements of the Free Dance, Seldon, A. S. Barnes.

# CHAPTER VIII

## THE BODY—AN INSTRUMENT OF EXPRESSION

In song we have the voice, in music we have the piano, violin or other instrument, in art we have the pen or the brush, while in dancing we have only the body through which to express our emotions. We may dress it in elaborate or simple costumes, but in either case, it is the body and its movements which speak in a language which all races understand.

It is important that a beautiful, supple body be developed, one which is neither too thin nor too heavy. Previous to dance training girls are frequently poorly poised and stiff. This should not discourage them. In truth, they need dancing more than the girl with a natural grace, for it is not the original material but the product in which they should be most interested. Many large students believe they cannot dance because of their size. This is not true. It is their strength, flexibility, and co-ordination which control their ability to dance. Often we see a large, well proportioned girl who is a beautiful dancer.

Size and type of build may be disregarded in an educational type of dancing where the interest lies in the development of personality and individuality rather than dancers. In work of this kind, a student is never encouraged to train beyond the normal limits of her own body.

There is in dancing, especially in ballet and acrobatics, a great danger of over-development. Modern creative dance, folk dancing, clog and tap, are all based on natural movements of the body, and in this work over-development is not usual. In ballet and acrobatics which demand intense stretching beyond natural limits and the strenuous practice of exercises which over-develop certain sets of muscles, we frequently find individuals who have, through dancing, developed an unattractive body.* The usual defects are large calf muscles, due to toe dancing; flat feet, due to improper positions of the feet; round shoulders, due to over-development of muscles of arms and shoulders (from acrobatics); and extreme hollow back (sway back), due to back bends, to supporting the body on toes, or merely to ignorance of a proper pelvic position. In all dance training constant attention should be paid to the use of the body and its control.

Chapter X describes a number of exercises for developing a usable body. These are a valuable aid in developing skill; however, their practice alone will not insure beauty of line and movement. This requires a sense of body position and a constant effort to maintain a balance within the body segments.

* See page 76.

To develop a well poised, well proportioned body, definite posture work is necessary. This cannot be general in character. The student must realize and maintain a definite mental picture of the ideal which she wishes to attain. She must constantly and consciously strive to adjust her balance and to control her

Frequently in dancing one will see unnatural body positions, similar to those shown above. These are inartistic; they express nothing. Though representing great skill and abnormal flexibility, continued practice frequently develops unattractive bodies, even deformities.

movements in an effort to acquire the most beautiful and most efficient use of her body. She must study the various movements possible in each joint of her body and must learn which muscle groups control these joints. She must set about definitely to stretch those muscles which are too short, to strengthen those which are too weak and to develop flexibility in joints where movement is abnormally limited.

In attempting to correct defects it is at the same time necessary to guard against over correction, to avoid large muscles, or flexibility beyond the point of control.

A strong kinesthetic sense should be developed so that one may be conscious of body position and movement. One must be able to sense the correct and incorrect

Today, the world's greatest dancers, including Martha Graham, Mary Wigman, Harald Kreutzberg, Yvonne Georgi, Doris Humphreys, Charles Weidman, and many others, find expression in natural body movements which represent marked skill, co-ordination, grace and strength.*

relation of body segments and must be able to localize a movement in one part of the body without affecting other parts.

The use of posture pictures or shadow drawings, mirrors, movies, where possible, conference with diagnosis and prescription of certain exercises and movements, will be of value to the student.

* These sketches, suggested by photographs of Mary Wigman, Yvonne Georgi and two Strauss dancers, were drawn by Maxine Bennett. Other sketches in this chapter are by Virginia Prudhomme.

Perhaps the region of the body where attention to control and balance is most required is that of the lower back and abdomen. Strong abdominal muscles, firm hip muscles, and a conscious control of the pelvis should be stressed in all types of activity. The person with sagging abdomen, hollow back, and relaxed hips is unattractive in sports clothes, bathing suit, or evening frock as well as in a dance costume. If she would express her true personality she should, through conscious effort, train her body that she may be as well poised entering a class

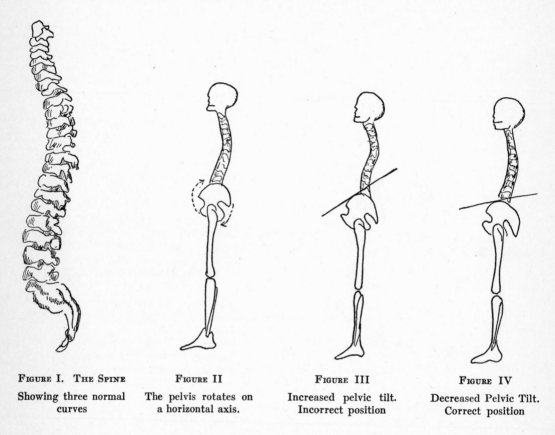

| FIGURE I. THE SPINE | FIGURE II | FIGURE III | FIGURE IV |
| --- | --- | --- | --- |
| Showing three normal curves | The pelvis rotates on a horizontal axis. | Increased pelvic tilt. Incorrect position | Decreased Pelvic Tilt. Correct position |

room, standing from her typewriter, or walking to the end of a diving board as she would be on a stage with bright lights.

One who carries herself with control, proper balance, and free relaxed movements impresses others with her grace, vitality, and alertness. On the other hand the individual with a forward head, depressed chest, round shoulders, and hollow back suggests indifference, ill health, over-work, and fatigue.

Body balance is principally controlled by the pelvis which regulates the position of the hips and lower spine and indirectly affects the position of the chest and upper back. The spine, while normally straight when viewed from the rear, is not normally straight when viewed from the side. Instead, it has three slight curves: at neck, upper back (near shoulders), and at the lower back (near waist). See Figure I. It is the over-exaggeration or obliteration of these curves which is abnormal, the common defects being an exaggerated hollow in lower back (commonly called sway back or hyperextension), an increased curve in the upper back (called round upper back or round shoulders), and an increased curve at the neck due to carrying the head forward.

The pelvis,* which is located between the spine and the legs, has been called

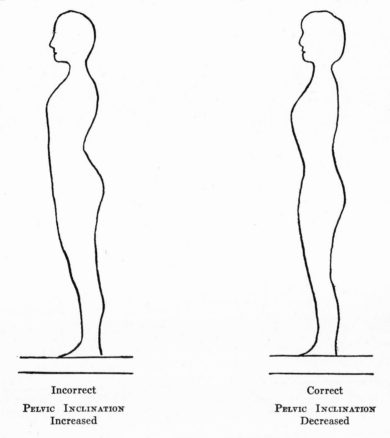

| Incorrect | Correct |
| --- | --- |
| Pelvic Inclination | Pelvic Inclination |
| Increased | Decreased |

the keystone of posture because its position greatly affects the other parts of the body. Especially does its position affect the curves of the spine. The pelvis rotates upon an imaginary axis which passes through it horizontally from right to left. Its movement is controlled by the abdominal and hip muscles and the anterior muscles of the lower spine (principally the quadratus lumborum). If these muscles are contracted and held firmly, the front of the pelvis is pulled upward, while the back of the pelvis is pulled down. (See Fig. II.) This rotates the pelvis so that its line of inclination is decreased. (See Fig. IV.) This is the proper position of the pelvis. If the abdominal muscles and the quadratus lumborum are

* The large bone which is sometimes called the hip bone. See Fig. I-IV, p. 78.

weak and relaxed and the hips are not held firmly, the pelvis is not properly controlled and it rotates into an incorrect position, with an increased tilt. (See Fig. III.) This causes an increased hollow in the lower back, which is often accompanied by a compensatory curve in the upper back.

To get the feeling of the proper position of the pelvis one may attempt to draw the front of the pelvis (the symphosis pubis) toward the breast bone (sternum). In doing this the knees relax but should not bend, and the abdomen will be drawn in so that it does not protrude beyond the line between the symphosis pubis and the sternum. In doing this the chest may be depressed. To complete the correct position of the spine, the chest should be lifted while the pelvis is held firmly in its proper position. Finally, the head should lift until the eyes are looking straight ahead.

The movement of the chest is dependent upon the strength of the posterior muscles of the upper spine. Likewise an appearance of freedom in the chest and shoulders depends upon the relaxation and length of the anterior chest muscles which are located on the front of the chest, extending from the breast bone to the tip of shoulder and upper arm. These muscles, commonly called the pectoral muscles, may be felt at the front of the arm pit. They are strong because they are used in the many movements common in our daily habits of eating, dressing, handling tools, etc.

If compensatory exercises are taken to stretch these muscles, they will maintain their normal length in spite of their constant use. However, if such stretching exercises are not taken these muscles tend to become tense and short. This condition combined with a weakness of the muscles of the upper back will pull the shoulders forward, depress the chest and produce round shoulders. Exercises such as "Arm Flinging" and "Chest Lifting" (see Chapter X) will aid in stretching the pectorals and at the same time will strengthen the muscles of the upper back and allow them to straighten the upper back and lift the chest.

The feet toeing straight is an important factor in dancing. The proper use of the foot demands a transference of body weight from the heel, through the outer border of the foot, ending with a push-off from ball and toe. Movements with the feet toeing outward result not only in an ugly line but in a weakening of the longitudinal arch, due to the fact that this position results in a transference of body weight from side of heel through the inner border of the foot to the ball and toe. In dancing it is very important to guard against this defect. It is important also to accustom one's self gradually to barefoot dancing, especially if high heeled shoes are frequently worn for walking. The abrupt change from high heels to bare feet will so stretch certain muscles and ligaments in the legs that pain as well as actual weakening of the arches may result.

Besides attention to the muscular and structural condition of the feet, one must also guard against infection. Recently much emphasis has been placed through advertising upon a foot condition called Ringworm. It is popularly, though incorrectly, termed "Athlete's Foot." It occurs as a cracking of the skin between the toes and small watery blisters on the skin of the foot. Many times a cracking of the skin may be due merely to hot weather or a frequent wet condition of the feet as about a swimming pool. In this case a thorough drying with the use of a foot powder will correct the difficulty.

Since ringworm of the foot is extremely infectious, it is wise to watch the feet carefully and to report any abnormal condition to the school physician. Remedies are many and vary with the individual and the stage of development of the infection. In the early stages ringworm may be cured by use of "Flowers of Sulphur." However, due to its rapid development and the great possibility of its becoming incurable as well as transferred to others, home remedies should be eliminated and medical attention sought immediately. Persons so infected should wear sandals when dancing and bathing shoes or clogs in and about showers and dressing rooms.

If the body is to be used as an instrument of expression, the work should be of a nature that will tend to free the individual from the limitations of her own physical and mental make-up. Frequently, even in schools, we find a dance group which is conducted and trained in a type of dance resembling the things we see in the moderate priced vaudeville. This sort of work is entirely out of harmony with the aims of modern education. The constant imitation of a leader destroys the student's tendency to create her own dance forms. The use of a definite vocabulary of movements results in a stereotyped effect which becomes monotonous not only to the dancer, but also to the spectator. An over-emphasis on group work, which refuses to allow any spark of spontaneity or individuality to burn for more than an instant, ruins all possibility of self-expression. In the theatrical type of work we frequently find gorgeous and ridiculously elaborate costumes, which fail in their effort to lend variety and interest because they so completely hide the body that the movements are still further limited in their expression. And, to complete the vicious circle, the audience becomes so accustomed to the cheap, gaudy brilliance, that an appreciation for sincere creative art is destroyed. Rather than being limited by superficial movements and an artificial expression, the dancer must be allowed to seek further into the possibilities of expressive movement within her own body. A sincere effort at self-expression, even though less finished than the one developed through imitation, is a stepping stone to artistic endeavor.

It is the dance instructor's privilege to be in a position to help the girl with a poorly poised body, and success in this alone should be recompense for a season's effort.

A head well poised above a high chest and relaxed shoulders, from which arms are controlled with graceful, strong movements; strong supple feet, toeing straight and supporting smoothly muscled legs and a slender, responsive body; these are the qualities which every intelligent person desires and which every dancer must possess.

# CHAPTER IX

ORGANIZATION OF CLASS WORK, MOTIVATION, COSTUME, ETC.

Through her introduction to dancing a student may enjoy and appreciate or she may hate and fear, one of the most valuable activities of the physical education program. If it is so presented to her that she dreads or dislikes it, she has been deprived of one of life's greatest pleasures and her personality may be forever cramped by the lack of this outlet for the expression of emotion.

The student's whole-hearted acceptance of dancing will depend greatly upon her first impressions of class work. For this reason the instructor should plan with great care the presentation of her first lessons and should watch for the reaction of the group, being ready to change her approach immediately if the student reaction is not desirable. This does not mean that the instructor should meet her class, trembling with the fear that they will not be in sympathy with her work. Her sincerity and self-confidence are absolute necessities.

Classification where possible into beginning, intermediate and advanced classes will be of great assistance in presenting class work in a way which will gain the confidence of the students. This can be done through simple tests, or merely through conversation with the student, questioning her concerning her interest, her previous training, her knowledge of music, and her other physical education work. The more advanced students then will not become disinterested because the class progresses too slowly, nor will the beginners be embarrassed because of the presence of the girls with previous training or better skill.

Beginners will come to their first lesson more eagerly, if they are assured in advance that they will not be asked to give solo dances, to "interpret spring" (as many think we do in dancing). It should be explained that the work in beginning classes is really only a study of body control and rhythm and that the class work will consist principally of rhythmic exercises to music. Many of them will have heard of "Original Dances." They should be assured that these are not required until intermediate or advanced work, that they will not be asked to create until they have acquired, as an instrument of expression, a trained, responsive body and a vocabulary of movements.

The costume worn by the class may be instrumental in setting the attitude. It must allow freedom of movement and be scant enough to allow the line of the body and limbs to be apparent. Its length and style will depend upon the student, her build and her personality, as well as the material used. In dance programs it will also depend upon the mood and nature of the dance in which worn. (See page 217.)

For class practice the costume worn may be a help or a hindrance. If possible it should be determined by class vote. It may be a simple dance tunic with underbody or shorts to match, a bathing suit, or a short romper suit.

Frequently, wearing a dance tunic will inhibit the already self-conscious person, who thinks that because she is so dressed, she is expected to immediately become graceful. In addition since dance costumes are usually furnished by the student, they are frequently made of material which will not drape softly, or they are poorly fitted and unbecoming. Also in the case of a poorly built person they are often unattractive. If the student is conscious of looking queer, she will be mentally inhibited and will be a difficult subject. Because of the wide use of the bathing suit today, many girls will feel more comfortable, mentally and physically, if this is used as the practice costume.

Unless there is a possibility of ringworm of the foot, or unless the floor is splintered, nothing should be worn on the feet. The bare foot on a clean, smooth (but not slippery) floor is not only extremely pleasurable, but it is safer as well as more efficient, than the foot encased in a slipper. The foot has in large amount the same type of sensibility as the hand, and this developed through use will make the dancer more sure-footed as well as able to carry herself over space with more freedom and joy.

When slippers are worn they should be the soft suede sandal, never a ballet slipper with stiff sole. In the case of tender feet which blister easily or any abrasions of the skin of the feet, sandals should be advised until this difficulty is corrected. The condition of the feet should be carefully checked, to prevent injury to arches and ankles or spread of infection.*

The instructor who knows her group, or who is a keen reader of faces and personality, will be helped in the presentation of dancing. With certain age groups, as in junior high school, or older students with previous training in dancing or music or art, she may approach dancing if she wishes from the standpoint of emotion. This approach, however, is most dangerous and should be reserved for advanced classes unless the group is plainly in sympathy. A presentation from the standpoint of rhythm, kinesiology or pure body control will in most cases be more successful, the first appealing especially to students of music, the second to those with a scientific turn of mind, while the athletic type of girl responds best to activity which tests her strength, co-ordination, and endurance.

No one of these methods of presentation should be continued alone throughout the term's work. If emotion is stressed throughout, the result is usually one of light, airy movements with no depth, no strength, for joy is the easiest emotion to express and the class will cling to this. If rhythm is stressed entirely the work is in danger of becoming limited by certain forms and patterns, with too little variation and spontaneity. A study of kinesiology without the modifying influence of a more idealistic approach, will result in a cold, intellectual attitude,

* See Chapter VIII, page 80.

while lessons purely on physical skills may become as confining as ballet or formal gymnastics. All these and any other approaches within the grasp of the instructor should be introduced whenever the occasion is opportune.

It has been found successful in the author's experience to demand participation by all. Everyone is required to dress in costume in order to be counted present. If a student is not well enough to do this, as in case of menstrual pain or severe cold, she may consult the instructor before class and may be sent to a rest room or to her home.

Every student who comes to class comes with the agreement of taking part mentally throughout the period and physically whenever the work is not too vigorous. In beginning classes, the instructor herself participates in activity as a member of the class, thus acting as a leader and example of correct activity, and at the same time dispelling the fear of criticism which beginners feel from observers.

To keep the lesson from approaching the stereotyped form of a gymnastic day's order, exercises * should be presented according to need and the need explained. For example, walking and running may be used as an introductory activity for general warming up to avoid muscle injury due to too sudden vigorous muscular activity. Foot exercises, with an explanation of the arches of the foot and the proper use of foot and ankle, may be used for developing strength and flexibility. These might be followed by exercises to develop a kinesthetic sense of controlled relaxation, follow-through, and body position.

Exercises may be introduced as a progression toward a complete dance movement; for example, in teaching a spiral turn, a progression starting by work in partners turning under arms (see Progression in Teaching Slide and Turn, page 114) may be used; on the other hand, an exercise may come as the result of a definite need seen in the execution of a more advanced movement or of a dance study; as, for example, if a spiral turn is poorly done, the instructor may suggest that the class practice Body Rotation or Roll with Arm Lead in order to sense the position of the body in a relaxed Follow Through.

If these exercises are repeated day after day, in exactly the same manner, to the same music, one will be developing little machines instead of personalities. They should be presented in a variety of ways and with a progression from easy to more difficult, and may be combined into simple patterns or compositions by the instructor and later by the students. Scarfs or balloons may be used to stimulate arm work without self-consciousness.

Simple dance studies † based on the fundamentals learned in class may be taught in beginning and intermediate classes as the students become ready for them. These may be group dances with more stress on foot pattern and floor pattern than upon body movement or interpretation. Later a greater variety of

* See Chapter X.                              † See Chapter XI.

foot patterns may be introduced with emphasis on body movement. These may gradually develop into individual patterns danced by the class in unison.

Motivation in Dance Creation requires careful attention to the effect on the individual. It must not be too forced, but on the other hand, if never demanded may never be received. One might quote an old adage—"Necessity is the mother of invention."

Creation by a group is most easily introduced, for no one individual need feel responsible for the result. To divide the class into small groups, assigning a bit of music, a theme, or a poem, has been found a satisfactory method of exposing the students to the necessity of leading themselves. Later each group may choose its own music and theme and finally, as individuals, each may bring into the dance laboratory some bit of her own creation, not to be presented in the spirit of exhibit, but as a "give and take" between members of the class.

Dance studies for use in beginning or intermediate class may be created by the instructor or by advanced classes. A number of such studies with suggestions for presenting, are included in Chapter XI. For additional material, see list, Page 131.

Grading students in Creative Dance classes is a difficult problem. The sympathetic instructor realizes that many times it is her least skilled students who are working the hardest. The individual with poor motor control or with a marked self-consciousness is at a great disadvantage when she is compared to a girl who has been allowed to express herself and who has no inhibitions. The former, however, is the one who needs dancing most and who should be encouraged to keep working until she is able to overcome at least a good part of her embarrassment. If her grades are consistently low she will become discouraged and will avoid dancing classes even though she has a sincere desire to improve her skill and personal poise.

This situation may be met in several ways. If possible, groups should be classified into beginning, intermediate and advanced. Even a more elementary group may be formed as a class in the Fundamentals of Rhythm. Then too, some arrangement should be made in the class work to test the effort of the poorer student. Open practice hours may be arranged for those who desire extra help. Outside reading may be assigned, or students may be asked to create something of an original nature, related if possible to dancing. In answer to such a request the author has received some very commendable poems, themes, sketches, posters, bits of music and in one case of an ingenious student the plan for an advertisement, which she stated was her "main interest and necessitated original and creative thought as well as balance, proportion and rhythm."

In grading classes in Creative Dance an effort should be made to make the tests as objective as possible. Tests on skills can scarcely be made except with the subjective judgment of the instructor but these can be made more valid and accurate if charts are kept and if the tests are a definite part of the class hour rather than consisting merely of a vague mental picture in the instructor's mind as she sits in her office some hours later. Some may argue that such tests will spoil the spontaneity of the work but in the author's experience it has led to greater interest and more earnest work, and seems particularly necessary, at least in a moderate degree, if academic grades and credits are to be given. Frequently in these tests a person is discovered who is doing exceptionally creditable work, but who was not noticed in the group because she was not outstandingly poor nor was she good enough to show up to advantage in comparison to the exceptionally skilled members of the class. Also by such tests one may isolate those students whose seriousness and effort justifies their passing the course but who are at the same time so poor in skill that they should be recommended to repeat the same course rather than entering a more advanced section.

In addition to such tests on skill, one may use the written examination as an opportunity to determine the seriousness and interest of the students. The following examination is given as an example of the objective and essay types of tests. The material contained in this test may be amplified by questions based on judgment of mood, time, and phrasing of music played during the examination, or by questions on rhythm or step patterns, group formations and figures, or upon dances which have been learned in class. Since questions of that type have been included in the tests on Rhythm, Tap and Clog and Folk Dancing, similar ones will not be included here.

The examination given below is based upon class work and informal class discussion and upon the following references which the students were asked to read outside of the class period; Chapters on Rhythm from "The Psychology of Musical Talent" by Seashore and from "Art in Everyday Life" by Goldstein and chapter one from "The Dance and Its Place in Education" by H'Doubler.

## BEGINNING DANCING

### Final Examination

Use blank sheets at back in answering questions I, II, and III.

  I.  Should children be given dance training? Discuss the reasons for your viewpoint.

 II.  Why do educators allow dancing to be taught as a part of an educational curriculum?

III.  Discuss the values of rhythm in everyday life.

IV.  Name exercises which are used in dancing class to accomplish the following: (Name more than one if you can)
   a. To stretch muscles on back of legs and hips.
   b. To stretch muscles at front of shoulders.
   c. To limber the shoulder joint and develop arm control.

    d. To strengthen the abdominal muscles.

    e. To stretch and relax muscles of neck and allow complete extension of upper body and head.

V. Place a check (√) at left of the correct phrase.

    a. During the back circle in the "Figure-Eight Standing," one relieves strain in the lower back by:

       _____Allowing the head to fall back as far as possible.

       _____Bending the knees.

       _____Bending backward at the waist.

       _____Swinging the arms above the head.

    b. In executing a dance fall we avoid landing hard on the knees by:

       _____Bending at the hips as we begin.

       _____Landing on first one knee and then the other.

       _____Leaning backward from the knees to balance weight.

       _____Catching the weight on the hands.

    c. In running:

      1._____The hips should be tilted backward.

       _____The hips should be tilted forward.

      2._____The legs should reach forward.

       _____The legs should extend backward.

      3._____The body should rise and fall.

       _____The body should be carried forward without a pronounced rise and fall.

      4._____The run should be made on whole of foot, heel down.

       _____The run should be entirely on toes.

       _____A push-off should be made from ball of foot and toes.

      5._____The landing from each step of the run should be on toes.

       _____The landing from each step of the run should be on heels.

       _____The landing from each step of the run should be on balls of feet.

    d. In running as the length of step increases the hips are carried:

       _____higher.

       _____lower.

       _____same height from floor as with small steps.

    e. In turning:

      1._____the body is held rigid.

       _____the body is completely relaxed.

       _____the body is relaxed, but well controlled.

      2._____the body turns as one unit.

       _____the body turns as a series of units, with a follow-through so that one part follows another.

      3._____the head falls back as chest lifts.

       _____the head is held erect.

_____the head remains facing forward and is turned quickly after body has almost completed turn.

4._____various leads may be used; for example, we may follow the arms, or chest or the turn may be initiated by the legs.

_____only one lead is possible.

f.  In the abdominal lift, as upper body lifts from floor:

1._____the back is rounded and abdomen hollow.

_____the lower back is hollow and the abdomen stretched and bulging.

2._____the hips are tilted backward so weight rests as in sitting position.

_____the hips are rolled forward under body so weight rests on lower spine.

3._____the head drops back with relaxed neck.

_____the head is held forward.

g.  In arm movements:

1._____we endeavor to make the shoulder and upper body initiate the movement.

_____the arm moves as a single unit independent of the rest of the body.

2._____elaborate movements are made with the fingers and wrists.

_____the fingers and wrists are used only as a part of the arm to add to the completion of the movement.

h.  In the Cross-Polka:

1.  During the reach of the leg:

_____the hips are tilted backward.

_____the hips are pushed forward.

2.  The backward leaning of the body:

_____should come as a result of the arms being carried above the head.

_____should come as a result of the reach of the free leg.

_____should be an independent movement.

3.  The arms are carried above the head:

_____to aid in balance as the leg reaches forward.

_____to cause the backward leaning.

4.  The head drops back:

_____as a result of relaxation and follow-through from chest and upper back extension.

_____as an independent movement because it looks better.

i.  Modern dance movements:

1._____are based on natural movements of the body.

_____are based on unnatural movements of the body.

2._____stress extreme backward bends.

_____require excessive stretching.

_____demand moderate flexibility which is under control.

3._____tend to develop poor posture.

_____stress the elements of good posture.

4._____include the use of arms and legs as separate units.

_____demand a follow-through of body parts.

j. In the modern dance, the feet:

1._____toe straight ahead, except in movements where definite foot effects are desired.

_____toe out, except in movements where definite foot effects are desired.

2._____are strengthened through barefoot work.

_____are supported and protected by slippers which contain stiff arches.

k. Modern educational dance:

1._____stresses imitation of others.

_____individual creation of dances.

2. Aims to develop:

_____personality.

_____creative ability in other lines of art.

_____appreciation of jazz.

_____appreciation of good music.

_____self-consciousness.

_____poise.

3. Is planned for:

_____only the exceptional dancers.

_____all students needing to develop poise.

VI. For instructor's information; not part of examination, please answer the following questions:

1. Why did you take dancing?

2. Have you enjoyed it enough to want to take more dancing at a future time, or do you finish with the feeling of "never again"?

3. What suggestions can you make to the instructor?

   Is the work monotonous—too advanced—too elementary?

   Are the skills too difficult?

   Is too much or too little time spent on a skill?

4. Have you received anything besides mere skill in dance technique?

# CHAPTER X

In developing skills to be used in dancing, the following exercises may be used. They have been chosen by the author from the long list of exercises which she uses in class work. Some of them were originated by Margaret Newell H'Doubler, Professor of Dancing and Head of the Department of Dancing, at the University of Wisconsin; others by Martha Graham, formerly a Denishawn dancer, now head of the Graham Studio of the Dance in New York City. Others come from Danish Gymnastics, while some are merely a simple series of movements developed by experimentation.

The student must clearly realize that these exercises are used as a means of developing dance technique and must not be confused with dances. Very satisfying patterns may be arranged by a combination of exercises, by class grouping or by floor plan and if variety is introduced the student will find great enjoyment in the execution of these movements. However, if the distinction between technique and dancing is not clearly defined by the instructor, she will find that the studies which the students later create will be artificial and superficial as well as lacking in individuality and real emotional or dramatic content.

Music for use with these exercises * is suggested in each instance. Other selections should be chosen by the instructor in order to avoid monotony, to give more rhythmic experience and to develop a broader appreciation of music. For source of suggested music see list below.

It is assumed that the elementary forms of locomotion, the walk, run, skip, leap, gallop and slide as well as the polka, schottische, two-step, mazurka and waltz, are all clear. If not, an analysis may be found in Chapters IV, V and XVI.

A. Exercises for stretching muscles and ligaments of shoulder and arm.†

* Music—Reference is to the list on page 131.
        (1)—Wisconsin Blue Print.
        (2)—Music by Louis Horst.
        (3)—Masterpieces of Piano Music.
        (4)—Gems of Melody and Rhythm.
        (5)—Dance Music by Garland.
        (6)—Dance Music by Steel and Petersen.
† See page 80.

I. Arm Flinging

Music—"Sorrentina" (1)
"Waltz-Faust" (3) (4)
"Arm Flinging" (6)

a. Sitting, legs extended to right, left hand resting on floor; fling right arm upward and backward at right angles to the body, vigorously enough to stretch the anterior chest muscles. Allow trunk to twist and head to fall back as eyes follow hand. The return move-

FIG. 1. ARM FLINGING

ment should be a relaxed rebound. Continue 4 or 8 times, then repeat on opposite side. See Figure 1.

b. Same exercise, lifting hips from the floor, weight supported on lower leg, knee, and left hand. Repeat on opposite side. See Figure 2.

FIG. 2. ARM FLINGING WITH A LIFT OF THE HIPS

| Rhythm of arm pattern | L | L |
|---|---|---|
| | Fling | Relax |
| Count with music—3/4 | 1 2 3 | 1 2 3 |
| 6/8 | 1 2 3 | 4 5 6 |

II. Head Circling

Music—"Elevation" (1)
"Slumber Song" (3) (4)
"Rotation" (6)

a. Sitting, allow head to circle slowly, dropping forward, then swinging to the side. (Try to touch ear to shoulder.) As head drops backward, lift chest and allow head to hang back heavily so as to stretch the muscles on the front of neck. Complete circle and repeat. Reverse direction frequently to avoid dizziness.

b. Double Circle or Figure Eight

Sitting, drop head forward, then swing head in half circle to left. When head reaches back position, bring it forward and make half circle toward right. Continue until movement of head describes a figure eight. Repeat several times with as much relaxation as possible. Repeat same exercise starting with head back and changing direction by a backward movement of head.

III. Chest Lifting                          Music—"Elevation" (1)
                                                  "Träumerei" (3) (4)
                                                  "Rotation" (6)

a. Sitting with head dropped forward on chest, lift the chest slowly and steadily, allowing head to remain forward until chest pushes it past dead center and it falls back. (Stimulate a strong stretch in the anterior neck muscles and avoid hunched shoulders.) Pull chest down allowing head to follow. Repeat. See Figure 3.

Fig. 3. Chest Lifting

b. Same exercise lying on back, knees bent, feet on floor. Contract abdominal muscles, flattening lower back to floor; hold this position of lower back and lift the chest. (Do not allow lower back to leave the floor as the chest is lifted.) Relax and repeat.

c. Chest Lifting taken while standing or walking.
In this case an effort must be made to avoid hyperextension * of the lower spine.

d. Chest Lifting followed by a strong extension of arms to overhead position. Let the impulse for arm raising come from chest. This may be accomplished by localizing the movement in the upper arm, the rest

* Hollow lower back. See pages 75-79.

of the arm in easy extension at the elbow. (Avoid stiff arms and bent elbows and wrists.) See Figure 28f.

IV. Arm Swing

Music—"Arm Swing in
Horizontal Plane" (6)

a. Horizontal Swing. Sitting on the floor, extend legs toward right, left hand on the floor, right arm hanging relaxed. Pull right shoulder across in front of body as far as possible. Pull backward as far as possible. Repeat moving shoulder in horizontal plane. When flexibility of shoulder has been established, allow arm to follow shoulder, still localizing the pull in the shoulder with the arm taking the follow through. Thus the arm (pulled by shoulder) swings across body toward left; then following a backward pull of the shoulder the right arm swings toward right. The strong pull of the shoulder rotates the arm so that back of hand faces in the direction in which arm is moving. Repeat same exercise with opposite arm and shoulder.

b. Vertical Swing.
Same exercise moving shoulder up and down, allowing arm to follow.

c. Arm Swing with Reach
Same exercise. The feeling of an extra reach is produced at the end of each swing by pulling shoulder back slightly, bending and then extending elbow and wrist.

d. Repeat all arm swings with both arms moving together or in opposition and in both horizontal and vertical directions.

e. Same exercise may be done standing or with an easy run allowing direction of arm swing to determine floor pattern.

f. The same exercise done standing may be developed into a spiral turn with an arm lead. Starting with the right arm behind the back and the left reaching across in front, pull the body into a turn left by a horizontal swing of left arm. As left arm swings behind the body complete the turn by swinging right arm to the side and across in front of body. Finish with a backward pull of the right shoulder followed by a strong reach of the right arm. Repeat same to the right. In this turn the body completes a turn and one-half or a turn and a quarter.

V. Shoulder and Arm Moving
in Figure Eight

Music—"Waltz Excerpt" (1)
"Sea Gardens"—Cook
"12/8 Rhythm"—(5)
"Figure Eight"—(6)

a. Sitting on the floor, extend legs toward right, left hand on the floor, right arm hanging relaxed; localizing the movement in the shoulder,

Fig. 4. Shoulder Movements in a Figure Eight

Fig. 5. Shoulder and Arm Movements in a Figure Eight

circle the right shoulder forward and up, then diagonally down backward. Continue backward into another circle, carrying the shoulder up and then diagonally down and forward. In this movement the tip of the shoulder describes a figure eight. (Complete figure takes six counts of music.) See Figure 4.

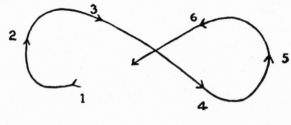

| Shoulder pattern | L | | | L | | |
|---|---|---|---|---|---|---|
| | Forw. | up | relax | Back | up | relax |
| | Forward circle | | | Backward circle | | |
| Count with  3/4 | 1 | 2 | 3 | 1 | 2 | 3 |
| music      6/8 | 1̱ | 2 | 3 | 4̱ | 5 | 6 |

Change position and repeat series of Figure Eights with the left shoulder

b. Same exercise using shoulder and arm. Fingers describe a large figure eight; impulse comes from the shoulder.

c. Same exercise adding movement of chest and head. As arm circles forward, chest and head fall forward; as arm circles backward, chest lifts and head falls backward. Head and chest should not move independently, but move as a result of the movement of shoulder and arm. See Figure 5.

d. Same exercise kneeling on one or both knees or standing, using one arm at a time; then both simultaneously. When both arms move together, they cross in front, then circle backward, swinging apart. When standing, in order to avoid hyperextension of the lower spine, during the backward circle, bend the knees slightly, pushing the hips forward.

e. Same exercise in four counts, taking a forward and a backward step on counts 1 and 3, with the opposite foot stepping in place on counts 2 and 4. The forward circle, with body bending forward at hips, is made on counts 1 and 2. The backward circle, pulling the body up into extension, is made on counts 3 and 4. See Figure 6.

f. Same exercise on a moving base, using a waltz run. Each circle is completed in three counts, during three steps. (First of each three steps is accented.) The complete figure eight takes six counts, two measures of waltz music.

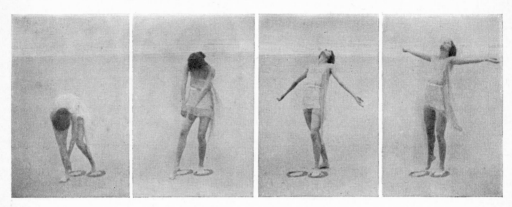

Fig. 6. Arm and Shoulder Movements in Figure Eight Pulling Body into Flexion and Complete Extension

g. Same exercise turning in place.

h. Same exercise (with waltz run) done with partner, right hands joined, left arms circling in figure eight. Turn in small circle with partner, keeping elbow straight and pulling away on back circle, so that balance results.

B. Exercises for Stretching Muscles of Legs

I. Foot Flexion and Extension            Music—"Foot Flexion" (6)

a. Sitting on floor with knees straight. (1) Flex the ankle as much as possible, lifting toes from floor. (Get feeling of trying to touch toes to front of leg. (2) Relax; then extend toes toward the floor. Repeat (1) and (2).

b. Same exercise standing.

c. Same exercise standing with toes over edge of stair. Extend ankles; then slowly relax (being careful not to lose balance). Lower heels until they are below level of stair, and a stretch is felt in tendon at back of heel.

II. Trunk Springing            Music—"Andante Celebri" (4)
                              "Ecossaisen" (1)
                              "Trunk Springing" (6)

a. Sit with the legs extended and apart. Keeping knees straight and trying to touch head and elbows to the floor, bend forward at the hips with quick springy movements. Relax as much as possible. The rhythm is even, with a spring on each count of the music. Relax between counts. See Figure 7a

FIG. 7. TRUNK SPRINGING

b. Same exercise, standing with feet apart and the trunk bent forward at the hips. Keeping knees straight, repeatedly touch fingers to the ground by means of quick springy movements of the trunk; later touch palm of hand to floor. See Figure 7c.

c. Same exercise, standing with feet together. Alternate each spring of the trunk with a squat position, hands on the floor. See Figure 8 (a and b).

d. Same exercise in four counts, "Squat, Spring, Fling, Spring." Cross arms under body as trunk springs on count 2.
Fling arms sideward, head up, on count 3. See Figure 8 (a, b, c, d).

FIG. 8. SQUAT-SPRING-FLING-SPRING

III. Trunk Springing with Trunk Rotation.
   a. Sitting with legs extended and apart and keeping knees straight, bend forward and sideward trying to touch head to right knee. Same exercise to left. See Figure 7b.

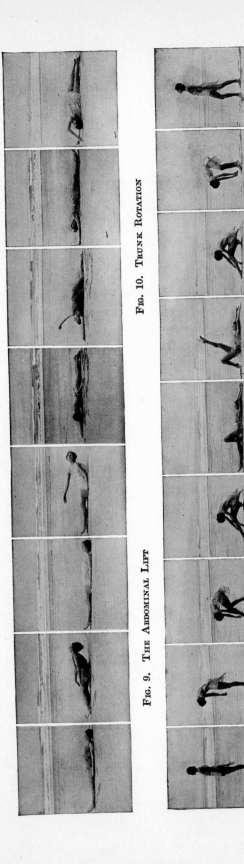

Fig. 10. Trunk Rotation

Fig. 9. The Abdominal Lift

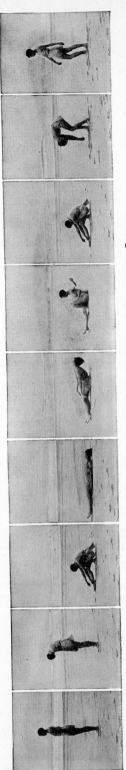

Fig. 11. Lying Down and Getting Up with Leg Swing

Fig. 12. Lying Down and Getting Up with Abdominal Lift

b. Same standing, feet apart, trunk hanging forward from hips. See Figure 7d.

IV. Trunk Swinging

Music—"Waltz Excerpt" (1)
"Trunk Swinging" (6)
"Humoresque" (3) (4)

a. Standing with feet apart, arms and upper body relaxed; swing arms from side to side, increasing the range of movement, allowing trunk to bend forward until hands touch floor as arms swing.

b. Same exercise, continuing fourth swing into a complete circle, lifting body through complete extension. (Avoid bending backward.)

| Rhythmic pattern of trunk and arms— | Long | | Long | | |
|---|---|---|---|---|---|
| | Swing left | | Swing right | | |
| Count of music—3/4 | 1 2 3 | | 1 2 3 | | |
| 6/8 | 1 2 3 | | 4 5 6 | | |

C. Exercises to Develop Abdominal Muscles and Quadraceps

I. Abdominal Lift

Music—"Pleading" (2)
"Abdominal Lift" (6)

a. Lying on back, arch lower back slightly in preparation; then suddenly contract abdominals, flattening lower back and lifting upper body from floor. Localize movement in abdominals and allow head to hang back relaxed. Arms lift weakly. Come up only few inches from floor, hold, then relax and fall back. See Figure 9.

b. Same exercise lifting one arm and shoulder at a time, relaxing in between. See Figure 9.

II. Lift with Arm Swing

Music—"Swinging Variante" (2)
"Arm Swing" (6)

Sitting on floor, left leg extended forward, right knee bent, right foot on floor. (1) Extend arms sideward, chest up, back arched. (2) Depressing chest, swing arms forward upward and straighten right knee slightly to lift body off floor; keep left leg extended forward. Hold, relax and repeat.

III. Backward Leaning

Music—"Back Lean" (6)

a. Standing on knees, hips held firmly under trunk, lean backward from the knees, hold, and return to position. Do not bend at hips or lower spine. See Figure 13.

FIG. 13. BACK LEAN

**b.** Same exercise, toes tucked under. Lean back until knees lift from the floor. Continue to lift to standing position, using a steady push of hips. Do not bend at hips. See Figure 14.

FIG. 14. BACK LEAN TO STAND

D. Exercises for Strengthening Legs and Feet
   (Movements of the legs and feet are made more efficient by localizing the movement in the larger muscles of upper leg and hip.)

I.  Pendulum Swing of Leg                     Music—"Pendulum Swing" (6)

   a. Standing on one foot, other leg extended backward. By a combined action of the gluteal and abdominal muscles and the quadratus lumborum (see page 77), reduce the tilt of the pelvis, thus causing the free leg to swing forward. Relax and allow free leg to swing back. Repeat rhythmically until there results a definite pendulum swing of the leg caused by hip action. (If unsteady, use chair, wall or partner for support.) See Figure 15.
   b. Same exercise, hopping on supporting leg. Chest is depressed as leg swings forward, elevated as leg swings back. Arms swing in opposition. (Avoid outward rotation of leg.) See Figure 16.

FIG. 15.  PENDULUM SWING OF LEG

FIG. 16.  PENDULUM SWING OF LEG WITH HOP

II. Walking                        Music—"Coronation March" (3) (4)
                                       "Running Motive" (2)
                                       "Country Gardens"—Grainger
                                       "Walking" (6)

   a. Practice walking, causing free leg to swing forward due to muscle
      action as in Pendulum Swing of Leg, and to a lift of the heel of the
      supporting foot.  Fall forward on to the free leg and repeat.  (This
      may give one the feeling of walking with stiff legs.)
   b. Develop (a) into a normal walk, with relaxed knees, but continue to
      use a contraction of the hip muscles.
   c. Develop (b) into an easy run by bending, then immediately straight-
      ening each knee as the leg takes the body weight.  This will tend to
      lift the body until the walk changes to an easy leap which, when ac-
      celerated, becomes a run.

III. Running                       Music—"Running Motive" (2)
                                       "Big Run" (2)
                                       "Run" (6)

   a. Long Stride.
      Run with a strong contraction of the gluteal muscles, carrying the
      hips low and well under trunk.  (Sit down slightly as you run.)  This
      position of the hips allows the legs freedom of movement forward.
      Keep the body erect, leaning neither forward nor back.  This keeps

FIG. 17.  RUNNING

the chest in a favorable position for easy breathing.  Attempt to take
very long steps.  Keep the feet near the floor and avoid waste of energy by eliminating all vertical movements of the body.  See Figure
17.

b. **Joyous Run.** Music—"Trio from 'Minuet in G' " (3)
"Joyous Run" (6)

Starting with a carefree buoyant walk, gradually accelerate to running. As speed increases, allow chest to lead, gradually lifting until in full extension at the finish.

IV. **Leaping.** Music—"Leap" (2)
"Uneven Leap" (6)

a. Leap in uneven rhythm, stamping on longer, strong count, and leaping on the next. The stamp is a strong step into the ground for the purpose of lifting the body. Get a wide stretch of the legs on the leap, contracting the gluteal muscles while in the air. The opposite arm swinging forward during the leap will aid in getting height.

| Rhythm of uneven leap | L | s | L | s |
|---|---|---|---|---|
| Foot pattern | stamp | leap | stamp | leap |
| Count with music, 3/4 | 1 | 2 3 | 1 | 2 3 |

See Figure 19b.

b. **Even Leap.**

A high leap on each count of music. The stamp is eliminated and all force for lift must come from flexion and extension of leg upon which landing is made.

c. **Leap in Waltz Rhythm.** Music—"Waltz Arabesque"—B *
"Waltz Leap" (6)

A high leap is made on the first count (the accent) of each measure, followed by two easy leaps on counts 2 and 3.

V. **High Skip** Music—"High Skip" (6)
"Sorrentina" (1)
"Blue Danube Waltz" (4)

Skip in slow uneven rhythm, attempting to lift the body by extension in upper trunk. The free leg may be carried forward, backward, or may hang relaxed under body. See Figures 18 and 19a.

VI. **High Skip Alternating with Leap** Music—"Skip and Leap" (6)
"Sorrentina (1)
"Leap" (2)

Alternate a high skip with a leap. In each case allow the arm opposite the free leg to swing forward with a shoulder pull to aid in gaining height.

* See page 127.

| L | s | L | s | L | s | L | s |
|---|---|---|---|---|---|---|---|
| Step | hop | step | leap | Step | hop | step | leap |
| Rt | Rt | Lt | Rt | Lt | Lt | Rt | Lt |

See Figure 19.

FIG. 18. HIGH SKIP, FREE     FIG. 20. JUMPING
LEG HANGING RELAXED

VII. Jumping          Music—"Fanfare" from William Tell (4)
                               "Prancing" (2)
                               "Prancing" (6)

a. Use the gluteal muscles as you spring from both feet. Knees and ankles flex as you land, extend as you lift. Continue rhythmically.

a                  b
FIG. 19. HIGH SKIP ALTERNATING WITH LEAP

    b. Same, alternating feet so that the push comes from left foot, then right, etc. This becomes prancing or leaping in place.

    c. Jump on both feet, spreading the legs forward and back, or sideward, after every fourth count.

    The rhythm is even, with a jump on each count. See Figure 20.

E. Exercises for Developing Trunk Movements Based on Pelvic Control

The basic movement of this series of exercises is a change in the curve of the spine by use of the abdominals, quadratus lumborum and gluteal muscles. In posture work, the movement is called "pelvic tilt," because in it the tilt or inclination of the pelvis is changed. When the above named muscles contract, the inclination of the pelvis is reduced, the hips are pulled under the trunk, the abdomen (and often the chest) is depressed, and the curve in the lower spine is reduced to as straight a line as possible. When these muscles relax, the pelvic inclination is increased and the curve in the lower spine increases.

  I. Back flexion and extension.          Music—"Elevation" (1)
                                                               "Rotation" (6)

    a. Standing on hands and knees, relax muscles of lower back, and allow back to sag until lower back is quite hollow. This movement should lift the head. Reverse the position by a strong contraction of the muscles on the front of the spine. Continue the contraction until the hollow is entirely removed and the back is humped, instead. Allow the head to fall forward, neck relaxed. Repeat the relaxation and contraction.

    b. The same exercise may be done allowing the elbows to bend during the first movement and at the same time extending the upper spine so that the chest is pushed forward.

    c. Kneeling, sitting back on heels, repeat same trunk movement as in "b." Allow the extension of the lower back to lift the chest and head as the upper body moves forward. In the return movement, as the lower back is rounded, allow the contraction of the anterior spine and ab-

FIG. 21. BACK FLEXION AND EXTENSION

dominal muscles to depress the chest and pull the head down.  See Figure 21.

d. Standing with the feet slightly apart, one foot placed ahead of the other, repeat the same trunk movement as "c."

II.  Hip Swing                                     Music—"Body Swing" (2)
                                                   "Hip Swing" (6)

a. Place one hand on the wall for support, arch back and bend forward, with free arm outstretched forward.  (See a, Figure 22.)  Bend the knees, bringing the hips toward the heels as the arms swing downward.  (See b, Figure 22.)  Lowering the knees, push the hips forward and upward, using a strong contraction of the gluteal muscles. At the same time the arms swing back and upward.  (See c, Figure 22.)  The abdominal muscles are strongly contracted in the final position, the lower back is flat and the hips are well under the body. Release the tension of the gluteal and abdominal muscles, and return through position b to the initial position a.  Repeat the movement and continue rhythmically.  One should have the sensation of swinging the hips in pendulum fashion from position a to c and back to a.

b. The same exercise should be done without support, both arms swinging together.  See Figure 22.

| Rhythmic pattern of hip | L | L |
| movement | Swing forward | Relax backward |
| Count of music 3/4 | 1    2    3 | 1    2    3 |

a                       b                       c

FIG. 22.  HIP SWING

III.  Hip Swing with a Lift                        Music—"Lift" (2)

The initial movement is a flexion and an immediate extension of the spine which causes the body to go from a position of complete extension to a position of flexion at the hips, with arms extended backward.  (See a, b, and c, Figure 23.)  From this position the hips swing forward, as in E, II, with the arms swinging forward.  (See d and e, Figure 23.)  In the final movement, the abdominal and gluteal muscles relax and the body is lifted into extension by a strong contraction of the extensors of the spine. See Figure 23.

FIG. 23.  HIP SWING WITH A LIFT

IV.  Hip Swing Kneeling, Followed by a Lift and Turn

Music—"Swing and Turn" (6)

The starting position is kneeling on left knee, right knee bent, upper body relaxed forward.

(1) Extend right knee, allowing hips to sit back on left heel, head and upper body low with arms crossed over chest.

(2) Push hips forward, allowing extension of back muscles to lift chest, head falling back.  This movement extends left knee as right is bent.

(3) Sit back as in (1).

(4) Push hips forward with body extension as in (2).  At the same time fling the arms sideward.

(5) Pull hips back and up, pulling body to standing position, feet apart, weight on left.  The movement of hips and body causes arms to swing upward to left, and turns body to face toward left.

(6) Swing hips sideward toward right.  Pull of body causes arms to swing as pendulum toward right and shifts the weight to right foot.

(7) Momentum caused by (6) causes body to make a three-quarter turn toward right, ending facing direction opposite that faced at beginning.  Weight at end of turn is on left foot, which is now in back.

(8) Kneel to position on left knee and repeat.  Repetition of exercise will turn body again toward right, bringing one to original position.

F.  Falls (to teach control in falling and getting up)

I.  Spiral Fall

Music—"Falling in a Circle" (2)
"Nocturne in F" (4)
"Spiral Fall" (6)

This fall may be analyzed in eight counts and completed in eight counts of music.  (See Figures 24 and 25.)

a    b    c    d    e    f    g

FIG. 24.  THE SPIRAL FALL

h    i    j    k    l    m    n

FIG. 25.  THE LIFT FROM A FALL

o    p    q    r    s    t

FIG. 26.  THE BACK FALL

1. Standing with arms overhead, bend to the right. (See b, Figure 24.)
2. Leaning backward from the knees, with hips well under the body, fall slowly to the knees, and sit to the left of feet. The hips must not flex until just as knees reach the floor. (See c, d and e.)
3. Allow upper body to fall forward, face down, over the knees. (See f.)
4. Roll over onto back. (See g and h.)
5. Arch the back and return to position as in 3, except with right leg extended backward. (See i and j.)
6. As if crawling bring the right foot forward, the body bending over right knee, left knee on floor. (See k.)
7. Lift the hips, allowing the upper body to remain relaxed forward. (See l.)
8. Lift the body into extension by an easy forward swing of the pelvis. This movement results in a pendulum swing of the left leg so that a step forward is taken. (See m and n.)

Repeat Spiral Fall as a continuous movement instead of by count.

## II.  Back Spiral Fall

This fall is an adaptation of the Spiral Fall, using a half turn in place. It may be analyzed in six counts and completed to two measures of waltz music.

(1)  Standing with arms extended upward to left, swing arms in pendulum fashion down and up to right.
(2)  Swing arms as pendulum toward left.
(3)  Swing arms toward right and allow body to lift on toes and twist toward right, following arms. Body ends facing opposite direction.
(4)  Leaning backward as in 2 of Spiral Fall, kneel and sit to left side of heels.
(5)  Allow upper body to fall forward over knees, arms extended above head.
(6)  Keeping arms and head close to floor, circle body toward left until lying on back.

## III.  Back Fall

a. Preliminary Exercise. Before practicing the back fall, an easy fall from the knees should be mastered. Standing on the knees, with the pelvic inclination decreased, lean back slowly as in Figure 13. At the same time reach for the floor with the left hand. When the fingers touch the floor allow the hand to slide sideward away from the body (see s and t, Figure 26), letting the body fall easily backward. The hips must not flex or the result is one of sitting down rather than fall-ing. The body relaxes completely upon reaching the ground. (See t, Figure 26.)

b. Completed Fall. Lift the arms and tense all body muscles, heels on the ground in strong position. Contract the abdominal muscles and at the same time gradually relax the muscles of the chest, legs, and upper back, allowing the arms to fall and the knees to bend. Lean backward from the knees, reaching for the floor with the left hand, and keeping the hips forward. As the left hand touches the floor, it slides sideward. The body drops to the knees and falls backward as in preliminary exercise. See Figure 26.

c. Execute a Back Fall with a slight turn toward the left.

IV. Falling from a Lift on One Foot.          Music—"Sorrentina" (1)
                                              "Slide and Lift" (6)

This fall may be used following a Slide and Lift. (See I, 1, page 112.)

a. Lift body with a hop on right foot, left leg relaxed and slightly in back. As right foot returns to floor, relax body, allowing left knee to take the weight. Lower right knee to the floor, sit to the left and complete the movement as in Spiral Fall. (See Figure 24.)

b. Lift the body with a hop on right foot, lifting left knee. Reach for-ward and across body with left leg (as in Cross Polka, page 116), causing an extension in upper body. Continue reaching forward until body begins to lose balance. Land on front of instep, lower leg and knee of forward leg, leaning backward from the hips to maintain bal-ance as long as possible. As left knee touches the floor, lower right knee, sit to left of heels, and allow upper body to fall forward, relaxed. Finish as in Spiral Fall. This is an extremely difficult fall and should be taught to advanced students only.

V. Fall from a Run          Music—"Running and Falling" (2) (6)

Run forward and jump, landing on both feet. Fall as in I.

VI. Fall from a Whirl          Music—"Whirl and Fall" (6)

Start low, body hanging forward from hips. With shoulders and arms leading, whirl, taking fast steps in place. While whirling, gradually bring arms and shoulders higher and higher until arms are extended up-ward. Without discontinuing body movement, break with feet and allow twist of body to carry on into Fall I. See Figures 24 and 28.

G. Exercises to Develop a Follow Through    Music—"Träumerei" (3) (4)
   in Body Rotation                                  "Elevation" (1)
                                                     "Schmetterling" Merkel
                                                     "Rotation" (6)

   I. Trunk rotation. See Figure 10.
      a. Lying on back, relaxed, reach across body with left leg, keeping
         shoulders on floor. Continue reach until trunk is pulled into ro-
         tation and left shoulder starts to leave floor. Stretch throughout
         body; then relax and return to original position. Repeat on oppo-
         site side.
      b. Same exercise from face lying position.
      c. Lying on back, relaxed, reach across body with arm until trunk ro-
         tation results, stretch, and relax.
      d. Same as c, lying face down.

   II. Roll                                    Music—Same as G-1.
    Lying on floor completely relaxed, cause the body to roll over, using vari-
    ous leads, the rest of body hanging back as dead weight and moving only
    when it is pulled by the moving part.
      a. Lying on back, arms over head. Leg lead—Left leg reaches across
         right and extends along floor until it pulls left hip from floor. As it
         continues to reach, the trunk is twisted, the left shoulder finally be-

FIG. 27. THE SPIRAL TURN WITH A SHOULDER AND ARM LEAD

    gins to move, until whole body rolls over face down. Head is last to
    be affected.
      b. Lying face down, arms over head. Arm lead—Reach across behind
         body with left arm, until shoulder leaves floor. As it continues to
         reach, chest is elevated and head falls back. Movement next affects

trunk which twists toward left.  Finally hip and leg move, and body completes roll over.

III.  Spiral—same movement as roll except standing, taking turn in air.  A chest and shoulder lead should be used.  The head drops back.  In the follow-through, the trunk is rotated, and the feet are last to be affected by the movement.  See Figure 27 and also Figure 28 d.

IV.  Spiral Whirl                                    Music—"Whirl and Fall" (6)
Start low, body hanging forward from the hips.  With the shoulders and arms leading, whirl taking small steps in place.  As steps accelerate in speed, gradually bring the arms and shoulders higher and higher until the arms are extended upward.  Finish with a lift to complete extension or continue into a Spiral Fall.  See Figure 28.

H.  Lying down and getting up without use of arms.

I.  Relax upper body, allowing trunk to bend forward; extending one foot in front, sit down and lie backward, one leg straight, other bent.  Swing straight leg and arms over head, then forward, pulling self up to position on both feet, body bent forward over knees.  Lift hips; then extend hips lifting body to erect position.  See Figure 11.

II.  Lie down as in above exercise.  With both legs straight and arms at sides, lift as in abdominal lift.  As the body comes to sitting position, bend one knee and arch the back, swinging the arms sideward.  Get up by flexing the upper spine and swinging the arms forward.  See Figure 12.

I.  Exercises with the Body Moving Through Space

"Slide and Lift" (6)
I.  Slide and Lift                    Music—"Blue Danube" (4)
"Sorrentina" (1)
"Swing Song" (4)
The step pattern is three steps and a hop, the second step shorter than the other two.  During the three steps the body is upright with slight flexion in the cervical and upper dorsal region of the spine.  The arms are carried at shoulder height.  On the hop, the body is lifted with a vigorous extension of the upper back and neck and a strong lift of the chest.  As a result of this lift, the head falls back.  The free leg hangs relaxed.  The arms aid the chest-lift by moving sideward upward, the arm movement originating in the shoulders.  The rhythm is uneven;

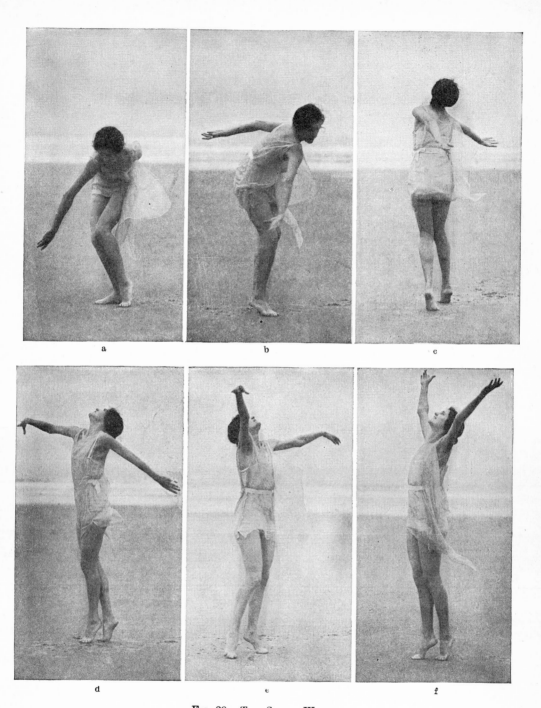

FIG. 28.  THE SPIRAL WHIRL

long—short—long—short.   Best adapted to music written in 3/4 or 6/8 time.   See Figure 29.

| Foot pattern | L | | s | L | | s |
|---|---|---|---|---|---|---|
| | Step | | close | step | | hop |
| Count with music | 1 | 2 | 3 | 1 | 2 | 3 |
| | 1 | 2 | 3 | 4 | 5 | 6 |

FIG. 29.   SLIDE AND LIFT

II.   Slide and Turn                                              Music *

The step pattern is four steps, the second and fourth shorter than the others.   During the first two steps the direction is sideward, the body upright with slight flexion in cervical and upper dorsal region.   The arms are carried at about shoulder height.   During the third and fourth steps a spiral turn with shoulder lead is executed.   If the pattern is started toward the left, the turn is made by lowering right shoulder and swinging right arm across in front of body; at the same time the left arm moves backward behind body, the upper body twisting to left and pulling rest of body into complete turn.   See Figure 27.   The rhythm is uneven, long, short, long, short.   Music best adapted is 3/4 or 6/8.

Progression in teaching.

a.   In partners, practice the childhood pattern called "Wring the Dishrag."   Couples facing hold hands and turn under both arms.   One person turns right, while other turns left.

b.   Same as (a), preceded by a slide in the direction in which the turn is made.

c.   Same as (b), except that the hands are unjoined at completion of the turn.

* Same music as that used for Slide and Lift.

d.  Practice Slide and Turn, facing partner, without joining hands.

e.  Practice (d), emphasizing a shoulder and chest lead.

NOTE: This same progression may be used in teaching the "Slide and Lift, Turning." In the latter, however, the foot pattern is Hop-step-close-step (polka), instead of Step-close-step-step. This results in an alternation of direction in turning; that is, if the first turn is toward the left, the second is toward the right.

III.  Slide and Leap Turn                                    Music *

Same as Slide and Turn except that on the turn the chest lift is done vigorously enough to lift the body off the floor so that the third step becomes a leap.

IV.  Slide and Lift Turning                                  Music *

Same as Slide and Lift, except that during the lift a spiral is executed, shoulder leading. The turn is alternately left and right, taken to the side of foot which takes first step. The turn may be either a half or whole turn. If a half turn is made, the slide is taken sideward. If a complete turn is made the slide should be backward.

V.  Slide and Lift with Leg Lead Turn                        Music *

Same as Slide and Lift, except that during the lift the free leg is carried forward and a turn is made toward the side of supporting leg. The turn leaves the free leg extended backward. See Figure 30.

FIG. 30.  SLIDE AND LIFT
WITH A LEG LEAD TURN

* Same music as that used for Slide and Lift.

VI.  Slide and Lift, Crossing (Cross Polka)          Music *

This movement includes an extension in chest and upper back which results from the reach of leg.  To gain this, practice slowly with support, the following: Lift right knee up to chest, head down.  Extend leg forward reaching across body.  As leg reaches forward, the hips are pulled forward.  The extension continues up spine and upper body leans back to balance, but not enough to retard forward movement of leg.  Chest lifts at end and head falls back.  (The entire movement in upper back must not occur independently, but as a result of reach of right leg.)  Body relaxes forward at end.  See Figure 31.  This, taken with a slide, and step-hop, occurs in place of chest lift in I, the complete pattern being as follows:

| L | s | L | s | |
|------|-------|------|-----|---|
| Step | close | step | hop | (Lifting right leg |
| Lt | Rt | Lt | Lt | across in front) |

After the right leg has reached forward, it takes the weight, this being the first step of a slide right.

FIG. 31.  THE CROSS POLKA

VII.  The High Jump (as adapted to dancing)  Music—"Atalanta" †
                                              "Sorrentina" (1)

A variation of the Slide and Lift with Leg Lead Turn.
Just before the turn, the free leg is lifted vigorously and as high as possible in front of the body.  As the turn is made the supporting leg is lifted as if attempting to clear the bar of a jumping standard.  In landing from the jump, the body is in a nearly horizontal position, and immediately after the supporting foot touches the ground, the weight is partially transferred to the hands.  The chest is brought toward the bent knee of the supporting leg.  The other leg is extended backward, the knee and instep resting lightly on the floor.  The head is up to give

---

* Same music as that used for Slide and Lift.          † See page 133.

the appearance of alertness. (The position assumed on landing is held momentarily. During this time the feet may exchange positions if it is desired that the following jumps be taken to same side. If the feet are not changed the jump is taken alternately right and left.)

VIII. The Discus Throw (As adapted to dancing)       Music—"Atalanta"

    a. Starting position
       Left foot 12 to 18 inches in advance of right, weight on left. Left arm hanging relaxed, right arm lifted slightly forward. Body erect over left foot, trunk twisted slightly to the left.

    b. Movement
       (1) Right arm swings backward, then forward and back; at the same time, the weight is transferred alternately right, left, right.
       (2) Right arm is then thrown vigorously forward and across body, leading the body in a spiral toward the left. As the turn is made three steps, left, right, left, are taken. (This is called a three-step turn; second step is short in time value.)

    c. Finish
       Follow-through of arm movement as if throwing discus, brings body into position similar to that assumed at start.

| | L | | L | | L | | L | |
| --- | --- | --- | --- | --- | --- | --- | --- | --- |
| Arm pattern | backward | | forward | | backward | | forward turning body into spiral | |
| Count 4/4 | 1 | | 2 | | 3 | | 4 | |
| 3/4 | 1 2 3 | | 1 2 3 | | 1 2 3 | | 1 2 3 | |
| 6/8 | 1 2 3 | | 4 5 6 | | 1 2 3 | | 4 5 6 | |

It is difficult to locate records of classical music which are suited for use with exercises due to the fact that few maintain a constant tempo. Records of some of the music referred to in this chapter are available in record form and may be used by adjusting the speed at which reproduced. When one wishes to use a part of a record, the place where victrola needle is to be placed or lifted may be marked by holding a piece of chalk against the revolving record.

The Victor record, Rhythm Medley, Number 20526, has been used with success for exercises when an accompanist was not available. This record is divided into sections which may be clearly heard. On page 118 is a list of exercises with which this record may be used:

| Suggested Exercise | Tempo of count | Counts per phrase | Phrases in section | Times exercise is done |
|---|---|---|---|---|
| **20526-A** | | | | |
| 1. Walk, run, whirl and fall | Moderate | 8 | 4 | 1 |
| 2. Arm flinging (with or without lift of hips) | Slow | 8 | 4 | 16 |
| 3. Head circling, chest lifting, body rotation, back lean | Count as 6/8 time, 4 meas. per phrase | | 6 | varies |
| 4. Arm swing with lift of body | Moderate | 16 | 2 | 8 |
| 5. Shoulder and arm in Figure 8 (sitting or with waltz run) | Slow | 8 | 4 | 16 |
| 6. Jumping (on both feet or alternating) | Moderate | 8 | 4 | 32 |
| 7. Same as 1 | | | | |
| **20526-B** | | | | |
| 1. Squat—spring—fling—spring | Moderate | 16 | 4 | 8 |
| 2. Jumping (on both feet or alternating) | Moderate | 8 | 4 | 32 |
| 3. Chest flexion and extension | Slow | 8 | 4 | 4 |
| 4. Pendulum swing of trunk and arms, continuing fourth swing into complete circle | Very slow | 4 | 8 | 8 |
| or | | | | |
| Pendulum swing of arms continuing third swing into spiral turn | Very slow | 4 | 8 | 8 |
| 5. Shoulder and arm in Figure 8 | Moderate | 16 | 8 | 32 |
| or | | | | |
| High Skip | Moderate | 16 | 8 | 64 |
| or | | | | |
| Polka | Moderate | 16 | 8 | 64 |

# CHAPTER XI

## DANCE STUDIES WITH RHYTHMIC ANALYSIS

The following are included as examples of simple dance studies which may be created by the instructor or the advanced classes and used in beginning and intermediate classes. They may serve not only as a recreational part of the daily lesson but also as an example from which the student may get her first inspiration for creating.

I. Chopin Waltz in G♭ major—Op. 70 ♯1.*
   Group dance.
   Formation, circle all facing in.
   Skills necessary.
      Slide and turn.
      Slide and half turn.
      Grand right and left in waltz rhythm.
   For analysis, see page 120.

II. Chopin Waltz in C♯ minor—Op. 64 ♯2.*
   Dance study for two or more.
   Formation in partners, inside arms crossed in back at waist, outside arm free.
   Skills necessary.
      Polka.
      Slide and turn.
      Waltz run.
      Waltz run turning in place with partner.
      Spiral whirl.
   See page 121.

III. Valse Lente (Coppelia) Delibes.†
   Formation, singly or in threes (hands joined) facing front.
   Skills included.
      Slide and Lift, Crossing.
      Waltz backward.
      Spiral Whirl.
   See page 122.

---

* May be bought in single copy or in collection of Chopin Waltzes, Volume 27, Schirmer's Library, G. Schirmer, N. Y.
   † Contained in collection "Masterpieces of Piano Music."

I

CHOPIN WALTZ IN G FLAT MAJOR

(Omit 1st Movement)

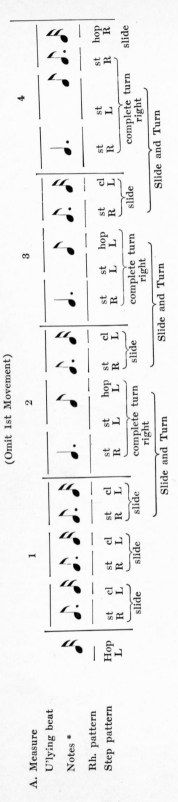

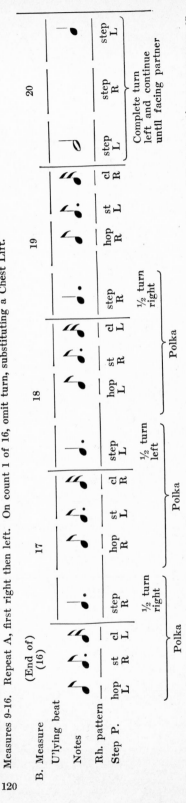

Measures 5-8. Same as 1-4, except executed toward the left.

Measures 9-16. Repeat A, first right then left. On count 1 of 16, omit turn, substituting a Chest Lift.

Measures 21-24. Give right hand to partner. With waltz step, move around circle with a "Grand Right and Left," meeting new person on count 1 of each measure. (Pass four persons, including partner.)

Measures 25-32. Face toward center of circle and repeat A, measures 1-8. Finish with a lift toward center.

* Notice that the rhythmic pattern is not identical with the note pattern.

120

II

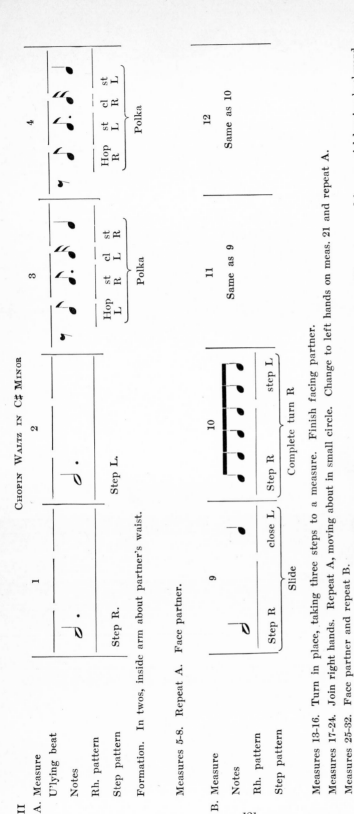

A. Measure | 1 | 2 | 3 | 4

U'lying beat

Notes

Rh. pattern

Step pattern | Step R. | Step L. | Hop st cl st / L R L R — Polka | Hop st cl st / R L R L — Polka

Formation. In twos, inside arm about partner's waist.

Measures 5-8. Repeat A. Face partner.

B. Measure | 9 | 10 | 11 | 12

Notes

Rh. pattern

Step pattern | Step R    close L | Step R    step L | Same as 9 | Same as 10
| Slide | Complete turn R

Measures 13-16. Turn in place, taking three steps to a measure. Finish facing partner.
Measures 17-24. Join right hands. Repeat A, moving about in small circle. Change to left hands on meas. 21 and repeat A.
Measures 25-32. Face partner and repeat B.
C. Measures 33-40. Join partner, arm about waist. Waltz Run turning in place on measures 39-40. (Turn is caused by one girl leaning backward, continuing steps in place, while partner makes a complete circle.)
Measures 41-44. Waltz Run with partner.
Measures 45-46. Turn in place as on 39-40.
Measures 47-48. Break away and whirl apart.
Measures 49-56. Join right hands with partner, turning in small circle with Waltz Run. Whirl away on 55-56.
Measures 57-64. Join left hands. Waltz Run turning in small circle, measures 57-60. Break away on 61 and whirl apart. Continue whirl until end of music, gradually decreasing speed. Finish in lifted position.

121

# VALSE LENTE (COPPELIA)

III

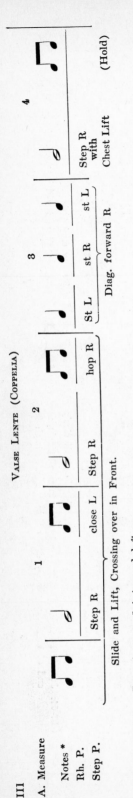
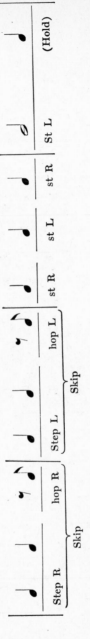

A. Measure
Notes *
Rh. P.
Step P.

| Step R | close L | Step R | hop R | St L | st R | st L | Step R with Chest Lift |
|---|---|---|---|---|---|---|---|

Diag. forward R

Slide and Lift, Crossing over in Front.

Measures 5-8.  Repeat meas. 1-4 toward left.
Measures 9-12.  Waltz backward, starting right.
Measures 13-16.  Slide and Turn R. meas. 13-14.  Step R and hold, meas. 15-16.
Measures 17-32.  Same as 1-16.

B. Measures 33-36.

| Step R | hop R | Step L | hop L | st R | st L | st R | St L |
|---|---|---|---|---|---|---|---|

Skip      Skip

(Hold)

Measures 37-40.  Whirl slowly in place with a waltz accent.
Measures 41-48.  Same as 33-40.
Measures 49-52.  Continue to whirl.
Measures 53-56.  Omit these measures.
Measures 57-60.  Gradually decrease speed of whirl and finally stop.
Measures 61-92.  Repeat A (1-32) using measures 91-92 for exit.

* Notice that the rhythmic pattern is not identical with the note pattern.

Waltz Arabesque

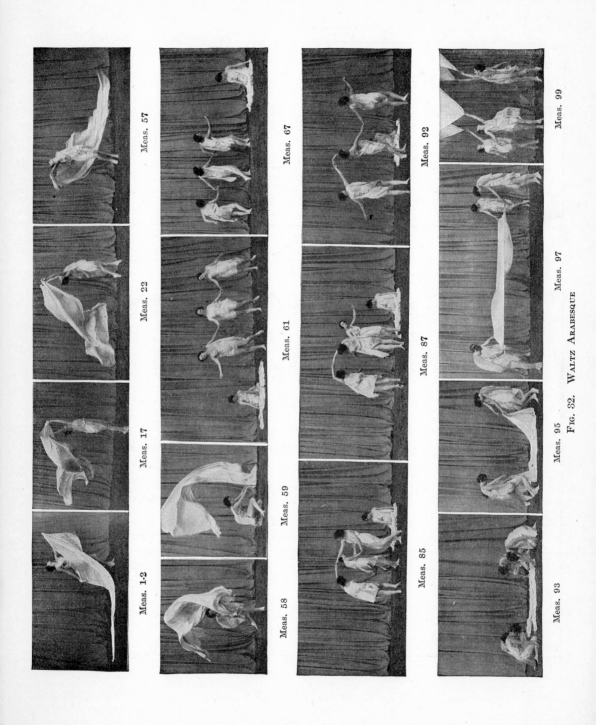

Meas. 1-2  Meas. 17  Meas. 22  Meas. 57

Meas. 58  Meas. 59  Meas. 61  Meas. 67

Meas. 85  Meas. 87  Meas. 92

Meas. 93  Meas. 95  Meas. 97  Meas. 99

Fig. 32.  Waltz Arabesque

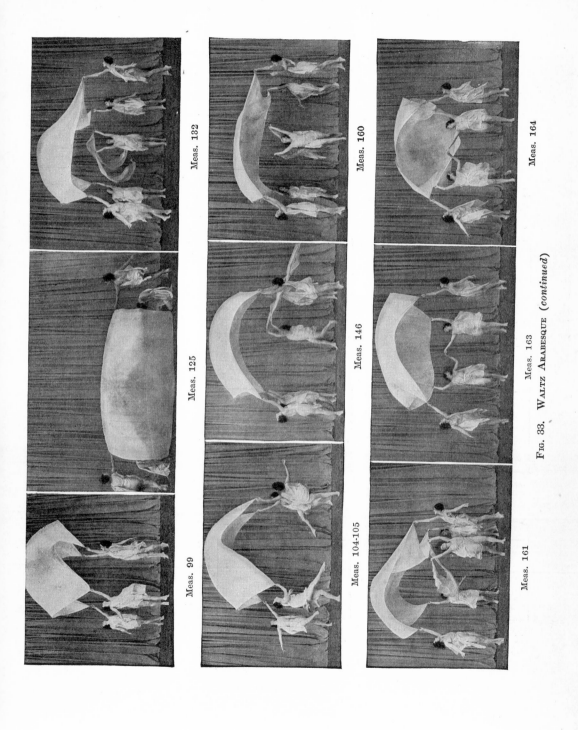

Meas. 99   Meas. 125   Meas. 132

Meas. 104-105   Meas. 146   Meas. 160

Meas. 161   Meas. 163   Meas. 164

FIG. 33. WALTZ ARABESQUE (*continued*)

~ Diagrams representing the floor pattern of Waltz Arabesque ~

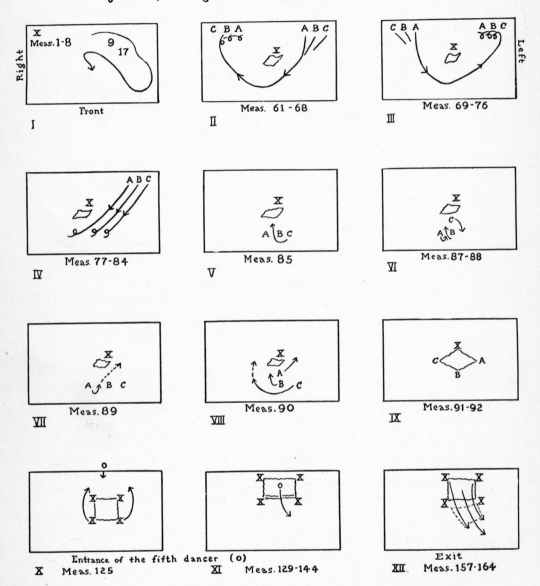

Front

I

II     Meas. 61 - 68

III    Meas. 69-76

IV     Meas. 77-84

V      Meas. 85

VI     Meas. 87-88

VII    Meas. 89

VIII   Meas. 90

IX     Meas. 91-92

X      Entrance of the fifth dancer (o)    Meas. 125

XI     Meas. 129-144

XII    Exit    Meas. 157-164

IV. Waltz Arabesque—Lack.*

> Group dance using scarfs.† See Figures 32 and 33.
> One large scarf 5 yards square.
> Two small scarfs 3 yards long, 1 yard wide.
> Formation varies.
> > a. Single dancer using large scarf.
> > b. Three dancers without scarfs.
> > c. Four dancers using large scarf.
> > d. Five dancers, four using large scarf, single dancer using two small scarfs.
> Costume—Dancers wear short tunics of same color as scarfs.

A. Meas. 1-4.    Single dancer enters from right with slow step (one step each two measures). Scarf is held high, drapes across body and drags on floor.

Meas. 5-8.    Dancer increases speed of steps (one step each measure).

Meas. 9-17.    Dancer runs (three steps to measure) in large circle about stage and finishes with a lift, center stage. (See diagram I, page 126.)

Meas. 18-20.    Music held—Omit.

Meas. 21-44.    Single dancer using large scarf moves about stage using various patterns; as skips, slide and lift, cross polka, etc. She finishes by running forward to center stage, throwing scarf forward over her head, and sitting down with scarf on floor in front of her.

Meas. 45-60.    Omit.

B. Meas. 61-64.    Three dancers enter left, hands joined; leap diagonally forward to center stage, three leaps to measure, first of each three, a high leap to give accent. (Begin on right foot.)

Meas. 65-68.    Three dancers run, following leader, to back right corner of stage. Dropping hands, each turns in place to face front. (See diagram II.)

Meas. 69-76.    Repeat Measures 61-68, moving left and finishing in back left hand corner. (Begin on left foot.) (See diagram III.)

Meas. 77-82.    Three, side by side (hands joined), waltz forward to center stage. (Begin on right foot.) (See diagram IV.)

Meas. 83-84.    Dropping hands, each turns in place (right) and finishes with lift forward.

Meas. 85-88.    Hands joined; waltz balance, "C" turns under raised hands of "A" and "B" (Meas. 85), "B" turns under raised arms of

---

* Music—"Waltz Arabesque" by Lack is published by G. Schirmer and by Century Music Publishing Co.

† Scarf material must be very light in weight. China silk has been found very satisfactory. It may be ordered by the bolt from Lawrence Textile Co., 105 E. 29th St., New York City. Fifty-yard bolt—@ 50¢ yd.—$25.00.

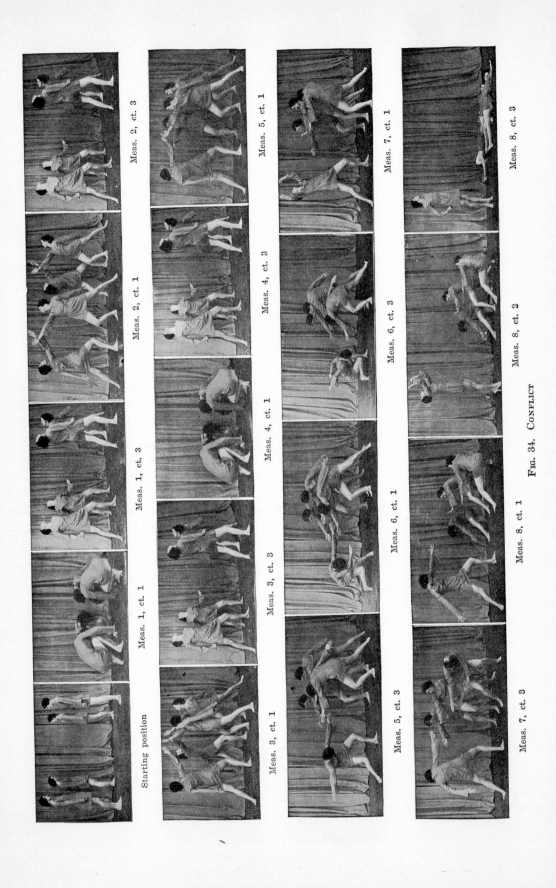

Starting position    Meas. 1, ct. 1    Meas. 1, ct. 3    Meas. 2, ct. 1    Meas. 2, ct. 3

Meas. 3, ct. 1    Meas. 3, ct. 3    Meas. 4, ct. 1    Meas. 4, ct. 3    Meas. 5, ct. 1

Meas. 5, ct. 3    Meas. 6, ct. 1    Meas. 6, ct. 3    Meas. 7, ct. 1

Meas. 7, ct. 3    Meas. 8, ct. 1    Meas. 8, ct. 2    Meas. 8, ct. 3

Fig. 34. Conflict

"A" and "B" (Meas. 86), "A" follows "B" (Meas. 87), all finish facing front.   (See diagrams V and VI.)

Meas. 89-92₂.*  "A" turns under raised arms of "C" and "B."   (Meas. 89.) "B" turns in place following "A," while "C" moves right, passing around group.  (Meas. 90.)   All facing back move toward single dancer and drop to knees, ready to pick up corner of scarf.   (See diagrams VII, VIII, IX.)

C. Meas. 93-104.  Four dancers rise slowly stretching scarf and holding it low until count 1 of measure 99 when each lifts to full extension allowing scarf to float high.   Dancers on left of stage hold scarf in right hand, other two hold it with left.   The scarf is pulled down on meas. 101, but lifted again on 103, reaching the floor on count 1 of 102, and in full extension on count 1 of meas. 104.

Meas. 105-108.  Holding corner of scarf in left hand, dancers move about circle to right with step pattern, two high skips and six running steps.

Meas. 109-124.  C is repeated on measures 109-124.

D. Meas. 125-128.  Two dancers in front run backward to outside of other two who kneel, holding back corner of scarf close to floor.   As scarf folds over itself, fifth dancer slips through break in curtain and bends low under scarf as it falls (see diagram X).

Meas. 129-144.  As four dancers lift scarf, single dancer lifts to full extension, then runs out from under scarf and dances alone as others allow scarf to sink slowly.   (See diagram XI.)

Meas. 145-148.  Four dancers lift scarf, keeping it stretched as a canopy as single dancer runs under from one side to other.

E. Meas. 149-164.  Scarf sinks slowly and is lifted once more. (Meas. 157) as single dancer runs under, lifts to full extension, then skips forward followed by dancers holding back corners of scarf. These three all carrying scarfs exit forward leaving other two who have dropped scarf, standing in full extension.   (See diagram XII.)

V. Conflict.

Music:   "Stride," Louis Horst,† or "Conflict," Eunice Steel.‡ Throughout this problem, movement occurs on counts 1 and 3 and the pose is held on counts 2 and 4.

---

* 92 ₂ is second ending of Part B of music.

† Louis Horst, Dance accompanist at the Graham Studio, New York City.  See I 2, p. 131.

‡ Eunice Steel, Dance accompanist, Oregon State College, Dept. of Physical Education.  See I 6, page 133.

Meas. 1—On count 1 the four people standing on the corners of an imaginary square, step forward R into center, arms brought strongly over the head, and down into a crouching position.  Count 3, step back R, turning toward R to face out, into strong standing position broad base, arms at side, fists clenched.

Meas. 2—Partners lunge toward each other, stepping R, arms crossed at wrists, heads back.  Count 3, repeat action of Count 3, Meas. 1.

Meas. 3—Step R into circle, R arms raised, L down.  Count 3—repeat as in Meas. 1.

Meas. 4—Repeat action of Meas. 1.

Meas. 5—Three members of group step into line opposing the "fourth" who faces them.  Step R, R arm raised.  Count 3—Step forward L, L arm forward.  "Four" steps back R into low position with L arm forward.

Meas. 6.—The three step forward R, R arm forward, "Four" steps back L, both arms forward (the position is one of retreat).  Count 3—The three step forward L.  "Four" steps back R into crouching position, head down, both arms back, fists clenched.

Meas. 7—"Four" stands erect with strong push from hips, arms raised.  The three step back R in retreat.  Count 3—"Four" steps forward R, R arm out.  The three step back L.

Meas. 8—"Four" steps forward L, L arm forward.  The three step back R into crouching position.  Count 3—"Four" raises both arms and brings them down strongly, fists clenched.  The three fall backward, R knee bent, L straight, arms overhead.

For illustration of positions, see Figure 34.

VI. Cinderella—A dance dramatization of the familiar fairy tale.
Music—arranged from the following:

Melodie—Massenet.
Gavotte—Gossec.
Fifth Nocturne—Leybach.
Loin Du Bal—Gillet.

The story is suggested entirely through natural dance movements and pantomime.  An attempt is made to keep movements from being too realistic.

A. Cinderella on floor—arm movements suggest scrubbing—body and facial expression as if day-dreaming.
Music Melodie
Meas. 1-9

B. Sisters enter and demand help in dressing for ball.
Gavotte
Stepmother enters and demands attention.
Meas. 1-16
Sisters and mother admire each other and pantomime dancing at the ball.  Cinderella looks on longingly as they leave.
(No repeats)
Meas. 17-24
Meas. 25-48

C. Cinderella mourns.                                                      Fifth Nocturne
                                                                          Meas. 1-9

    Fairy God-mother enters, dances about Cinderella who can
scarcely believe her eyes.                                                Meas. 10-28
God-mother dresses Cinderella and calls coach.                            Meas. 29-40
God-mother teaches Cinderella to dance.                                   Meas. 41-56

D. At the ball.  Two sisters and mother are present and notice-           Loin du Bal
ably waiting for attention.                                               Meas. 1-4
Prince approaches and asks one sister to dance.                           Meas. 5-8
Prince and first sister dance, finishing near mother and second
sister, who have been waiting their turn expectantly.                     Meas. 9-28
Prince and second sister dance.                                           Meas. 29-48
Prince invites stepmother to dance.                                       Meas. 49-52
Prince and stepmother dance during which time Cinderella
enters.  Prince sees her and watches her as he finishes the
dance and thanks stepmother.                                              Meas. 52-83
Prince invites and dances with Cinderella.                                Meas. 84-129
Cinderella hears the clock chime twelve.                                  Meas. 130-133
Cinderella runs away.  Prince following picks up her slipper.             Meas. 134-145

E. Prince and Page come to Cinderella's home to find one whom             Gavotte
slipper fits.  They announce their errand.                                Meas. 1-8
They try the slipper on first sister with no success.                     Meas. 9-16
Second sister unable to force foot into slipper.                          Meas. 17-24
Mother tries.                                                             Meas. 25-32
Page finds Cinderella in corner.  Brings her to Prince who
fits slipper and recognizes her.                                          Meas. 33-48

F. Prince and Cinderella, reliving the ball, dance together while         Loin du Bal
mother and sisters exit in a "huff."                                      Meas. 52-83

For other music which may be used in creating dance studies from a rhythmic
approach see Page 133.


Suggested References:
    I. Music for class work (The numbers 1-6 used in connection with music in
                Chapter X, refer to the following list)
        1. Wisconsin Blue Print—(for fundamentals)—order from Department
           of Physical Education—University of Wisconsin.
        2. Music for Martha Graham's work, written by Louis Horst, Dance
           Accompanist at Graham Studio, New York City.
        3. Masterpieces of Piano Music, M.U.M.I.L. Publishing Co.
        4. Gems of Melody and Rhythm for Young People—Steenman—Theo.
           Presser Co., Philadelphia.

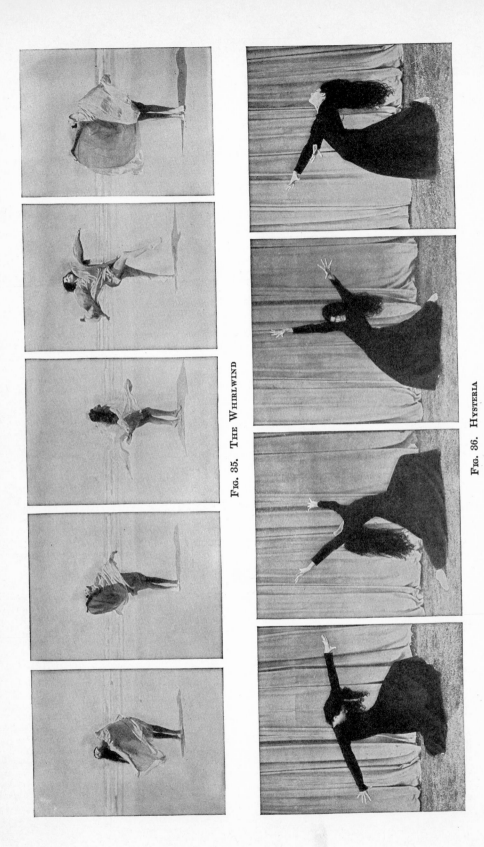

Fig. 35. The Whirlwind

Fig. 36. Hysteria

5. Music for Natural Dancing—Ruth Garland—G. Schirmer Inc., N. Y.
6. Music for Exercises in Creative Dance—Eunice Steel and Thelma Petersen.
   This collection includes music for each exercise described in Chapter X and was composed expressly for use with dance classes. For price list write to Department of Physical Education for Women, Oregon State College, Corvallis, Oregon.

II. Music and Dances
7. Natural Dance Studies—Helen Smith—A. S. Barnes and Co.
8. Rhythms and Dances for Elementary Schools—Dorothy LaSalle—A. S. Barnes and Co.
9. A.B.C. of Children's Rhythm—Elizabeth Waterman—Clayton-Summy Publishing Co.
10. Natural Rhythms and Dances—Gertrude Colby—A. S. Barnes & Co.
11. The Dance in Education—Marsh—A. S. Barnes and Co.
12. Dance Studies Analyzed *—Betty Lynd Thompson and Margaret Jewell.

III. Suggested Music for Dances (not included in above)

|  | Suggestions for some of the possible movements. |
|---|---|
| † Atalanta—Hellebrandt | —Vigorous—running, slide and lift turning, discus throw and other athletic events. |
| Camp of Gypsies—Behr | —Light, joyous—skips, polkas, slides. |
| Caprice Viennois—Kreisler | —Slow, smooth—turns. Vigorous—lifts and whirls. |
| † Dance Sonata—Hellebrandt | —Vigorous—runs, leaps, whirls. Slow—soft flowing movement. Gay—skips, polkas, etc. Vigorous, heavy—leaps, runs. |
| Dream Tango—Melderen | —Vigorous—tango, lifts, turns, etc. |
| Espanita—Rosey | —Vigorous waltz—slide and lift, turns, high skips. |
| * Fireworks—Debussey | —Vigorous—Leaps and whirls, falls. Includes scarf work. |
| Folk Dance—E. German | —Fast, folk spirit—schottische, polka, folk dance steps and formations. |
| Juba—Dill | —Syncopated joyous frenzy of Negro. |

* May be purchased direct. Address Department of Physical Education for Women, Oregon State College, Corvallis, Oregon. Music is not included in text, but is available in familiar collections or in single copies.
† Music in blue print form may be obtained through the Department of Physical Education, Women's Division, University of Wisconsin, Madison, Wisconsin.

King's Breakfast—Fraser Simson—Gay, comedy—pantomime and rhythmic interpretation.

Kuiawaik—Weiniaski          —Vigorous—mazurka, leaps, lifts, turns.

Liebeslied (Love's Sorrow)  
Liebesfreud (Love's Joy)    }—Kreisler—Contrasting mood.

Les Sylphes—Bachmann        —Fast, gay—excellent for scarf work.

* Mazurka from Ballet Coppelia—  
                 Delibes—Fast, vigorous—mazurka, lifts, turns.

Minor and Major—Spross      —Contrasting sadness and joy.

† Moods of the River—Hellebrandt—Light, fast—skips, whirls.  
                      Slow, flowing—excellent for scarf work.

‡ Moods of the Nations—Petersen—Folk characterizations.

Old Refrain—Kreisler        —Slow flowing movements.

Overture—(from Poet and Peasant)—F. von Suppe        —Vigorous, strong—leaps, whirls, etc.

* Polish Dance—Scharwenka    —Vigorous mazurka.

Preludes—Chopin 1-24 op. 28  —Strong movement.

Prelude in G minor—  
           Rachmaninoff—Heavy—strong movement.

Prophet Bird—Schumann       —Weird—slow movements with accurate rhythmic interpretations.

* Romance—Rubenstein         —Dance Orchestration for 50-100 students.

* Sea Gardens—Cook           —Soft flowing movements with contrast of vigor.

* Skaters Waltz—Waldteufel   —Vigorous—skips, turns, waltz runs.

* Sing-a-Song—Steele         —Comedy based on nursery rhyme.

* Turkish March—Beethoven    —Vigorous heavy work.

Valse Lente (Coppelia)—Delibes—See Page 119.

Valse Triste—Sibelius       —Sad—vigorous.

Voices of Spring—Strauss    —Slow slides and turns, etc.

Waltz Arabesque—Lack        —See Page 127.

* Waltz Brilliante—Chopin    —Vigorous waltz.

Waltz in C♯ Minor—Chopin    —See Page 119.

Waltz in G Flat Major—Chopin—See Page 119.

Waltz No. I and II—Jensen   —Gay, light.

Whirlwind—Krantz            —Vigorous, fast—movements suggesting caprice of whirlwind. (See Figure 35.)

---

* Described in Dance Studies Analyzed. See II, 12, page 133.  
† See footnote †, page 133.  
‡ See I 6, page 133.

IV. Music for Dance Dramas

"Life of Dance"—depicting History of Dance—Kornhouser.*

"The Little Princess Who Couldn't Dance"—Hellebrandt.*

"The Juggler"—(Christmas Story)—Bertha Ocshner.*

"Sleeping Beauty"—Eunice Steel. Address Department of Physical Education for Women, Oregon State College, Corvallis, Oregon.

V. Theory

The Dance and Its Place in Education—H'Doubler—Harcourt Brace and Co.

Creative Activities in Physical Education—Horrigan—A. S. Barnes & Co.

The Dance in Education—Marsh—A. S. Barnes & Co.

The Importance of Being Rhythmic—Pennington.

Elements of the Free Dance—Selden—A. S. Barnes & Co.

Eurhythmics, Art and Education—Dalcroze—A. S. Barnes & Co.

Expression Gymnastics—Bode—A. S. Barnes & Co.

Dancing in the Elementary Schools—Dance Committee A.P.E.A.—A. S. Barnes & Co.

* These and others may be obtained by writing to the Department of Physical Education, Women's Division, University of Wisconsin, Madison, Wisconsin.

# TAP, CLOG, AND FOLK DANCING

# CHAPTER XII

## FUNDAMENTALS OF TAP DANCING AND CLOGGING

Tap dancing and clogging are two of the most popular rhythmic activities today, not only to the young boy and girl, but also to college students and adults. Wherever they are offered, a large group of enthusiasts will be found, be it in school, studio, or community house. Large groups of men, women, and children, from all walks of life will find a common interest in these two types of dancing.

Through tap dancing and clogging the student gains excellent rhythmic training as well as a certain skill and co-ordination. If well analyzed neither activity is difficult, and the person who cannot learn at least simple routines is rare, while in a series of ten or twelve lessons the person of average skill will become fairly proficient.

These activities are especially enjoyable because they can be performed either by a group or by a single individual, either in class with instructor and accompanist or at home by radio, victrola, or vocal accompaniment. Also, after certain fundamentals are mastered (a vocabulary, as it were), each individual may invent his own combinations and routines.

Tap dancing differs from clogging only slightly. It is more fascinating because it is more irregular, more syncopated, and when mastered is performed more rapidly. Also, tap routines are usually worked out so that they will fit any music of similar time and tempo, while clogs are usually planned for a definite piece of music.

The fundamentals are essentially the same except that they are performed in a different rhythm. Since the rhythm in either tap or clogging is extremely important, it seems logical to teach the fundamentals through this approach.

The most elementary skill is the *rattle*. This consists of a brush of the foot, forward and back, making two sounds. Standing on the left foot, with right knee and hip slightly bent to keep right heel off the floor, right foot is brushed forward and slapped backward. The foot is relaxed at the ankle so a clear sound (not a scrape) is made in each direction. (It is helpful to have aluminum taps nailed to toe of each shoe, which should be light in weight and flexible with a low heel. On the other hand, the metal taps, unless of a good grade and well attached, frequently scratch the floor very badly. For use with large groups in a gymnasium, ordinary sport oxfords with leather soles have been found very satisfactory. In situations where the same floor is later being used by sports classes or by dance classes in bare feet the students in tap and clog classes should

139

be requested to keep a clean pair of shoes for indoor use only.)  The feet are kept close together and the rattle made just under and slightly in front of the body.  It is a fault to let the foot swing through too wide an arc.  The rattle may be done in an even or uneven rhythm—being used evenly for clogging but either way for tap.

Evenly the rhythm is

|  |  |  |  |  |  |  |  |  |
|---|---|---|---|---|---|---|---|---|
| 1 | 1 | 1 | 1 , | | | | or | ♩ ♩ ♩ ♩ |
| brush | slap | brush | slap | br. | sl. | br. | sl. | br.  sl.  br.  sl. |

rattle

Unevenly the rhythm is

|  |  |  |  |  |  |  |  |  |
|---|---|---|---|---|---|---|---|---|
| s | l | s | l , | | | | or | ♪ ♩. ♪ ♩. |
| brush | slap | brush | slap | br. | sl. | br. | sl. | br.  sl.  br.  sl. |

rattle

Clap each rhythm until it is mastered; then duplicate that rhythm.  In doing the rattle the weight remains always over the same foot, so when the right foot gets tired of doing the rattle, change and practice on the left.

The next fundamental is the *shift* or the *one* as it is called.  Since it is a one-part pattern it has no rhythmic pattern, being given a long or short value at will.  Usually in clogging it is given a value twice as long as a brush or a slap; that is, as long as the two combined.

Practice the shift slowly doing a succession of "ones" in even rhythm.

| Long | Long | Long | Long | | | | |
|---|---|---|---|---|---|---|---|
| Shift | Shift | | | ♩ | ♩ | ♩ | ♩ |
| Right | Left | Right | Left | Right | Left | Right | Left |

Standing with the weight on the left foot, a shift (or a "one") is accomplished merely by changing the weight to the right foot.  This may be done in place (as marking time in marching) by placing whole of right foot on floor and lifting heel of left foot; it may be done moving forward or back (it is then simply walking); or it may be done as running in place, lifting the knees high.

Now practice a succession of shifts in uneven rhythm.

| s | l | s | l | | | ♪ ♩. ♪ ♩. |
|---|---|---|---|---|---|---|
| Rt Lt | Rt Lt | Rt | Lt | Rt | Lt | Rt Lt  Rt Lt |

In doing two shifts in uneven rhythm, it helps to place the toe of the foot, which takes the short unit, behind the other foot.  On the short unit the weight is shifted only momentarily to the toe of rear foot, then to the whole of the front foot for the long unit.  In the above diagram, since the right foot is taking the short unit of the rhythmic pattern, it would be placed in back of the left foot and the right toe only would take the weight.

The "shift" or "one" is essentially a "step" and may be referred to as any of these terms.

Combinations of "Rattles" and "Ones"

Practice a series of three rattles and a "one" in this rhythm

(a)
s   s   s   s   s   s   1

Rat tle   rat tle   rat tle   shift

Rt       Rt       Rt       Rt

Then repeat on opposite foot.   Continue first right, then left.

Next practice two rattles and a shift, and repeat in this rhythm

(b)
s   s   s   s   1   s   s   s   s   1

Rat tle   rat tle   shift   rat tle   rat tle   shift

Rt       Rt       Rt       Left     Left     Left

Practice one rattle and a shift and repeat in this rhythm

(c)
s   s   1   s   s   1   s   s   1

Rat tle   shift   rat tle   shift   rat tle   shift

Rt       Rt     Left   Left     Rt       Rt

This combination of a rattle and a shift is called a *three* for it makes three sounds.   Notice that the "shift" or the "one" takes twice as long as either of the first two sounds and that it gets the accent.   Note also that if the first "three" is done with the right foot, the next "three" is done with the left foot, and so on alternately right and left.

In doing these combinations to music, we will let each short equal an eighth note, and each long will equal a quarter note.

The rhythm will equal then—

(a)   s   s   s   s   s   s   1 = ♪♪ ♪♪ ♪♪ ♩  $\left(\frac{4}{4}\right)$

Rattle   Rattle   Rattle   Shift

(b)   s   s   s   s   1       = ♪♪ ♪♪ ♩  $\left(\frac{3}{4}\right)$

Rattle   Rattle Shift

(c)   s   s   1       = ♪♪ ♩  $\left(\frac{2}{4} \text{ or } \frac{4}{4}\right)$

Rattle   Shift

The first will equal one measure of 4/4 time, the second will equal one measure of 3/4 time, and the third will equal one measure of 2/4 time or one half a measure of 4/4 time.

Practice these to music and you will discover that (b) is more satisfying done to 3/4 time (waltz) while (a) and (c) fit either 2/4 or 4/4 music.

You will also notice that (a) and (c) can be used interchangeably within the same music, but that a better grouping is felt if (c) is repeated so as to equal (a); for example,

> "rattle step rattle step rattle rattle rattle step"

is more satisfying than

> "rattle step rattle rattle rattle step rattle step"

while "rattle step rattle rattle rattle step" is not good because it does not complete a phrase and leaves an unfinished feeling.

A "three" followed by a step is called a *four*. It is more easily executed if the final step of the "three" is done on the ball of the foot, or if the foot taking the "three" is placed in back of the foot which takes the final step of the "four."

The four may be analyzed as:

| s | s | s | s | | s | s | s | s |
|---|---|---|---|---|---|---|---|---|
| Rat- | tle | shift | shift | | Rat- | tle | shift | shift |
| | Rt | Rt | Lt | | Rt | Rt | Lt | |

Three

Four

When a number of "fours" are repeated in succession they all begin on the same foot.

Another fundamental which fits 4/4 time is a *seven*. Its rhythm is the same as (a) s s s s s s l, but the step pattern is like two "three's" and a "one," or like a "three" and a "four," namely,

| Rat | tle | shift | rat | tle | shift | shift |
|-----|-----|-------|-----|-----|-------|-------|
| Rt | Rt | Rt | Lt | Lt | Lt | Rt |

Three    Three    One

Four

| rat | tle | shift | rat | tle | st | st |
|-----|-----|-------|-----|-----|----|----|
| Lt | Lt | Lt | Rt | Rt | Rt | Lt |

Three    Four

Seven

We may call it two "three's" and a "one" without a pause after the "three." It may be counted "one, two, three, four, five, six, seven"—with a silent pause on "eight."

Notice that on counts "six" and "seven" you have two shifts in uneven rhythm. Do these with your toe in back on count "six" and it will be easier and will also give a stress to count "seven."

Note also that (as in "threes") if the first "seven" is started on the right foot, the next "seven" begins on the left.

"Threes" and "sevens" may be used interchangeably but 2 "threes" and 1 "seven" make a better combination than 1 "three" and 1 "seven."

Another pattern which fits 4/4 time and may be used with "threes" and "sevens" is a combination of a "three" and two steps done in this rhythm:

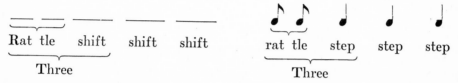

It has five sounds but is called a "plain five" to distinguish it from a "waltz five."

In doing threes, fours, sevens and plain fives with 4/4 music, one must synchronize the accent of the foot pattern with the accent of the music. The following diagram should illustrate on which count the fundamental begins and which part is accented. Since in 4/4 music we have an accent on count one with a sec-

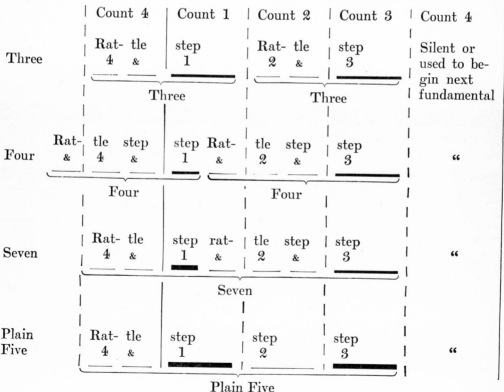

ondary accent on count three, the above fundamentals are executed so that the accenting foot steps on those counts. In all of the above fundamentals the final step is accented, therefore the other units with which the fundamental begins must come on some count previous to one or three.

The *Waltz Five* commonly referred to as a "Five" has the same rhythm as pattern (b). (See Combinations of "rattles" and "ones," page 141.)

The foot pattern of a "five" is a step, a "three" and a step or it might be called a step-rattle-step-step, or it may be considered a step followed by a "four."

| Step | rat- tle | step | step | | Step | rat- tle | step | step |
| Lt | Rt | Rt | Lt | | Rt | Lt | Lt | Rt |

It may be counted "one, two, three, four, five," with count "six" a silent pause. On count four the toe is placed in back as on count six in a "seven."

To bring out the waltz time of the music, count the Five, "one, and, two, and, three."

| 1 | and | 2 | and | 3 | | 1 | and | 2 | and | 3 |
|---|-----|---|-----|---|---|---|-----|---|-----|---|
| Step | rat- tle | step | step | | | Step | rat- tle | step | step | |

A waltz five * should be done only to waltz music as its complete pattern equals a measure of 3/4 music. It cannot be used interchangeably with "threes" or "plain fives" as these do not fit 3/4 music.

As you practice these fundamentals notice that combinations which equal two or four measures sound best when repeated because they fit the phrasing of the music. Therefore the following combinations will be satisfying to 4/4 music:

(1) 2 "threes" and 1 "seven," repeated.
(2) 4 "threes" and 2 "sevens," repeated.
(3) 2 "threes," 1 "plain five," 2 "threes," 1 "seven," repeated.

Or to 3/4 music.

(1) 4 "Waltz Fives."
(2) 2 slow skips and 2 "Waltz Fives."
(3) 4 slow skips and 4 "Waltz Fives."
(4) 3 slow skips and 1 "Waltz Five."
(5) 3 "Waltz Fives" and 1 slow skip.

* For progression in teaching see page 164.

Having mastered the above fundamentals it should not be difficult to understand the clogs from such books as:

"The Clog Dance Book"—Helen Frost.

"Clogs and Character Dances"—Helen Frost.

"Simple Clogs and Athletic Dances"—Hillas and Knighton.

"Oriental and Character Dances"—Helen Frost.

"Clogs and Jigs"—Mary Wood Hinman.

It will help in the correct execution of all clogs if time is taken to analyze clearly just how the steps fit the music. By marking off the counts by measures and fitting the step pattern and its rhythm into this form, one will be more conscious of the correct timing of the steps with the music. Below is an example of how this might be done.

Analyze your original dance by measures as follows:

*Example from Clementine—3/4 music*

| | Measure | | | Measure | | |
|---|---|---|---|---|---|---|
| Count 3 | Count 1 | Count 2 | Count 3 | Count 1 | Count 2 | Count 3 |
| Step L / Brush R | Rock on R heel | Step L | Step R  Brush L | Rock on L heel | Step R | Step L  Brush R |
| 3  & | 1 | 2 | 3  & | 1 | 2 | 3  & |
| | Rock R  Step L | Brush Back R / Rock Back R toe | Step L  Brush R | Rock forward on R heel | Step Left | Step R  Brush L |
| | 1  & | 2  & | 3  & | 1 | 2 | 3  & |

*Example from Reuben Taps—4/4 music*

| | Measure | | | | Measure | | | |
|---|---|---|---|---|---|---|---|---|
| Count 4 | Count 1 | Count 2 | Count 3 | Count 4 | Count 1 | Count 2 | Count 3 | Count 4 |
| Rat- tle L L | Tap Toes | Rat- tle L L | Tap Toes | Rat- tle L L | step rat L R | Seven  tle step R R | step L | Rat- tle R R  etc. |
| 4  & | 1 | 2  & | 3 | 4  & | 1  & | 2  & | 3 | 4  & |

# CHAPTER XIII

## TAP ROUTINES

Tap Dancing is no harder than clogging except that usually the fundamentals are combined into longer and more difficult patterns. Tap Dances are usually classified as Waltz Tap, Buck and Wing, or Soft Shoe.

Waltz Tap includes routines done to Waltz music, that is to a three-part underlying beat; Buck and Wing is done to 4/4 music, as a fox-trot—four-part underlying beat; Soft Shoe is usually done to 6/8 time, having a six-part underlying beat.

The following routines have been taught to classes of beginners, both men and women, with definite success. Clap these rhythms slowly, then try the foot patterns. When the foot pattern of each phrase has been mastered practice it in the rhythm given. (When counting keep the count regular.) Later combine the phrases into the routine as analyzed.

WALTZ TAP

Music—"Monterey"
"Dancing with Tears in My Eyes"
"Let Me Call You Sweetheart"

The fundamental step of this routine is a "waltz six," which resembles a "waltz five" except that it is preceded by a brush, and is uneven in rhythm.

| Music ...... | | | | | | | | | | | | |
|---|---|---|---|---|---|---|---|---|---|---|---|
| Count ...... | (& | 1 | & | 2 | & | 3) | (& | 1 | & | 2 | & | 3) |
| Rhythm .... Step pattern | Brush Lt | step Lt | rat- Rt | tle Rt | step Rt | step Lt | Brush Rt | step Rt | rat- Lt | tle Lt | step Lt | step Rt |

Waltz Six
(beginning left)

Waltz Six
(beginning right)

The Waltz Six may be learned as follows:

(1) Place left toe behind right and practice a double shift in uneven rhythm.

| s | L | s | L | s | L | etc. |
|---|---|---|---|---|---|---|
| step Rt | step Lt | step Rt | step Lt | step Rt | step Lt | |

146

(2) Standing on right foot practice an uneven rattle with left foot.

|  s | L |  s | L |  s | L |  |
|---|---|---|---|---|---|---|
| rat- | tle | rat- | tle | rat- | tle | etc. |

(3) Now add double shift to rattle, thus:

|  s | L |  s | L |  s | L |  s | L | etc. |
|---|---|---|---|---|---|---|---|---|
| Rat- | tle | step | step | Rat- | tle | step | step | |
| Rt | Rt | Rt | Lt | Rt | Rt | Rt | Lt | |

(Four)            (Four)

This may be called a "four."

(4) Now practice (1), (2) and (3) starting on opposite foot, that is, rattle left, step left, step right and repeat in uneven rhythm.

(5) Practice stumbling in uneven rhythm. A stumble, also called a spank, is a quick brush forward, followed by a step on the same foot; repeat on opposite foot.

|  s | L |  s | L |  s | L |  s | L |
|---|---|---|---|---|---|---|---|
| Brush | step | brush | step | brush | step | brush | step |
| Lt | Lt | Rt | Rt | Lt | Lt | Rt | Rt |

(6) Now do a stumble Lt and a "Four" Rt in uneven rhythm and you have a "Waltz Six."

| Brush | step | rat- | tle | step | step |
|---|---|---|---|---|---|
| Lt | Lt | Rt | Rt | Rt | Lt |

Stumble            Four

Waltz Six

You finish with your weight on the left foot ready to do a "six" on the right.

Continue slowly until you have mastered the "Waltz Six." Practice with music, starting just before the first count of the measure. (The first brush comes just at the last of the preceding measure.) Keep it uneven so that beats 1, 2, 3 of the music get the longer and heavier sounds in the tap.

In tap dancing a pattern which is used at the end of each verse or chorus is called the *break*. The "break" for this Waltz Tap consists of two "waltz six's" —one left, one right, followed by

| & | 1 | & | 2 | & | 3 | & | 1 | & | 2 | 3 |
|---|---|---|---|---|---|---|---|---|---|---|
| Brush | step | rat- | tle | hop | step | stum- | ble | stum- | ble | jump to |
| Lt | Lt | Rt | Rt | | back | forward | | forward | | both feet |
| | | | | | Lt | Rt | Lt | Lt | Rt | Rt |

Stumble

| 1 | | 2 | | 3 |
|---|---|---|---|---|
| Place R toe across | and | Make a complete turn to the left | and | Bring weight to R |

FIG. 37.  TURN ON TOES—WALTZ TAP

| 1 | 2 | 3 | 1 | 2 | 3 |
|---|---|---|---|---|---|
| Step left | Brush R forward | Brush R across | Brush R forward | Step right | Touch left toe |

FIG. 38.  WALTZ TAP—PART C

The whole break takes one 4-measure phrase of music.

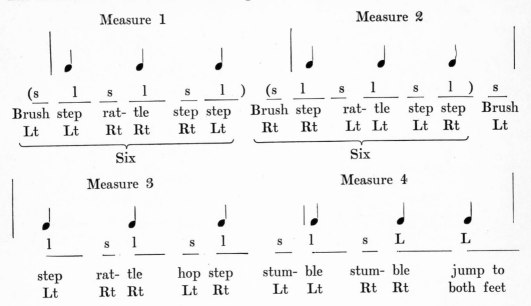

|        | Measure 1 |      |       |       |       |     | Measure 2 |       |      |       |       |       |
| (s | l | s | l | s | l ) | (s | l | s | l | s | l ) | s |
| Brush | step | rat- | tle | step | step | Brush | step | rat- | tle | step | step | Brush |
| Lt | Lt | Rt | Rt | Rt | Lt | Rt | Rt | Lt | Lt | Lt | Rt | Lt |

Six        Six

| Measure 3 | | | | | | | Measure 4 | |
| l | s | l | s | l | s | l | s | L | L |
| step | rat- | tle | hop | step | stum- | ble | stum- | ble | jump to |
| Lt | Rt | Rt | Lt | Rt | Lt | Lt | Rt | Rt | both feet |

Throughout this waltz tap routine there are six parts of four phrases each and one final part of eight phrases.

The final phrase of each part is the "break." Each phrase takes four measures of waltz music, and the first two measures of each phrase are used for two "six's," left and right. The final two measures of each phrase vary as follows:

|  |  |  |  | PHRASE I | | | | | | Phrases 2, 3 & 4 |
|  | Measures 1 & 2 | | Measure 3 | | | Measure 4 | | | |
| ¾ | | | Count 1 | Count 2 | Count 3 | Count 1 | Count 2 | Count 3 | Repeat Phrase 1 twice, and follow by the "break" |
| Part a. | Six L | Six R | Step L | Swing R across | Hop L | Step R across | Hop R | Hop R | |
| b. | " | " | " | " | " | Place R toe across | Turn on toes (complete turn) | Place wt. on R heel | " |
| c. | " | " | Step L | Brush R forward | Brush R across L | Brush R across R | Step R | Touch L toe to R hand | " |
| d. | " | " | Stumble Lt (Face left) | rattle Rt | hop Lt | step back Rt | stumble Lt (complete turn to left to face front) | stumble Rt | step Lt | step Rt | " |

Count 1          Count 2          Count 3          Count 4          Count 5          Count 6
Step left     Brush right forward     Step forward right     Step left in place     Brush right backward     Step back right

FIG. 39. SOFT SHOE FUNDAMENTAL

Step across on right on count 1     Swing left leg sideward     Spring from right clicking heels     Land on right on count two     Step across on left on count 3

FIG. 40. HEEL CLICK—WALTZ TAP

| e. | Six " | Six " | Step L | Swing R across | Hop L | Step R across | Hop R | Hop R | " |
|---|---|---|---|---|---|---|---|---|---|

(make complete turn left)

| f. | " | Stumble " L | rattle R | hop back L | tap R toe in back | stumble R | rattle L | hop R | tap L | " |
|---|---|---|---|---|---|---|---|---|---|---|

Part g. contains eight measures.

| Measure 1 | Measure 2 | | | Measure 3 | Measure 4 | | |
|---|---|---|---|---|---|---|---|
| Six L | Step R across in front | Hop R clicking heels to left | Step L across in front | Six R | Step L across in front | Hop L click heels to right | Step R across in front |

| Measure 5 | Measure 6 | Measure 7 | | | Measure 8 | | |
|---|---|---|---|---|---|---|---|
| Six L | Six R | Jump feet apart | click heels landing on both feet | pause after landing | Jump feet apart | click heels landing on both feet | pause after landing |

Repeat g twice (three times in all) then repeat measures 1, 2, 3 and 4 of g and finish with the break.

At end of final break make uneven jump instead of both feet at once.

NOTE.—Part d is just like the break, except that a complete turn left is executed during measures 2 and 4—also last jump is uneven. Part e is just like part a, except that a complete turn left is made during two final hops.


SIMPLE BUCK AND WING

Music.—Any slow 4/4 with uneven rhythm in melody. As—
"Beneath a Shady Nook,"
"Uhn—um."

The fundamental step pattern in this routine is a "rattle hop step" in rhythm —s l s l.

| s | L | s | L | s | L | s | L | etc. |
|---|---|---|---|---|---|---|---|---|
| Rat- | tle | hop | step | Rat- | tle | hop | step | |
| Rt | Rt | Lt | Rt | Lt | Lt | Rt | Lt | |

Practice until this becomes very easy. It is done in place with an uneven rattle, a quick hop, and an accent on the step. Try it with music. With 4/4 time the rattle hop comes on the counts "and 4 and" while the step comes on the first beat of the measure.

| 1 | & | 2 | & | 3 | & | 4 | & | 1 | & | 2 | & | 3 | & | 4 | & | 1 |
|---|---|---|---|---|---|---|---|---|---|---|---|---|---|---|---|---|
|   |   |   |   |   | Rat- | tle | hop | step | Rat- | tle | hop | step | Rat- | tle | hop | step |

When this has been accomplished the rest of the routine is easy.

The "Break" is accomplished by alternating the above pattern with two slow steps. The break then is

| & | 4 | & | 1 | 2 | 3 | & | 4 | & | 1 | 2 | 3 |
|---|---|---|---|---|---|---|---|---|---|---|---|
| rat- | tle | hop | step | step | step | rat- | tle | hop | step | step | step |
| Rt | Rt | Lt | Rt | Lt | Rt | Lt | Lt | Rt | Lt | Rt | Lt |

The break is used on the last phrase of each part, and each part contains four phrases of 2 measures each. Parts (a), (b) and (c) each begin with a "rattle hop step" done three times, followed by steps in place.

(a) = 3 "rattle hop steps" and two slow steps. Repeat twice and add break; then repeat all of (a) on opposite side. Rhythm of each of first three phrases of Part (a) is as follows:

| s | 1 | s | 1 | s | 1 | s | 1 | s | 1 | s | L | L | L |
|---|---|---|---|---|---|---|---|---|---|---|---|---|---|
| Rat- | tle | hop | step | Rat- | tle | hop | step | Rat- | tle | hop | step | step | step |
| Rt | Rt | Lt | Rt | Lt | Lt | Rt | Lt | Rt | Rt | Lt | Rt | Lt | Rt |

(b) = 3 "rattle hop steps" and four fast uneven steps. Repeat twice and add break, then repeat all of (b) on opposite side.

| s | 1 | s | 1 | s | 1 | s | 1 | s | 1 | s | 1 | s | 1 | s | 1 |
|---|---|---|---|---|---|---|---|---|---|---|---|---|---|---|---|
| Rat- | tle | hop | step | Rat- | tle | hop | step | Rat- | tle | hop | step | step | step | step | step |
| Rt | Rt | Lt | Rt | Lt | Lt | Rt | Lt | Rt | Rt | Lt | Rt | Lt | Rt | Lt | Rt |

(c) = Part (c) is exactly the same as part (b) except that a complete turn, to side of accenting foot, is made during the four fast uneven steps.

(d) = Part (d) begins on count "and" after 4.

| & | 1 | 2 | & | 3 | 4 | & | 1 | & | 2 | & | 3 | & | 4 | & |
|---|---|---|---|---|---|---|---|---|---|---|---|---|---|---|
| Brush left across | step across on left | hop left click-ing heels to right side | Brush right across | step across on right | hop R click-ing heels to left side | brush Lt forward | step Lt | rat- Rt | tle Rt | hop Lt | step Rt back | brush L | step forward | |

stumble (under "brush Lt forward step Lt")    stumble (under "brush L step forward")

Repeat (d) twice, starting right then left—(three times in all) and finish with "Break 2"—which is

| & | 1 | & | 2 | & | 3 | & | 4 | & | 1 | 2 | 3 | 4 |
|---|---|---|---|---|---|---|---|---|---|---|---|---|
| brush step forward Rt | rat- Lt | tle Lt | hop Rt | step back Lt | rat- Rt | tle Rt | hop Lt | step back Rt | step Lt | step Rt | | |

stumble (under "brush step forward Rt")

(e) = Part (e) begins also on count "and" after 4.

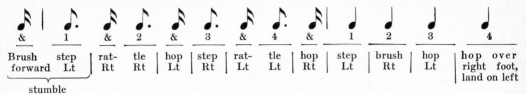

| Brush forward | step Lt | rat- Rt | tle Rt | hop Lt | step Rt | rat- Lt | tle Lt | hop Rt | step Lt | brush Rt | hop Lt | hop over right foot, land on left |
|---|---|---|---|---|---|---|---|---|---|---|---|---|
| & | 1 | & | 2 | & | 3 | & | 4 | & | 1 | 2 | 3 | 4 |

stumble

Repeat twice, starting right, then left and finish with "Break 2."

SIMPLE SOFT SHOE ROUTINE          Music—Slow 6/8, "Swanee," "Captain Jinks."

Underlying beat—six count.

| | Measure 1 | | | | | | Measure 2 | | | | | | |
|---|---|---|---|---|---|---|---|---|---|---|---|---|---|
| a. | 1 | 2 | 3 | 4 | 5 | 6 | 1 | 2 | 3 | 4 | 5 | 6 | etc. |
| | step | brush forward | step fwd. | step | rat- | tle | step | brush forward | step fwd. | step | rat- | tle | alter-nating |
| | Lt | Rt | Rt | Lt | Rt | Rt | Rt | Lt | Lt | Rt | Lt | Lt | |

See Figure 39—Counts 1-4

In measure one the weight stays over the left foot, being placed only momentarily on right on count 3. In measure two, the weight stays over the right foot except on count 3.

| | Measure 1 | | | | | | Measure 2 | | | | | |
|---|---|---|---|---|---|---|---|---|---|---|---|---|
| b. | 1 | 2 | 3 | 4 | 5 | 6 | 1 | 2 | 3 | 4 | 5 | 6 |
| | step | brush forward | step fwd. | step | slap back | step back | step | brush forward | step fwd. | step | rat- | tle |
| | Lt | Rt | Rt | Lt | Rt | Rt | Lt | Rt | Rt | Lt | Rt | Rt |

See Figure 39—Counts 1-6

Repeat (b) starting on right foot and ending with rattle with left. Continue, alternating.

In (b) weight stays over left foot for two measures. It is shifted to right only momentarily on counts 3 and 6 of first measure and count 3 of second measure.

On repeat starting right, the weight stays over right foot for two measures except counts 3 and 6 of first and 3 of second measure.

I. When (a) and (b) have each been mastered, combine them in this order: a (Lt), a (Rt), b (Lt), a (Rt), a (Lt), b (Rt) and repeat.

II. Alternate with small skips, using 3 counts for each skip: Skip (Lt), skip (Rt), a (Lt), skip (Rt), skip (Lt), a (Rt), a (Lt), a (Rt), b (Lt).

Repeat same on opposite side.

III.  Repeat II skipping backward.

IV.  Later try this order:

Skip (Lt), skip (Rt), a (Lt), skip (Rt), skip (Lt), a (Rt), skip (Lt), skip (Rt), bb (Lt). (bb is done just as b except that measure "one" is done twice then followed by measure "two.")

| 1 | 2 | 3 | 4 | 5 | 6 | 1 | 2 | 3 |
|---|---|---|---|---|---|---|---|---|
| step | brush | step, | step | slap | step, | step | brush | step |

bb

| 4 | 5 | 6 | 1 | 2 | 3 | 4 | 5 | 6 |
|---|---|---|---|---|---|---|---|---|
| step | slap | step, | step | brush | step, | step | rat | tle |

Repeat (IV) starting on Rt foot. Finish on count 4, omitting final rattle.

V.  Try (I), (II), (III) and (IV), with 6/8 music. This routine should be done lightly with heels off floor.

ADVANCED BUCK AND WING ROUTINE    Music.—Any slow foxtrot—4/4 "Should I," "Following You."

I. Rhythm

| Step pattern | Rat-<br>Rt | tle<br>Rt | hop<br>Lt | rat<br>Rt | tle<br>Rt | step<br>Rt | brush<br>Lt | step<br>Lt | step<br>Rt |
|---|---|---|---|---|---|---|---|---|---|
| Count | 1 | and | 2 | and | 'a' | 3 | and | 4 | and |

Repeat five times (six times in all) starting on alternate feet (L, R, L, R, L), and finish with "Break."

**Break**

Rhythm

| Step pattern | Rat-<br>Rt | tle<br>Rt | hop<br>Lt | rat<br>Rt | tle<br>Rt | step<br>Rt | brush<br>Lt | slap<br>Lt | step<br>Lt |
|---|---|---|---|---|---|---|---|---|---|
| Count | 1 | and | 2 | and | 'a' | 3 | and | 4 | and |

Rhythm

| Step pattern | Rat-<br>Rt | tle<br>Rt | hop<br>Lt | brush<br>Rt | step<br>Rt | step<br>Lt | tap<br>Rt | (keep wt.<br>on Lt) |
|---|---|---|---|---|---|---|---|---|
| Count | 1 | and | 2 | and | 3 | and | 4 | |

II. (a)

| Rat- | tle | hop | rat | tle | hop | rat | tle | hop | pause |
|------|-----|-----|-----|-----|-----|-----|-----|-----|-------|
| Rt | Rt | Lt | Rt | Rt | Lt | Rt | Rt | Lt | |
| 1 | and | 2 | and | 'a' | 3 | and | 'a' | 4 | |

(b)

| Rat- | tle | hop | rat | tle | step | brush | step | step |
|------|-----|-----|-----|-----|------|-------|------|------|
| Rt | Rt | Lt | Rt | Rt | Rt | Lt | Lt | Rt |
| 1 | and | 2 | and | 'a' | 3 | and | 4 | and |

Repeat (a) and (b) on opposite side.
Repeat (a) twice and follow by the "Break."

III. Begin on the "and" after count 4 at end of "Break."

| rat | tle |
|-----|-----|
| Rt | Rt |
| and | 'a' |

(4)

| Step Rt | | step | rat | tle | step Rt | step | rat | tle |
|---------|--|------|-----|-----|---------|------|-----|-----|
| (Lift L leg | | Lt | Rt | Rt | Left leg | Lt | Rt | Rt |
| across R) | | | | | lifted across | | | |
| 1 | | 2 | and | 'a' | 3 | 4 | and | 'a' |

| Step | brush | slap | hop | tap | step |
|------|-------|------|-----|-----|------|
| Rt | Lt | Lt | Rt | Lt | Lt |
| | | | | (in rear) | |
| 1 | 'a' | 2 | 'a' | 3 | 4 |

Repeat III twice (three times in all) and follow by the break.

IV. Face left and move backward.

| Rat- | tle | hop | rat | tle | step | slap | hop | rat | tle |
|------|-----|-----|-----|-----|------|------|-----|-----|-----|
| Rt | Rt | Lt | Rt | Rt | Rt | Lt | Rt | Lt | Lt |
| 1 | and | 2 | and | 'a' | 3 | and | 4 | and | 'a' |

| step | slap | hop | step | slap | hop | step |
|------|------|-----|------|------|-----|------|
| Lt | Rt | Lt | Rt | Lt | Rt | Lt |
| 1 | and | 2 | and | 3 | and | 4 |

Repeat IV twice (3 times in all) face front and follow by the break.

V.  Begin on "and" after count 4 at end of break.

|  | rat tle |
|--|---------|
|  | Rt Rt |
| 4 | and 'a' |

| Step Rt (lift left leg across) | Step Lt (letting Rt leg slide back) | Step Rt (in front of Lt) | Tap Lt toe in back |
|-------------------------------|-------------------------------------|--------------------------|--------------------|
| 1 | 2 | 3 | 4 |

| step Lt | tap Rt in rear | (Pause) | hop Lt | place Rt heel forward | (Pause) |
|---------|----------------|---------|--------|-----------------------|---------|
| 1 | and | | and | 3 | 4 |

Repeat V twice (3 times in all) and follow by the break.

VI.  Begin on "and" after count 4 at end of break.

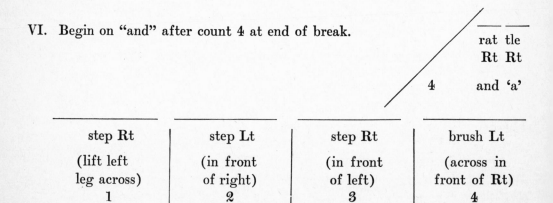

|  | rat tle |
|--|---------|
|  | Rt Rt |
| 4 | and 'a' |

| step Rt (lift left leg across) | step Lt (in front of right) | step Rt (in front of left) | brush Lt (across in front of Rt) |
|-------------------------------|------------------------------|-----------------------------|----------------------------------|
| 1 | 2 | 3 | 4 |

| hop Rt | pause | hop over Lt foot | step Lt |
|---|---|---|---|
| 1 | 2 | 3 | 4 |

Repeat VI twice (3 times in all) and follow by the break.

VII. Begin on the "and" after count 4 of break.

|  | rat tle Rt Rt |
|---|---|
| 4 | and 'a' |

| tap Lt heel | brush Rt | tap Lt heel | slap Rt | step Rt |  | Pause | rat tle Lt Lt |
|---|---|---|---|---|---|---|---|
| 1 | and | 2 | and | 3 |  | 4 | and 'a' |

| tap Rt heel | brush Lt | tap Rt heel | slap Lt | step Lt |  | Pause |
|---|---|---|---|---|---|---|
| 1 | and | 2 | and | 3 |  | 4 |

| brush Rt | slap Rt | brush Rt | slap Rt | step Rt | step Lt across | step Rt behind | step Lt across |
|---|---|---|---|---|---|---|---|
| 1 | and | 2 | and | 3 | and | 4 | and |

| brush Rt | slap Rt | tap Lt heel | step Rt | brush Lt | step Lt | step Rt |
|---|---|---|---|---|---|---|
| 1 | and | 2 | and | 3 | and | 4 |

Repeat VII three times (4 times in all) starting on alternate feet.

MILITARY TAP                 Music—"National Emblem March," by Bagley.

Planned for groups of four. If more take part, they should be grouped by fours and the individuals in each group should stand as close together as comfortable.

The following patterns should be learned before the dance is put together:

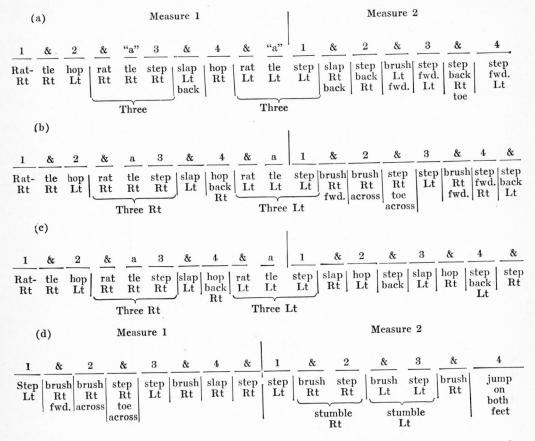

**(a)**

Measure 1 | Measure 2

| 1 | & | 2 | & | "a" | 3 | & | 4 | & | "a" | 1 | & | 2 | & | 3 | & | 4 |
|---|---|---|---|---|---|---|---|---|---|---|---|---|---|---|---|---|
| Rat- Rt | tle Rt | hop Lt | rat Rt | tle Rt | step Rt | slap Lt back | hop Rt | rat Lt | tle Lt | step Lt | slap Rt back | step back Rt | brush Lt fwd. | step fwd. Lt | step back Rt toe | step fwd. Lt |

(*Three* under "rat tle step"; *Three* under "rat tle step")

**(b)**

| 1 | & | 2 | & | a | 3 | & | 4 | & | a | 1 | & | 2 | & | 3 | & | 4 | & |
|---|---|---|---|---|---|---|---|---|---|---|---|---|---|---|---|---|---|
| Rat- Rt | tle Rt | hop Lt | rat Rt | tle Rt | step Rt | slap Lt | hop back Rt | rat Lt | tle Lt | step Lt | brush Rt fwd. | brush Rt across | step Rt toe | step Lt | brush Rt fwd. | step fwd. Rt | step back Lt |

(*Three Rt*; *Three Lt*)

**(c)**

| 1 | & | 2 | & | a | 3 | & | 4 | & | a | 1 | & | 2 | & | 3 | & | 4 | & |
|---|---|---|---|---|---|---|---|---|---|---|---|---|---|---|---|---|---|
| Rat- Rt | tle Rt | hop Lt | rat Rt | tle Rt | step Rt | slap Lt | hop back Rt | rat Lt | tle Lt | slap Rt | hop Lt | step back | slap Lt | hop Rt | step back Lt | step Rt | |

(*Three Rt*; *Three Lt*)

**(d)**

Measure 1 | Measure 2

| 1 | & | 2 | & | 3 | & | 4 | & | 1 | & | 2 | & | 3 | & | 4 |
|---|---|---|---|---|---|---|---|---|---|---|---|---|---|---|
| Step Lt | brush Rt fwd. | brush Rt across | step Rt toe across | step Lt | brush Rt | slap Rt | step Rt | step Lt | brush Rt | step Rt | brush Lt | step Lt | brush Rt | jump on both feet |

(*stumble Rt*; *stumble Lt*)

Note.—In (d) on counts "and three" of measure 1, the right foot remains across left as weight is shifted right, and then back to left.

The same is true of measure 2 in (b).

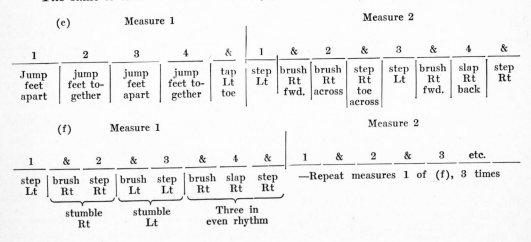

**(e)**

Measure 1 | Measure 2

| 1 | 2 | 3 | 4 | & | 1 | & | 2 | & | 3 | & | 4 | & |
|---|---|---|---|---|---|---|---|---|---|---|---|---|
| Jump feet apart | jump feet together | jump feet apart | jump feet together | tap Lt toe | step Lt fwd. | brush Rt | brush Rt across | step Rt toe across | step Lt | brush Rt | slap Rt back | step Rt |

**(f)**

Measure 1 | Measure 2

| 1 | & | 2 | & | 3 | & | 4 | & | 1 | & | 2 | & | 3 | etc. |
|---|---|---|---|---|---|---|---|---|---|---|---|---|---|
| step Lt | brush Rt | step Rt | brush Lt | step Lt | brush Rt | slap Rt | step Rt | | | | | | |

(*stumble Rt*; *stumble Lt*; *Three in even rhythm*)

—Repeat measures 1 of (f), 3 times

(g)

| 1 | 2 | & | a | 3 | & | a | 4 | & | a | |
|---|---|---|---|---|---|---|---|---|---|---|
| Fall on Lt foot sliding Rt backward | step back Rt | rat Lt | tle Lt | step Lt | rat Rt | tle Rt | step Rt | rat Lt | tle Lt | Repeat 3 times always falling on left foot. |

Three Lt     Three Rt

(h)

| 1 | & | 2 | & | 3 | & | 4 | a | 1 | & | 2 | & | 3 | & | 4 | a |
|---|---|---|---|---|---|---|---|---|---|---|---|---|---|---|---|
| Step Lt | brush Rt | brush Rt across | step Rt toe across | step Lt | brush Rt | slap Rt back | hop Lt | step Rt | brush Lt | step Lt across | step Lt toe across | step Rt | brush Lt | slap Lt back | hop Rt |

| 1 | & | 2 | a | 3 | & | 4 | a | 1 | & | a | 2 | & | 3 |
|---|---|---|---|---|---|---|---|---|---|---|---|---|---|
| step Lt | brush Rt | slap Rt | hop Lt | step Rt | brush Lt | slap Lt | hop Rt | step Lt | rat Rt | tle Rt | step Rt toe | step Lt | step Rt |

Three

(In the above rhythms when we have split a unit marked "and," the two portions are marked "and" "a.")

When all of the above patterns have been mastered, the military routine may be executed to the above music by using two measures of music for each measure of rhythm. Put the parts together in the following order:

Music *
Introduction
    Measure 1-8.    No activity.
    Measure 9-10.    Mark time with four stumbles Rt, Lt, Rt, Lt.
A—Entrance. In single file, each close behind one in front, moving across stage from left to right.
    Measure 1-16.    a. a. c. d. Starting with right foot. On last count each jumps to face front by making one quarter turn left—this leaves all persons standing side by side.
    Measure 1-16.    (Repeat) a. a. c. d. starting with right foot. Remain facing front at end.
B—
    Measure 1-32.    b. a. b. a. b. a. c. d. As line moves forward or back attempt to stay side by side and in straight line with the precision of a military unit.
    Measure 1-32.    (Repeated)—same as above.

* For convenience, the music has been divided into an Introduction (first 10 measures)—A (next 16)—B (next 32)—C (last 34 measures). Also for the purpose of slow practice the step pattern has been analyzed so that four counts of step pattern equal two measures (or eight counts) of music.

C—

Measure 1-4.     All of e.

Measure 5-10.    All of e. with second measure of e. repeated.

Measure 11-12.   All of f.

On last count of f., the person on left end of line makes a quarter turn right and continues in that direction while others proceed forward. This makes him moving behind line toward right end. As in diagram 2.

No. 4 turns Rt

Diagram 1                Diagram 2

Measure 13-14.   All of f. On last count, No. 3 turns right while others go forward. This makes No. 4 and No. 3 side by side. See Diagram 3.

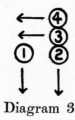

Diagram 3

Measure 15-16.   All of f. with No. 2 turning on last count.

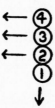

Measure 17-18.   All of f. and on last count numbers 2, 3 and 4 make quarter turn left finishing behind No. 1.

Note.—In marching this figure is called "Evading"—the turn must be done on exactly the right count, and the marching continued without interruption.

The whole figure looks like this

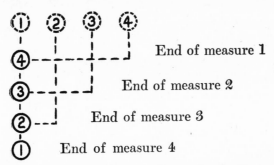

End of measure 1

End of measure 2

End of measure 3

End of measure 4

Measure 19-26. All of g. done 4 times, single file moving backward.
Measure 27-34. All of h.  Still in single file.

C—

Repeated—follow same routine except on repeat of e., all make a quarter turn
left on second jump (count 3).  This puts them side by side moving across room.

On measures 11-18. Repeat "Evading" No. 4 turning right
and marching straight forward, while others march on toward left.
Numbers 3, 2 and 1 turn successively and final figure leaves group
side by side facing front with No. 4 now at the right end of line.

Evading the second time has been done as follows:

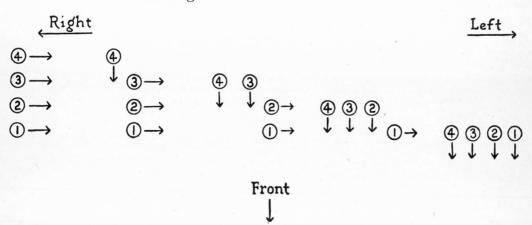

# CHAPTER XIV

## SUGGESTIONS FOR LESSONS AND TESTS

The student will gain more skill, more rhythmic training, and more knowledge with the ability to work alone, if the work in clogging or tap dancing is well analyzed. It is a grave mistake to stand in front of the class and say, "Do this as I do it," allowing the class to imitate. The student may be able to do the activity well while in class, but will be unable to repeat it alone or to choose proper music or to invent new routines.

A certain amount of demonstration is good, either performed by the instructor, or by several of the better students, or by a group, but this must be reinforced by an analysis of step pattern, rhythmic pattern, music, and phrasing. When demonstrating a fundamental or a pattern to the class, it is confusing, as instructor faces group, if she asks them to move right as she moves right, for this makes her move in the opposite direction or with opposite foot. Either she should tell them to begin right, and she herself begin left—or better still, she should stand with her back to the class as she demonstrates during difficult parts. This latter gives them the clearest picture of what they are to do with their feet.

It is well to have the class sit and listen to the music and phrasing, and to clap the rhythm of patterns which are written on the board or done by instructor. Chanting the step pattern as they clap the rhythm is also a good method of learning a fundamental. The student must know what she is doing so that her mind, not her eyes, control her feet.

It is also well to let the music control the activity as much as possible. That is, instead of saying to the class, "Do four Waltz Five's to this music," say "Do Waltz Five's for one phrase and stop as music goes on," or "Do Waltz Five's for one phrase, then a slow skip for one phrase, Five's again for a phrase, etc."

In order to insure that the student gets the work accurately, it is a great help to have the material which is taught in class typed and posted on the bulletin board in the gymnasium, so that the student can check on anything which he forgets, or does not understand, or misses due to absence. Or if the interest is great enough the dances may be mimeographed and sold for a few cents a copy (money to cover cost of mimeographing).

In classes, where it is desired to cover a large amount of material in a short time, as in the case of a college class of professional physical education students, it is well to sell * or post copies of all material taught and to require students to perfect certain of these dances outside of class. In this way the time available for class work may be used in analyzing new dances or learning difficult parts, while the order of steps is learned outside by each individual. After dances have been learned, they should be reviewed in class, so that each student may check to see if she is following the directions correctly.

In teaching dances which are to be done in circles, as "Country Dance" from Frost, it is well to teach the step patterns and phrases with all students facing front of room. Thus they will not be confused by seeing the students on the opposite side of the circle moving in another direction. Later, these can all be executed in a circle without confusion.

In giving signals for the next phrase, it should be understood between student and teacher that the signal will be given before the class is ready to begin a new phrase, thus giving time to think as they finish the phrase to which they are dancing, and to be prepared for the new phrase.

It is helpful, after a class has completed a dance, to have them do it in small groups with others watching. This brings out the correct performance and points out to the class mistakes against which they must guard.

In planning lessons it is well to teach as many dances as can be easily learned. Too much time spent on fundamentals will make the class a bore. It is wise to teach each day only enough of the fundamentals to enable the class to learn a new dance. For example, in the first lesson of thirty-five minutes, a class should be able to learn to rattle, a shift, and a three. After a few minutes practice these can be used in a simple clog, such as "Newsboy."† At the next lesson, "Newsboy" may be reviewed and part or all of "Country Dance ‡ taught. Several lessons should be spent on simple clogs using the "three" and "plain five," as, Rig-a-Jig-Jig, Lindy Lee, Sleigh Bells.

Next in order might come the "Seven"—this should be taught slowly at first so that each student gets the proper transference of weight. "University High Clog" or "Reuben" ¶ are excellent to teach for practice in doing sevens. Other simple dances which use the seven, or combinations of two "threes" and a "seven," are

"Yankee Doodle"—Frost  "Old Man"—Frost  "Dixie"—Frost

More difficult character dances are

"Reuben Taps"—Frost    "On Deck"—Frost

---

* To prepare and sell material which is on the market, is a violation of copyright laws, as well as an unnecessary expense to the professional student, who will prefer to buy the books for his personal property. In the case of selling copies of uncopyrighted material, which is not on the market, mimeographed material may be prepared for a few cents a copy and several students may buy one copy together, or the material may be posted where it may be studied.

† Athletic Dances and Simple Clogs—Hillas and Knighton.

‡ Clog and Character Dances—Frost.

¶ Clogs and Jigs—Hinman.

Before the "waltz five" is taught the class should be familiarized with 3/4 music. Let them clap it, sway with the measure, do a waltz balance, etc.

The "waltz five" may be taught from several approaches.

(1) From a waltz balance.

Leap on to left foot then shift weight twice, right, left; leap on to right foot and shift weight twice, left, right. Continue alternating left, right, left, right. This should all be done in place with the leap (a small one) coming as an accent on count "one" of each measure. Now add a rattle just after the leap. This becomes a step rattle step step. In practicing this, emphasize the rhythm —always having the initial leap (or accented step) on count one.

(2) The "waltz five" may be taught from a rhythmic approach.

Analyze rhythm as   s   s   s   s   L   .   Teach a "four." (See pages 148.) Have class clap count "one;" then on counts "and two and three" they execute a "four."

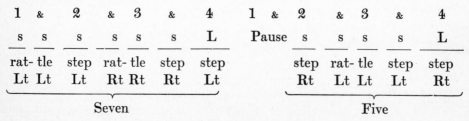

| 1 | & | 2 | & | 3 | |
|---|---|---|---|---|---|
| s | s | s | s | L | repeat on same foot. |
| clap | rat | tle | step | step | |
| | Lt | Lt | Lt | Rt | |
| | | | toe | | |

Later practice on opposite foot.

When the four has been learned, ask class to change from one side to other by taking a step forward on count "one" followed by a "four." They will then be doing a "waltz five" slowly.

| 1 | & | 2 | & | 3 | | 1 | & | 2 | & | 3 |
|---|---|---|---|---|---|---|---|---|---|---|
| s | s | s | s | L | | s | s | s | s | L |
| Step | rat- tle | step | step | | | step | rat- tle | step | step | |
| Lt | Rt Rt | Rt | Lt | | | Rt | Lt Lt | Lt | Rt | |

Four Rt           Four Lt

Five Lt           Five Rt

(3) The "waltz five" may also be taught from a "seven" by omitting the first rattle. When done to 3/4 time the time allowed for rattle is left out and the first step comes on count one instead of two.

| 1 | & | 2 | & | 3 | & | 4 | 1 | & | 2 | & | 3 | & | 4 |
|---|---|---|---|---|---|---|---|---|---|---|---|---|---|---|
| s | s | s | s | s | s | L | Pause | s | s | s | s | L |
| rat- tle | step | rat- tle | step | step | | | | step | rat- tle | step | step |
| Lt Lt | Lt | Rt Rt | Rt | Lt | | | | Rt | Lt Lt | Lt | Rt |

Seven           Five

In practicing the waltz five use combination of skips, turns, etc.

Later teach "Hurdy Gurdy Waltz."

After a sufficient amount of fundamentals and other step patterns as "wiggle sticks," "pigeon toe," "break your leg," etc., have been taught through the above dances, let the class try originating dances. Divide the class into small groups of 4-8, assign them different corners of the room, tell them to keep their backs to the other groups and plan a dance. Have the musician play short piece with definite rhythm. "Side by side"—4/4, "East Side, West Side"—3/4, are good for use in this, or music from any of the clogs which have not been taught in class. About five minutes before class period is over call for the dances and let each group perform for others. Discuss good points in phrasing, etc. At the next lesson let groups work again, this time for more finish, an entrance and exit, or a characterization. Later ask each person, working with one or two partners, to bring in an original dance, with music of their own choice. Emphasize the importance of phrasing, a good ending and simple, well executed steps, rather than difficult poorly executed patterns. Also ask for original combinations.

Each student may be required to write out an analysis of the steps of her original clog or tap dance, putting it into chart form similar to that given on page 145. This will help her to plan a dance which is correctly phrased and which fits the music. It is also an aid to grading as it gives credit to the girl who understands what she is doing, but is too awkward or self-conscious to give a perfect execution.

The author has found that when a written analysis is required that the students come to class much better prepared than when no analysis, or merely a brief outline of the steps, is required. It completely eliminates the person who might bring some music to class, depending upon her "inspiration of the moment."

It is well to stimulate practice, or for fairness in grading a large class to keep an accomplishment chart, on which each person is checked on all fundamentals which she learns. Such a chart would have across the top a list of fundamentals and step patterns to be learned, with space for grade on original dance, final exam, and dances tested. Down the left side would be an alphabetical list of names, grouped in squads, if class is large. (See chart, page 173.)

Instead of a plain check in each square, symbols such as     −   ⊥   +   ++
may be used to indicate degree of perfection.

− indicates incorrectly done or inability to do,

⊥ indicates done fairly well,

+ indicates done correctly,

++ indicates very well done.

Students should be checked frequently and later allowed to improve score. Tests may be made as class stands in formation for testing, all practicing fundamentals as instructor moves up and down line and checks each in turn, or they may be called upon in small groups or by individuals to demonstrate. The author has found it successful in testing large classes (for instance, eighty to one hundred students) to give frequent tests requiring a perfect performance of the dances which have been taught in class. Groups of fifteen or twenty students may be tested at once, if they are told that any one who makes a mistake must sit down immediately. In this way they check themselves and by the process of elimination and retests, the instructor is able to classify them into good, fair, or poor groups.

In scoring the symbols used may be given certain values, such as

$$(-) = 1 \text{ point}$$

$$(\perp) = 2 \text{ points}$$

$$(+) = 3 \text{ "}$$

$$(++) = 4 \text{ "}$$

These scores may be totaled at the end of term. This total can then be averaged with grades on original dance, other dances, and final written exam.

If time permits a written examination should be given at the end of the term, especially for the purpose of giving the poorly co-ordinated student a chance to show that she has been observing of class work, or, in a large class, in order to grade students more fairly.

A written examination of the objective type (see below) is both fairer and easier to grade. If this type is used copies of it should not be lost and it should be revised each term.

When examination is completed students may be asked to exchange and grade each other, then hand in to instructor; or papers may be handed in immediately and graded by instructor.

In planning lessons for tap dancing much the same procedure can be followed as suggested for clogging. In the case of long routines, several parts may be taught at each lesson. Charts, tests, and original dances will stimulate interest.

### WRITTEN EXAMINATION IN TAP DANCING

I.  In the blank at the left write the name of the fundamental which the sentence defines.

    1.  A _____ is a rattle step step.

    2.  A _____ is a shift in weight.

    3.  A _____ is a stumble rattle step step.

    4.  A _____ is a rattle step.

5. A _____ is a rattle step rattle step step.

6. A _____ is a brush and a slap.

7. A _____ is a brush and a step.

II. In the blank at the left insert the time signature of the music used for the following:

1. _____ music is used for Buck and Wing.

2. _____ music is used for Six's.

3. _____ music is used for Three's.

4. _____ music is used for Plain Five's.

5. _____ music is used for Waltz Tap.

6. _____ music is used for Waltz Five's.

7. _____ music is used for Soft Shoe.

8. _____ music is used for Seven's.

III. At the left of the rhythm write the name of the fundamental which it describes. Check with an X those rhythms which do not describe a fundamental.

1. A _____ is done in a rhythm s  s  L

2. A _____ is done in a rhythm s  s  s  L

3. A _____ is done in a rhythm s  s  s  s  L

4. A _____ is done in a rhythm s  s  s  s  s  L

5. A _____ is done in a rhythm s  s  s  s  s  s  L

6. A _____ is done in a rhythm s  L  s  L  s  L

7. A _____ is done in a rhythm s  s  L  L  L

IV. Complete the following sentences.

1. If the first three is begun with the left foot, the second is begun on the

   _____ .

2. If the first seven is begun with the left foot, the second is begun on the

   _____ .

3.  If the first four is begun with the left foot, the second is begun on the
    _____ .

4.  If the first waltz five is begun with the left foot, the second is begun on the
    _____ .

5.  If the first plain five is begun with the left foot, the second is begun on the
    _____ .

6.  If the first waltz six is begun with the left foot, the second is begun on the
    _____ .

7.  If the first rattle is begun with the left foot, the second is begun on the
    _____ .

8.  If the first stumble is begun with the left foot, the second is begun on the
    _____ .

9.  If the first rattle hop is begun with the left foot, the second is begun on the
    _____ .

10. If the first rattle hop step is begun with the left foot, the second is begun
    on the _____ .


V.  Six bits of music will be played four times. Listen carefully. As music is
    played second time write down in column one the fundamentals which could
    be used with it. As it is played the third time write the time signature and
    as it is played the fourth time count the number of phrases.

|         | Fundamentals to be used | Time Signature | Number of Phrases |
|---------|-------------------------|----------------|-------------------|
| Music 1 |                         |                |                   |
| Music 2 |                         |                |                   |
| Music 3 |                         |                |                   |
| Music 4 |                         |                |                   |
| Music 5 |                         |                |                   |
| Music 6 |                         |                |                   |

VI. In the following space describe the first step and break of the Waltz Tap learned in class.

VII. In the space below describe the fundamental used in the soft shoe which we did to Swanee.

VIII. In counting a "Three" with the music, one begins counting on count \_\_\_\_\_.

In counting a "Waltz Five" with the music one begins counting on \_\_\_\_\_.

In counting a "Plain Five" with the music one begins counting on \_\_\_\_\_.

In counting a "Seven" with the music one begins counting on count \_\_\_\_\_.

In counting a "Waltz Six" with the music one begins counting on \_\_\_\_\_.

IX. On a blank page make a diagram of measures as you did for your original dance and fill in the rhythms of the following fundamentals:

"Three" — "Waltz Five" — "Plain Five" — "Seven" — "Waltz Six"
Write the rhythm by means of long and short lines and indicate under each the count on which it comes; for example \_\_\_\_\_  \_\_\_\_\_  \_\_\_\_\_  \_\_\_\_\_

4          and          1          and

_____. Above the rhythm write the step pattern in terms of steps
2

and rattles and indicate which foot takes each count, using R to indicate right foot and L to indicate left foot.

X.  As the music for each dance is played, choose from the list at the right the steps with which that dance begins; then write the corresponding number in the blank space at right of dance name:

Music and Name of Dance

Choose from this list the step with which dance begins and place corresponding number in blank at left:

a. Clementine    _ _ _

b. Reuben Taps    _ _ _

c. Billy Magee    _ _ _

d. Lindy Lee    _ _ _

e. Hurdy Gurdy    _ _ _

f. Country Dance    _ _ _

1. Grapevine left.

2. Rattle tap, rattle tap, "Three," run, run.

3. Four slow "Threes" and four slap steps backward.

4. Four fast "Threes" in succession without a pause.

5. One waltz "Five," one "step-swing-hop."

6. Step L, brush R, rock forward on R heel, step L.  Repeat on opposite foot.

XI.  *Analyze Lindy Lee and Reuben Taps.*  Instead of writing out the descriptions, merely fill in each blank with a number corresponding to the description for that phrase.  All steps are described starting left.  If they are repeated to the right, repeat the number and place after it an R.  If your analysis is correct all blanks will be filled.

|                | *Lindy Lee* |  |  |  |                | *Reuben Taps* |  |  |  |
| --- | --- | --- | --- | --- | --- | --- | --- | --- | --- |
| A. | ___ | ___ | ___ | ___ | A. | ___ | ___ | ___ | ___ |
| B. | ___ | ___ | ___ | ___ | B. | ___ | ___ | ___ | ___ |
| C. | ___ | ___ | ___ | ___ | C. | ___ | ___ | ___ | ___ |
| D. | ___ | ___ | ___ | ___ | D. | ___ | ___ | ___ | ___ |
|    |     |     |     |     | E. | ___ | ___ | ___ | ___ |

1. Step L, "Three" R, Step L, brush R forward, hop L, place R heel forward.

2. Balance forward L, balance backward R, pause, then jump lifting heels in back of body.

3. Grapevine sideward left for seven counts.

4. "Break your leg," e.g., jump with feet apart, knees bent, body twisted toward left—jump, twisting body to face right—then repeat 3 times in faster rhythm.

5. Four skips forward.

6. Rattle L and tap toes, rattle L and tap toes, Three L, run, run.

7. Rattle L and chug on R heel; repeat twice, then fall onto L foot.
8. Four skips backward.
9. Squat and jump up, then make ½ turn left following L toe.
10. Rubber legs, starting by crossing L foot over R. Rock from side to side, then swing R foot to side as hop L, and repeat all with R foot crossed over L.
11. Rattle L, step L with toe pointed in. Twist L foot for three counts dragging R foot. Repeat on opposite foot.
12. Two "Sevens."
13. "Wiggle-sticks" for four slow counts.
14. "Wiggle-sticks" for seven fast counts.
15. Rattle L, place L toe on floor and lift R leg. Bring L heel down, then step R forward, click heels twice and step L.
16. Turn toes in pigeon-toed, bending body forward, then swing heels together lifting body; pause; then 2 runs, knees high.
17. Rattle L, place L toe on floor and lift R leg. Bring L heel down, then step forward R and follow by a "seven" L.

Material for teaching may be found in the following books:

| Name | Author | Publisher |
|---|---|---|
| The Clog Dance Book | Frost | A. S. Barnes and Co. |
| Clog and Character Dances | " | " " " " " |
| Oriental and Character Dances | " | " " " " " |
| Tap Caper and Clog | " | " " " " " |
| Athletic Dances and Simple Clogs | Hillas & Knighton | " " " " " |
| Tap Dancing | Hillas | " " " " " |
| Clogs and Jigs, Vol. V | Hinman | " " " " " |
| Tap Dancing | Ballweber | Clayton Summy Co. |
| Tap Dances | Duggan | A S. Barnes and Co. |

If piano is not available, a victrola may be used. In choosing records for clogging or tap, use those which are planned for dancing, which keep a regular tempo, and which are not interrupted by novelty choruses and vocal solos. Sometimes portions of a record will be found usable.

There are two records manufactured by the Victor Company for use in tap dancing:

1. 22386-A—Tap Dancing.
   22386-B—The Daughter of Rosie O'Grady—Waltz Clog.
2. 22228-A—Swanee River Medley.
   22228-B—Tap Dance.

Other Victor records are:

3. 20639    —Captain Jinks—Soft Shoe.
4. 19842-A—National Emblem March—Military Tap.
5. 35798    —Estudiantina  Waltz—Waltz Tap.
6. 21493    —Sidewalks of New York—Waltz Tap.
7. B-6134  —Johnny Robinson in a Tap Routine.

For others, see list on Page 180.

| Student | Threes | Plain Fives | Sevens | Waltz Fives | Wiggle Sticks | Rubber Legs | Single Pigeon-toe | Double Pigeon-toe | Lindy Lee | Reuben Tap | Hurdy Gurdy | Total Score on Steps and Dances | Execution of Original Dance | Analysis of Original Dance | Written Examination | Final Grade |
|---|---|---|---|---|---|---|---|---|---|---|---|---|---|---|---|---|
| Squad 1. | | | | | | | | | | | | | | | | |
| 1 Mary Astor | | | | | | | | | | | | | | | | |
| 2 Betty Burr | | | | | | | | | | | | | | | | |
| 3 Helen Carr | | | | | | | | | | | | | | | | |
| 4 May Coates | | | | | | | | | | | | | | | | |
| 5 Jane Frank | | | | | | | | | | | | | | | | |
| 6 Jean Good | | | | | | | | | | | | | | | | |
| Squad 2. | | | | | | | | | | | | | | | | |
| 1 | | | | | | | | | | | | | | | | |
| 2 | | | | | | | | | | | | | | | | |
| etc. | | | | | | | | | | | | | | | | |

# CHAPTER XV

### FOLK DANCING, ITS USE, SOURCE OF MATERIAL AND TESTS

A splendid rhythmic activity for us with individuals of all ages, up to grand-parents we might say, is found in the form of Folk Dancing.

The true folk dance has developed in many nations, just as its folk lore, being handed down from generation to generation. Much of it, until modern times, has been in no tangible form, the tunes and steps merely taught by father to son. In recent years a definite attempt has been made to preserve this wealth of ma-terial, and students of dancing have studied with the peasants and written down the dances and the music. Much of this has been translated into English; so there is available to the teacher or community leader a vast amount of valuable infor-mation on the dances of foreign lands as well as of our own pioneers. Elizabeth Burchenal and Mary Wood Hinman are two who have contributed a large num-ber of dances of various nations, while Cecil Sharp has given us a library of Eng-lish Country Dancing, Morris Dancing and English Sword Dancing, with a large vocabulary of terms and the descriptions of steps and music.

Many of these dances have been sorted, graded, and compiled in single vol-umes.* Thus, whether the leader desires to teach dances of one particular country or a series of dances from many countries she has only to go to one or more of the many books on Folk Dancing for her material.

Besides authentic folk dances we have, under the classification of Folk Danc-ing, a great number of singing games as well as athletic and character dances, many of which are more modern in origin but none the less popular for that.

Folk Dancing is excellent for use with children in the schools as well as for recreational work with all ages, including adults, because the skills are compara-tively simple and easily learned, and the rhythms and phrases are readily grasped. It is possible to find dances which will be hard enough to be stimulating to the age group with which working, or easy enough to be taught in a few minutes time for recreational purposes, as well as varied and interesting enough to appeal to a mixed group of individuals including a wide range of age and development. The socializing influence of Folk Dancing has been recognized as long as the activity has existed. One would have only to see a large group of peasants dancing to-gether on the village green, after the day's work, or be present at a barn dance in one of our own rural communities to realize the truth of this statement, while an

* See Bibliography of Folk Dance Books, page 177.

hour's participation would prove the recreational, rhythmic and physiological value of this activity.

Folk Dancing in the schools is often taught in correlation with other material as with geography, sociology, sewing, or music. It also furnishes a splendid activity in physical education. The manner in which it is presented would depend entirely upon the age group and the general objectives of the course. When taught in correlation with geography, teachers have planned their daily lessons so as to teach dances from the country about which the students are then studying. Pictures of the peasants in native costume are brought to class, and a short discussion of the occupation, habits, and temperament of the people may be indulged in. The Folk Dance Costume book will be found valuable in this situation.

In directing a lesson it is important that the teacher herself know the dance and the music thoroughly. She should point out the phrases and changes of mood in the music and give brief, clear directions for the steps and the rhythms. New or difficult steps should be isolated and practiced until mastered, and then combined into the dance patterns. (For teaching Folk Dance fundamentals with a rhythmic approach, see Chapter V and Chapter XVI.)

An attempt to preserve the spirit and spontaneity of the dance will aid in making it more interesting. If the class is large, it may be divided into smaller groups. There should be an agreement between students and teacher that a certain signal, a chord on the piano, a low whistle, or clapping of the hands will mean absolute silence and attention, in order that directions may be clearly given or corrections made. To preserve the play element, these should be given in the spirit of help and co-operation, and never in a dictatorial manner. As far as possible the children should control the discipline of the class. To give a clearer picture of the dance, one group may dance for the rest. In teaching a recreational group of individuals with varying abilities, it is well to have a group of those who have danced before act as a demonstration group, or to have the trained individuals scattered through the crowd as group leaders.

The dances taught should be simple enough (depending upon the objective) to be taught in one or two lessons, so that interest will not lag. Also a dance which has been learned should be occasionally reviewed so that the class may enjoy dancing it. Allowing the class to choose the dance which it wishes to review is a splendid way to complete the period's work.

In some situations it is interesting for the children to keep notebooks, but in the case of high school and college students it seems better to post directions for dances or to have books of reference for class use. Tests and accomplishment charts, as suggested in Chapter XIV, may be used to motivate interest or for testing. Folk Dance parties, programs, or festivals in costume are valuable also in stimulating interest. (See Chapter XVII.) In presenting material to a professional group who expect to teach folk dancing it is better to give a large amount of material, including a wide variety of skills, rather than to spend too much time in perfecting each individual dance. In this case the work in class should be supplemented by a list of references or by mimeographed material. (See Page 163, Chapter XIV.)

To facilitate grading of large classes or individuals with poor motor control, the class may be given a written examination at the end of the term. (See sample examination sheet, Page 190.) A practical examination on dances, with the students in simple costumes which they themselves plan, will also be of educational and recreational value. Original dances of the type learned in class will give the class opportunity to experience choice of appropriate music and step patterns as well as a use of their knowledge of rhythm, phrasing, and characterization.

Because the Physical Education library contains such a wealth of folk dance material, prepared in an interesting, clear manner with the accompanying music, it is thought unnecessary to include here material for use in class. Instead, a list of references has been prepared, in an effort to help the teacher locate the type of material which she wishes to present to her students. These books include music, but since many times one is found in a situation where a piano or an accompanist is unavailable, a list of records which may be used with victrola accompaniment has been included. These will be found very satisfactory as they have been recorded for use in folk dancing, and are, consequently, well phrased and well timed. The list of folk dance records has been arranged in chart form (see Page 180) so that by a horizontal reading one may locate the directions for a particular folk dance. One may also determine for which school grade a dance is adaptable and what foot pattern is most frequently used. Country dances which, for variety, depend more upon group formation than upon step pattern are listed as English (E. C. D.), American (A. C. D.), and Irish (I. C. D.). One may also, by a vertical reading, determine how many dances, for which victrola records are available, may be found in each book.

## Source of Material for Folk Dancing

| Number referring to List of Records | Name of Book | Author | Publisher | Remarks |
|---|---|---|---|---|
| 1 | Dances of Many Nations | La Salle | A. S. Barnes and Co., 1926 | Excellent. Wide variety music and dances. |
| 2 | Rhythms and Dances for Elementary Schools | Nielson and Van Hagen | A. S. Barnes and Co., 1930 | Excellent for general program. |
|  | Manual of Physical Education Activities for Elementary Schools |  |  | Includes games. |
| 3 I | Dances of the People | Burchenal | G. Schirmer, 1913 | Three books from a fine collection by Elizabeth Burchenal. |
| 3 II | Dances from Old Homelands | Burchenal | G. Schirmer, 1922 |  |
| 3 III | Folk Dances and Singing Games | Burchenal | G. Schirmer, 1909 |  |
| 4 I | Folk Dances and Games | Crawford | A. S. Barnes and Co., 1908 |  |
| 5 I | The Folk Dance Book | Crampton | A. S. Barnes and Co., 1909 | Graded collection. |
| 5 II | The Second Folk Dance Book | Crampton | A. S. Barnes and Co., 1916 |  |
| 6 | Social Games and Group Dances | Elsom and Trilling | Lippincott, 1919—Rev. 1927 | Good for Community Recreation. |
| 7 I | Solo Dances Revised | Hinman | 1930 | These are published as Gymnastics and Folk Dances, Volumes I-V. A. S. Barnes and Co. |
| 7 II | Couple Dances Revised | Hinman | 1930 |  |
| 7 III | Ring Dances Revised | Hinman | 1930 |  |
| 7 IV | Group Dances Revised | Hinman | 1932 |  |
| 7 V | Clogs and Jigs Revised | Hinman | 1930 |  |
| 8 I | Popular Folk Games and Dances | Hofer | A. Flanagan, 1907—Rev. 1914 | Paper edition, illustrated. |
| 8 II | Polite and Social Dances | Hofer | C. F. Summy Co., 1917 |  |
|  | Folk Dances for Boys and Girls | Shambaugh | A. S. Barnes and Co., 1929 |  |
|  | Folk Dances for Young People | Van Cleve | Bradley, 1916 |  |
|  | Outline of Physical Education for First and Second Grades | Anderson and McKinley | A. S. Barnes and Co. | Includes planned program. |
| 9 | The Playground Book | Sperling | A. S. Barnes and Co., 1929 | Includes playground and classroom games. |
| 10 | Physical Education Handbook | Wray (Editor) | A. S. Barnes and Co. | Sections printed in loose leaf form. |
| 3 IV | American Dances (Pioneer) | Burchenal | G. Schirmer, 1918 |  |
|  | American Country Dances | Burchenal | Boston Music Co., 1926 |  |
|  | Three Old American Quadrilles |  |  |  |
| 11 | Dances of Our Pioneers | Ryan | A. S. Barnes and Co., 1926 | Contains separate booklet of calls and directions. |
|  | Old Square Dances of America | Dunlary and Boyd | Recreational Training School, Chicago, 1925 |  |
| 12 | "Good Morning" | Mr. & Mrs. Henry Ford | Dearborn Pub. Co., 1925 | "Old Fashioned Dances Revived." |

## Source of Material for Folk Dancing—*Continued*

| Number referring to List of Records | Name of Book | Author | Publisher | Remarks |
|---|---|---|---|---|
| | **American Indian** | | | |
| 13 | The Rhythm of the Redman | Buttree | A. S. Barnes and Co., 1930 | Excellent Indian Material. Illustrations by Ernest Thompson Seton. |
| | American Indian and Other Folk Dances | Shafter | A. S. Barnes and Co., 1927 | |
| | **English Dances** | | | |
| 14 | Country Dance Book Vol. I-VI | Sharp | | H. W. Gray and Company, N. Y. agents for Novello Co., London. Tunes come in separate books. |
| | The Morris Book Vol. I-V | Sharp | Novello Co. | |
| | The Sword Dance Book Vol. I-III | Sharp | Novello Co. | |
| 15 | The English Country Dance Vol. I-VIII | Sharp | Novello Co. | Notation and music. |
| 16 | An Introduction to English Country Dance | Sharp | Novello Co. | |
| 17 | Single copies of dances from the above | Sharp | H. W. Gray | Contains description together with tunes of twelve dances. Single dances with music may be purchased. |
| 18 I | The Esperance Morris Book | Neal | G. Shirmer | |
| 18 II | The Esperance Morris Book Part II | Neal | Curwen & Son (London) | |
| | English Folk Song and Dance | Kidson and Neal | Macmillan | |
| | **Danish Dances** | | | |
| 3 V | Folk Dances of Denmark | Burchenal | G. Shirmer | Illustrations in native costumes. |
| | Danish Folk Dances | Bovbjerg | Recreational Training School (Chicago), 1917 | Music and description in separate volumes. |
| | **Other Nations** | | | |
| 3 VI | National Dancing of Ireland | Burchenal | A. S. Barnes and Co., 1924 | |
| 3 VII | Folk Dances of Finland | Burchenal | G. Schirmer, 1915 | |
| 19 | Swedish Folk Dances | Berquist | A. S. Barnes and Co., 1914 | Illustrations in native costume. |
| | Folk Dances of Czecho-Slovakia | Geary | A. S. Barnes and Co., 1922 | |
| | Russian Peasant Dances | Baum | C. F. Summy Co. | |
| | Folk Dances of Bohemia and Moravia | Spaech and Boyd | Saul Bro., 1917 | |
| 8 | Slavic Folk Dances | Geary | Womans Press, 1924 | Colored illustrations in native costume. |
| | Five Folk Dances from Austria, Germany and Holland | Burchenal | G. Schirmer | |
| | Philippine Folk Dances and Games | Rayes and Rames | Silver, Burdett Co. | |
| | Oriental and Character Dances | Frost | A. S. Barnes and Co., 1928 | |

| | Title | Author | Publisher, Date | Notes |
|---|---|---|---|---|
| | **Athletic and Character Dances** | | | |
| | Fifty Figure and Character Dances | Bell | A. S. Barnes and Co., 1925 | Illustrated in color. |
| | Twenty-five Figure and Character Dances | Bell | A. S. Barnes and Co., 1931 | Illustrated. |
| | Oriental and Character Dances | Frost | A. S. Barnes and Co., 1928 | |
| | Clog and Character Dances | Frost | A. S. Barnes and Co., 1924 | |
| | Tap, Caper and Clog | Frost | A. S. Barnes and Co., 1930 | |
| | Athletic Dances and Simple Clogs | Hillas and Knighton | A. S. Barnes and Co., 1928 | |
| | Recreative Dances for Classes in Physical Education | Beckley | O. Ditson, 1927 | |
| | **Singing Games and Child Rhythms** | | | |
| 5 III | Characteristic Rhythms for Children | Ashton | A. S. Barnes and Co., 1931 | |
| | Play Songs | Bentley | Laidlaw Bros., 1912 | |
| | The Song Play Book | Crampton and Wollaston | A. S. Barnes and Co., 1917 | |
| | Dramatic Games and Dances for Little Children | Crawford | A. S. Barnes and Co., 1914 | |
| 8 III | Rhythms of Childhood | Crawford and Fogg | A. S. Barnes and Co., 1925 | Music from Folk Melodies, for use in grades 1-4. |
| | Choice Rhythms for Youthful Dancers | Crawford and Fogg | A. S. Barnes and Co., 1925 | For grades 5-8. |
| | Mother Goose Nursery Rhymes set to Music | Elliott | McLaughlin | |
| | Children's Singing Games | Hofer | A. Flanagan, 1914 | Paper edition; illustrated. |
| | Singing Rhymes and Games | Davis | Clayton-Summy, 1901 | |
| | Swedish Song Games | Kastman and Kohler | Ginn & Co., 1913 | |
| 20 I | Rhythm Action Plays and Dances | Moses | M. Bradley, 1915 | |
| | Physical Education for Primary Schools | Ocher | A. S. Barnes and Co., 1926 | |
| 20 II | Physical Education for Second Grade | Ocher | A. S. Barnes and Co. | |
| 21 | Folk Games of Denmark and Sweden | Pedersen and Boyd | Saul Bro, 1915 | Contains colored illustration of costume. |
| 22 | Dramatized Rhythm Plays | Richards | A. S. Barnes and Co., 1927 | |
| | Rhythms for Children, I, II and III | Shafer and Moses | A. S. Barnes and Co., 1921 | |
| | Dramatic Dances for Little Children | Shafer | A. S. Barnes and Co., 1927 | |
| 28 | Games in Song for Little Folk | Steiner | A. S. Barnes and Co., 1921 | 1st Grade. |
| | New Song Plays to Old Tunes | Wood | A. S. Barnes and Co., 1924 | |
| | **Costumes for Folk Dancing** | | | |
| 24 | The Folk Costume Book | Haire | A. S. Barnes and Co., 1926 | Authentic costumes for many countries illustrated in color. |
| | **Festival Books** | | | |
| 25 | The Festival Book | Lincoln | A. S. Barnes and Co., 1912 | |
| | The Guild of Play Book of Festival and Dance | Kimmins | London | |
| | Folk Festivals | Needham | Viking Press | |
| | Folk Festivals for Schools and Playgrounds | Shambaugh | A. S. Barnes and Co., 1932 | |

179

CHART SHOWING VICTROLA RECORDS AVAILABLE FOR FOLK DANCING, WITH REFERENCES FOR LOCATING THE DIRECTIONS FOR DANCE PATTERNS, AND THE GRADE FOR WHICH THE DANCE IS BEST ADAPTED.

(Numbers below refer to Folk Dance Book in which Dance can be found.—See list above.)

| Name of Record for Folk Dancing | Number of Record | 1 LaSalle | 2 Nielson | 3 Burchenal | 4 Crawford | 5 Crampton | 6 Elsom and T | 7 Hinman | 8 Hofer | 9 Sperling | 10 Handbook | 11 Ryan | 12 Ford | 13 Sharp | 14 Sharp | 15 Sharp | 16 Sharp | 17 Sharp | 18 Neal | 19 Berquist | 20 Ocher | 21 Pedersen | 22 Richards | 23 Wood | 24 Lincoln | 25 Kimmins | Grade | Foot Pattern Used in the DANCE |
|---|---|---|---|---|---|---|---|---|---|---|---|---|---|---|---|---|---|---|---|---|---|---|---|---|---|---|---|---|
| Ace of Diamonds (Danish) | C-A3001 V-20989 | X | X | III V | | I | | | | | | | | | | | | | | | | | | | | | 3–4 | Polka |
| Arkansas Traveler (American) | V-20638 | | | IV | | | | | | | | | | | | | | | | | | | | | | | 7–9 | A.C.D. |
| Badger Gavotte (American) | C-5570 V-19910 | X | X X | | | | | | | | | | X | | | | | | | | | | | | | | 8 | Two-step |
| Bean Setting (English) | V-20640 | X | | | | | | II | | | | | | | I | | | | II | | | | | | | | 6–8 | Morris Stick Dance |
| Bleking (Swedish) | C-A3037 V-20989 | X | X X | I | I | I | | II | I | X | X X | | | | | | | | | X | | | | | | | 3–4 | Bleking |
| Black Nag (English) | V-20444 | | | | | | | | | | | | | II | | I X | I X | X X | | | | | | | | | 6–8 | E.C.D. |
| Bobbing Joe (English) | V-20642 | | | I | | | | | | | | | | III | | | | | | | | | | | | | 6–8 | E.C.D. |
| Boston Fancy (American) | V-20001 | | | IV | | | | | | | | | | | | | | | | | | | | | | | 5–8 | A.C.D. |
| Broom Dance (German) | V-20448 | | X | I | | | X | | | | | X | | | | | | | | | | | | | | | 3–4 | Polka |
| Bummel Schottische (German) | V-20448 | | | II | | | | | | | | | | | | | | | | | | | | | | | 4–7 | Polka |
| Captain Jinks (American) | V-20639 | X | | | | | X | | II | | | | | | | | | | | | | | | X | | | 8 | A.C.D. |

180

| Name of Record for Folk Dancing | Number of Record | 1 | 2 | 3 | 4 | 5 | 6 | 7 | 8 | 9 | 10 | 11 | 12 | 13 | 14 | 15 | 16 | 17 | 18 | 19 | 20 | 21 | 22 | 23 | 24 | 25 | Grade | Foot Pattern Used in the DANCE |
|---|---|---|---|---|---|---|---|---|---|---|---|---|---|---|---|---|---|---|---|---|---|---|---|---|---|---|---|---|
| Carrousel (Swedish) | C-A3032 V-20432 | | X | III | | I III | X | III | | X | | | | | | | | | | | I | | | | | | 2–3 | Slide |
| Chelsea Reach (English) | V-20746 | | | | | | | | II | | | | | III | | | | X | | | | | | | | | 6–8 | E.C.D. |
| Chimes of Dunkirk (Belgium) | C-A3061 V-21618 | X | X | | | I | | | III | X | X | | | | | | | | | | | | | | | | 1–2 | Run |
| Circle-Uncle Steve (American) | V-20639 | | | IV | | | | | | | | | | | | | | | | | | | | | | | 7–8 | A.C.D. |
| Come Let Us Be Joyful (German) | V-20448 | | X | I | | | | | | | | | | III | | | | | | | | | | | | | 4–6 | Step-hop |
| Confess (English) | V-20746 | | | | | | | | | | | | | III | | | | | | | | | | | | | 7–8 | E.C.D. |
| Country Gardens (English) | V-20642 | | | | | | | | | | | | | | I | | | | | | | | | | | | 6–8 | Morris Hand-kerchief dance |
| Crested Hen (Danish) | V-21619 | X | | I V | | II | | III | | | | | | | | | | | | | | | | | | | 5–7 | Skip |
| Csardas (Hungarian) | C-A3037 | | | III | | I | | IV | | | | | | | | | | | | | | | | | | | 5–7 | Social Dance |
| Cshebogar (Hungarian) | V-20992 | X | X | | | | X | | | X | | | | | | | | | | | | | | | | | 5–7 | Slide, Skip |
| Dance of Greeting (Danish) | C-A3039 V-20432 | | X | III | | I | X | | | X | X | | | | | | | | | | | | | | | | 1–2 | Run |
| Durang's Hornpipe (American) | V-20592 | | | IV | | | | | | | | | X | | | | | | | | | | | | | | 7–8 | A.C.D. |
| Farandole (French) | V-21685 | | X | II | | I | | | | | | | | | | | | | | | | | | | | | 1–4 | Run, skip |
| Finnish Reel | C-A3062 | | X | | | I | | | | | | | | | | | | | | | | | | | | | 5 | Run, hop |
| Gathering Peascods (English) | V-20445 | | | | | | | IV | | | | | | II | | I | X | X | | | | | | | | | 7–9 | E.C.D. |

181

**Numbers Below Refer to Folk Dance Book in Which Dance Can Be Found.—See List Above.**

| Name of Record for Folk Dancing | Number of Record | 1 | 2 | 3 | 4 | 5 | 6 | 7 | 8 | 9 | 10 | 11 | 12 | 13 | 14 | 15 | 16 | 17 | 18 | 19 | 20 | 21 | 22 | 23 | 24 | 25 | Grade | Foot Pattern Used in the DANCE |
|---|---|---|---|---|---|---|---|---|---|---|---|---|---|---|---|---|---|---|---|---|---|---|---|---|---|---|---|---|
| German Clap Dance (German) | C-2050 V-20641 | X | | I | | I | | | I | | | | | | | | | | | X | | | | | | | 1–3 | March |
| Girl I Left Behind Me | C-33058F | | X | | | | | | | | | | | | | | | | | | | | | | | | 8 | A.C.D. |
| Green Sleeves (English) | V-21619 | | | | | | | III | II | | | X | X | | | | | | I | | | | | | | X | 4 | Skip |
| Grimstock (English) | V-20444 | | | | | | | | | | | | | II | | | | X | | | | | | | | | 8 | E.C.D. |
| Gustaf's Skal (Swedish) | V-20988 | X | X | I | I | II, III | | IV | | | | | | | | | | | | X | | | | | | | 4–5 | Polka |
| Hansel and Gretel (German) | V-21620 | X | X | | | II, III | | | III | | | | | | | | | | | | | X | | | | | 3–4 | Polka |
| Hatter, The (Danish) | C-43000 V-20449 | X | | II, V | | | | | | | | | X | | | | | | | | | | | | | | 7 | Quadrille |
| Heel Toe Polka | C-555D V-19909 | | | | | | | | | | | | | | | | | | | | | | | | | | 8 | Slide Polka |
| Hewitt's Fancy (English) | V-21620 | | | | | | | | | | | | | | | | | | | | | | | | | | 7–8 | |
| Highland Fling No. 1 (Scotch) | C-A3000 V-21616 | X | | I, III | | I | | V | | | | | | | | | | | | | | | | | X | | 7–8 | Hop, cut, etc. |
| Highland Schottische (Scotch) | C-A3039 V-21616 | X | X | | I | I | | | I | | | | | | | | | | | | | | | | | | 5–6 | Schottische |
| Hopp Mor Annika (Swedish) | V-21618 | | | | I | I | | | | | | | | | | | | | | | | | | | X | | 6 | Skip Polka |
| How D'ye Do My Partner (Swedish) | V-21685 | | X | | | | X | | | | | | | | | | | | | | | | | | X | | 1 | Skip |
| Irish Lilt (Irish Washer-woman) | C-3061 V-21616 V-21749 | X | | | I | | II | V | | | X | X | | | | | | | | | | | | | | | 7–8 | Cut, hop also A.C.D. |

182

| Name of Record for Folk Dancing | Number of Record | 1 | 2 | 3 | 4 | 5 | 6 | 7 | 8 | 9 | 10 | 11 | 12 | 13 | 14 | 15 | 16 | 17 | 18 | 19 | 20 | 21 | 22 | 23 | 24 | 25 | Grade | Foot Pattern Used in the DANCE |
|---|---|---|---|---|---|---|---|---|---|---|---|---|---|---|---|---|---|---|---|---|---|---|---|---|---|---|---|---|
| I See You (Swedish) | C-A3041 V-20432 | | | III | | I III | | III | I | X | | | | | | | | | | | | | | | | | 2-3 | Skip Polka |
| Jenny Pluck Pears (English) | V-20446 | | | | | | | | | | | | | | | | | | | | | X | | | | | 7-8 | E.C.D. |
| Jig St. Patrick (Irish) | C-A3052 | | | III | | | | | | | | | | II | | | | X | | | | | | | | | 8 | Jig |
| Kinderpolka (German) | C-3052 V-20432 | | X | | | I | | | | X | X | | | | | | | | | | | | | | | | 1-2 | Slide |
| Klappdans (Swedish) | C-3036 V-20450 | | | I | I | I | X | III | I | X | | | | | | | | | | | | X | | | X | | 3-5 | Polka |
| Komarinskaia (Russian) | C-A3002 | | | III | | I | | | | | | | | | | | | | | | | | | | | | 6-8 | Russian steps |
| Lads a Bunchun (English) | V-20640 | | | | | | | | | | | | | | II | | | | | | | | | | | | 7-8 | Morris Stick Dance |
| Lady in the Dark (English) | V-20746 | | | | | | | | | | | | | III | | | | X | | | | | | | | | 6-8 | E.C.D. |
| Lady of the Lake (American) | V-20592 | | | IV | | | | | | | | | | | | | | | | | | | | | | | 6-8 | A.C.D. |
| Laudnum Bunches | C-A3052 | | | III | | I | | | | | | | | | I | | | | II | | | | | | | | 7-8 | Morris Corner Dance |
| Little Man in a Fix (Danish) | V-20449 | X | X | II V | | | | III | | | | | | | | | | | | | | | | | | | 6 | Run |
| Lott'ist Tod (Swedish) | V-20088 | | X | | I | | | II | | | | | | | | | | | | X | | | | | | | 6 | |
| May Pole Dance—Bluff King Hal (English) | C-A3038 V-20990 | | | III | | II | | III | | | | | | | | | | | | | | | | | | X | 4-8 | Skip |
| Medley of Flings (Scotch) | C-33051F V-79004 | X | | I III | | I | | V | | | | | | | | | | | | | | | | | | | 7-8 | Cut, hop |

Numbers Below Refer to Folk Dance Book in Which Dance Can Be Found.—See List Above.

| Name of Record for Folk Dancing | Number of Record | 1 | 2 | 3 | 4 | 5 | 6 | 7 | 8 | 9 | 10 | 11 | 12 | 13 | 14 | 15 | 16 | 17 | 18 | 19 | 20 | 21 | 22 | 23 | 24 | 25 | Grade | Foot Pattern Used in the DANCE |
|---|---|---|---|---|---|---|---|---|---|---|---|---|---|---|---|---|---|---|---|---|---|---|---|---|---|---|---|---|
| | | | | | | | | | | | | | | | | | | | | | | | | | | | | Numbers Below Refer to Folk Dance Book in Which Dance Can Be Found.—See List Above. |
| Medley of Hornpipes (Irish) | V-79005 | | | I V | | | | | | | | | | | | | | | | | | | | | | | | 7–8 | Polka and others |
| Medley of Jigs (Irish) | C-33019F C-33021F C-33026F V-79005 | | | III | | I | | | I | | | | | | | | | | | | | | | | | | | 7–8 | Jig steps |
| Medley of Reels (Irish) | C-33026F C-33042F V-79004 | | | | | | | | | | | | | | | | | | | | | | | | | | | | |
| Merry, Merry Milkmaids (English) | V-22380 | X | | | | | | | | | | | | III | | III | | | | | | | | | | | | | E.C.D. |
| Minuet—Don Juan (French) | V-20900 | | | | I | | | IV | II | | | | | | | | | | | | | | | | | | | 4–8 | Step point |
| Miss McCloud's Reel (Irish) | V-20447 | | | VI IV | | | | | | | | | | | | | | | | | | | | | | | | 7–8 | I.C.D. |
| Monkey Musk Nos. 1 and 2 (American) | C-231D V-20447 | X | | | IV | I | | | II | | | X | X | | | | | | | | | | | | | | | 4–7 | A.C.D. |
| Newcastle (English) | V-20444 | | | | | | | | | | | | | II | | IV | | X | | | | | | | | | | 8 | E.C.D. |
| Nigarepolska (Swedish) | V-21685 | | X | | | I III | | III | I | | | | | | | | | | | | | X | | | | | | 2 | Bleking-step |
| Norwegian Mountain March (Norwegian) | C-A3041 V-20151 | | X | V III | | I | | III | I | X | | | | | | | | | | | | | | | | | | 5–6 | Waltz run |
| Old Dan Tucker (American) | V-20447 | | X | II IV | | | | | I II | | | | X | | | | | | | | | | | | | | | 7–8 | A.C.D. |
| Old Mole, The (English) | V-22380 | | | | | | | | | | | | | III | | IV | | X | | | | | | | | | | 8 | E.C.D. |
| Old Noll's Jig (English) | V-36010 | | | | | | | | | | | | | VI | | VIII | | | | | | | | | | | | | E.C.D. |

| Name of Record for Folk Dancing | Number of Record | 1 | 2 | 3 | 4 | 5 | 6 | 7 | 8 | 9 | 10 | 11 | 12 | 13 | 14 | 15 | 16 | 17 | 18 | 19 | 20 | 21 | 22 | 23 | 24 | 25 | Grade | Foot Pattern Used in the DANCE |
|---|---|---|---|---|---|---|---|---|---|---|---|---|---|---|---|---|---|---|---|---|---|---|---|---|---|---|---|---|
| Old Zip Coon (American) | V-20592 | | | IV | | | | | | | | | | | | | | | | | | | | | | | | |
| Parson's Farewell (English) | V-20446 | | | | | | | II | | | | | | II | | VI | | X | | | | | | | | | | E.C.D. |
| Pop Goes the Weasel (American) | C-A3078 V-20151 V-20447 | X | X | IV | | | X | III | II | | X | | X | I | | V | | | I | | II | | X | X | X | | 4–8 | Skip |
| Poppy, The (Lithuanian) | V-20991 | | | II | | | | | | | | | | | | | | | | | | | | | | | 2 | Walk Pantomime |
| Plain Quadrille | C-50018D | X | | | | | | | | | | X | X | | | | | | | | | | | | | | 8 | A.C.D. |
| Quadrille—Figure 1 (Chillicothe, Virginny Shore) (American) | V-20638 | | | | | | | | | | | X | X | | | | | | | | | | | | | | 7–8 | A.C.D. |
| Quadrille—Fig. 2 (O Susanna, Arkansas Traveller) (American) | V-20638 | | | | | | | | | | | X | X | | | | | | | | | | | | | | 7–8 | A.C.D. |
| Quadrille—Fig. 3 (Captain Jinks, Rosin the Bow) (American) | V-20639 | | | | | | | | | | | X | X | | | | | | | | | | | | | | 7–8 | A.C.D. |
| Rakes of Mallow (Irish) | C-33049 V-20991 | | | II | | | | | | | | | | | | | | | I | | | | | | | | 7–8 | I.C.D. |
| Reap the Flax (Swedish) | C-A3301 | | | III | I | | | | | | | | | | | | | | | | | X | | | | | 5–8 | Run Pantomime |
| Rheinlander (Swedish) | C-A3050 | | X | | I | | | | | | | | | | | | | | | | | | | | | | 5–8 | Polka |
| Ribbon Dance (English) | V-21619 | | | | | | X | | | | | | | I | II | | X | | | | | | | | | | 5–6 | E.C.D. |
| Ripple, The | V-19907 | | | | | | | | | | | X | | | | | | | | | | | | | | | 8 | Slide Waltz |
| Roman Soldiers (English) | V-21617 | X | | II | | | | III | | | | | | | | | | | | | | | | | | | 2 | Walk Pantomime |

| Name of Record for Folk Dancing | Number of Record | Numbers Below Refer to Folk Dance Book in Which Dance Can Be Found.—See List Above. | | | | | | | | | | | | | | | | | | | | | | | | | Grade | Foot Pattern Used in the DANCE |
|---|---|---|---|---|---|---|---|---|---|---|---|---|---|---|---|---|---|---|---|---|---|---|---|---|---|---|---|---|
| | | 1 | 2 | 3 | 4 | 5 | 6 | 7 | 8 | 9 | 10 | 11 | 12 | 13 | 14 | 15 | 16 | 17 | 18 | 19 | 20 | 21 | 22 | 23 | 24 | 25 | | |
| Rufty Tufty (English) | V-20446 | | | | | | | IV | | | | | | II | | I | X | X | | | | | | | | | | E.C.D. |
| Sailor's Hornpipe (English) | C-A3054 V-21685 | | | I V | | II | | IV | | | | | | | | | | | | | | | | | | | 8 | Polka |
| Schottische | V-19907 | | | | | | | | | | | X | X | | | | | | | | | | | | | | 7–8 | Schottische |
| Sellenger's Round (English) | C-10009D V-20445 | X | | | | | | III | | | | | | IV | | III | | X | | | | | | | | X | 5–7 | E.C.D. |
| Seaside Polka (American) | V-19909 | | | | | | | | | | | | X | | | | | | | | | | | | | | 8 | Slide, run |
| Seven Jumps (Danish) | V-21617 | X | | I V | | | | II | | | | | | | | | | | | | | | | | | | 4 | Skip |
| Shepherd's Hey (English) | V-20641 | | | | | | | II | | | | | | | I | | | | | | | | | | | | 6–8 | Morris |
| Shoemakers Dance (Danish) | C-A3038 V-20450 | | | V III | | I | | III | | X | X | | | | | | | | | | I | X | | | | | 1–2 | Skip Polka |
| Sicilian Circle (American) | C-556D V-20639 | X | X | | | | X | | II | | | X | | | | | | | | | | | | | | | 8 | A.C.D. |
| Soldier's Joy (American) | V-20592 | | | | | | | | | | | X | | | | | | | | | | | | | | | 5–8 | A.C.D. |
| Speed the Plow (English) | V-36010 | | | IV | | | | | | | | | X | I | | | | | | | | | | | | | 8 | E.C.D. |
| St. Patrick's Day (Irish) | C-A3000 V-21616 | | | III | | | | | | | | | | | | | | | | | | | | | | | 8 | Jig |
| Sweet Kate (English) | V-20444 | | II | | | | | IV | | | | | | III | | | X | X | | | | | | | | | 8 | E.C.D. |
| Tantoli (Swedish) | C-A3054 V-20992 | | | I VII | | | | II | | | | | | | | | | | | | X | | | | | | 6 | Polka Step hop |
| Tarentella (Italian) | C-A3062 | | | III | | | | II IV | | | | | | | | | | | | | | | | | | | 8 | Run, slide hop |

| Name of Record for Folk Dancing | Number of Record | 1 | 2 | 3 | 4 | 5 | 6 | 7 | 8 | 9 | 10 | 11 | 12 | 13 | 14 | 15 | 16 | 17 | 18 | 19 | 20 | 21 | 22 | 23 | 24 | 25 | Grade | Foot Pattern Used in the DANCE |
|---|---|---|---|---|---|---|---|---|---|---|---|---|---|---|---|---|---|---|---|---|---|---|---|---|---|---|---|---|
| Trallen (Swedish) | C-A3002 | | | | | | | | | | | | | | | | | | | | | | | | | | 7–8 | Waltz run Dal step |
| Turn Around Me (Czecho-Slovakian) | V-21620 | | | II | | | | | | | | | | | | | | | | | | | | | | | 5–8 | Run |
| Uncle Steve (American) | V-20639 | | | II IV | | | | | | | | | | | | | | | | | | | | | | | 8 | A.C.D. |
| Varsovienne | C-683D V-19910 | | X | | | | | II | | | | X | X | | | | | | | X | | | | | | | 8 | Waltz |
| Virginia Reels (American) | C-50018D V-20447 | X | X | IV | | II | X | IV | | X | | X | X | | | | | | | | | | | | | | 7–8 | Walk, skip |
| Waves of Tory (American) | V-20991 | | | II VI | | | | | | | | | | | | | | | | | | | | | | | 8 | A.C.D. |
| Wheat, The (Czecho.) | V-20992 | | | | | | | | | | | | | | | | | | | | | | | | | | | See Folk Dances of Bohemia and Moravia |
| White Cochade (Irish) | V-20991 | | | VI IV | | | | | II | | | | | | | | | | | | | | | | | | | |
| Wind that Shakes the Barley (Irish) | V-20991 | | | II VI | | | | | | | | | | | | | | | | | | | | | | | | |
| Yankee Doodle (American) | V-20166 | | | | | | | | | | | | | | | | | | | | | | | X | | | | 7–8 | I.C.D. |
| Young America Hornpipe (American) | V-20592 | | | IV | | | | | | | | | | | | | | | | | | | | | | | | |

Numbers Below Refer to Folk Dance Book in Which Dance Can Be Found.—See List Above.

187

| Name of Record for Singing Games | Number of Record | — Numbers Below Refer to Folk Dance Book in Which Dance Can Be Found.—See List Above. |||||||||||||||||||||||| Grade | Foot Pattern Used in the DANCE |
|---|---|---|---|---|---|---|---|---|---|---|---|---|---|---|---|---|---|---|---|---|---|---|---|---|---|---|---|---|
| | | 1 | 2 | 3 | 4 | 5 | 6 | 7 | 8 | 9 | 10 | 11 | 12 | 13 | 14 | 15 | 16 | 17 | 18 | 19 | 20 | 21 | 22 | 23 | 24 | 25 | | |
| A-Hunting We Will Go (English) | V-22356 | X | | | | III | | III | | | X | | | | | | | | | | | | | | | | X | 2 | Skip |
| Can You Plant the Seeds? | V-22356 | | | | | | | | | | | | | | | | | | | | | | | | | | | | |
| Carrousel (Swedish) | V-20432 | | X | III | | I III | X | III | | X | | | | | | | | | | | I | | | | | | | 1-3 | Slide |
| Dance of Greeting (Danish) | V-20432 | | X | III | | I | X | | | X | | | | | | | | | | | | | | | | | | 2 | Run |
| Did You Ever See a Lassie (American) | C-10008 D / V-21618 | | X | | | III | X | | | X | | | | | | | | | | | I | | | | | | | 1 | Skip / Pantomime |
| Farmer in the Dell, The (American) | V-21618 | X | X | | | III | | III | III | X | X | | | | | | | | | | | | | | | | | 1 | Skip |
| Hickory Dickory Dock | C-100006D | | | | | | X | I | | | | | | | | | | | | | | | X | | | | | 1 | Run |
| Hansel and Gretel (German) | V-21620 | X | X | | | II III | | | III | | | | | | | | | | | | | | | | | | | 3-4 | Skip |
| How d'ye Do My Partner (Swedish) | V-21685 | | | | | III | | | | X | X | | | | | | | | | | I | | | | | | | | |
| Here We Go Round the Mulberry Bush (American) | V-20806 | | | | | | | | III | | | | | | | | | | | | | | | | | | | | |
| Holly, Holly, Ho, The (English) | V-22356 | | | | | | | | | | | | | | | | | | | | | | | | | | | | |
| I See You (Swedish) | V-20432 | | | III | | I III | | III | III | X | | | | | | | | | | | | | | | | | | 1-3 | Run, skip |
| Jolly is the Miller (English) | C-A3078 / V-20214 | | X | | | III | X | III III III | | X | X | | | | | | | | | | | | | | | | | 1-3 | Skip |

Numbers Below Refer to Folk Dance Book in Which Dance Can Be Found.—See List Above.

| Name of Record for Singing Games | | 1 | 2 | 3 | 4 | 5 | 6 | 7 | 8 | 9 | 10 | 11 | 12 | 13 | 14 | 15 | 16 | 17 | 18 | 19 | 20 | 21 | 22 | 23 | 24 | 25 | Grade | Foot Pattern Used in the DANCE |
|---|---|---|---|---|---|---|---|---|---|---|---|---|---|---|---|---|---|---|---|---|---|---|---|---|---|---|---|---|
| Kinderpolka (German) | V-20432 | | X | | | I | | | | X | | | | | | | | | | | | | | | | | 1–2 | Slide |
| London Bridge (English) | V-20806 | X | | | | | | III III | III III | | | | | | | | | | I | | | | | X | | | 1–2 | Skip, run walk |
| Looby Loo (English) | C-10008D V-20214 | X | X | | | III | | III III | III III | | X | | | | | | | | I | | | | X | | | | 1 | Skip, slide Pantomime |
| Muffin Man, The (New England) | V-20806 | X | | | | III | | III III | III III | | | | | | | | | | | | | | | | | | 1–2 | Skip |
| Needle's Eye, The (American) | V-20214 | | | | | | | | III | | | | | | | | | | | | | | | | | | | |
| Oats, Peas, Beans, and Barley Grow (English) | C-10008D V-20214 | | X | | | III | | | III III | X | X | | | | | | | | | | | | | | | | 2 | Skip, slide Pantomime |
| On the Bridge (French) | V-22356 | X | | II | | | | | | | | | | | | | | | | | | | | | | | 2 | Skip curtsey |
| Poppy, The | V-20991 | | | II | | | | | | | | | | | | | | | | | | | | | | | 2 | Walk Pantomime |
| Sally Go Round | V-22356 | X | | | | | | | | | | X | | | | | | | | | | | | | | | 1–2 | Skip, walk Run, slide |
| Soldier Boy (American) | V-20806 | | | | | III | | III | III | | | | | | | | | | | | | | | | | | 2 | March Pantomime |
| Today's the First of May (Swedish) | C-10009D | | | III | | II III | X | III | | | | | | | | | | | | | | X | | | | | 4 | Polka |
| Turn Around Me (Czecho.) | V-21620 | | | II | | | | | | | | | | | | | | | | | | | | | | | 5–8 | Run |

189

Final Examination—Folk Dancing.

Name ————————————————

Instructor ————————————————

Section ————————————————

I. Are the following terms characteristic of
"A"—American Country Dances?
"E"—English Country Dances?
(Encircle correct letter.)

—— A E Lead up to the right.

—— A E Reel.

—— A E Quadrille.

—— A E Forward and back a double.

—— A E Grand right and left.

—— A E Promenade.

—— A E Set.

—— A E Eight slips sideward.

—— A E Arming.

—— A E Do-ce-do.

—— A E Swing your Partner.

—— A E Siding.

—— A E Alemande left.

—— A E Turn single.

II. In blank at left of above terms place number corresponding to correct definition: *

1. Hook right arm with partner and turn about.

2. Leap to right, place left toe behind right and shift weight twice.

3. Four steps forward, four steps backward.

4. Back to partner give left hand to next person, right to next, etc.

5. Set of eight persons in square.

6. Walk or skip with partner in circle.

7. Give partner left hand, turn about give right hand to next person, left to next, etc.

8. Move sideward about circle, keeping feet close to floor.

9. Arms about partner, turn in place.

10. Give partner right hand, left to next person, right to next, etc.

11. Meet partner and return to place passing back to back.

12. Turn in place with four short leaps.

13. Back to partner, give next person left hand, turn once about and give right hand to partner left to next, etc.

* Extra definitions and descriptions have been added to test student's discrimination.

14. Balance in front of couple.

15. Right hand to partner turn once and half around, left hand to next, right to partner, left to next, etc.

16. Couple move right to face next couple.

III. Beside the following terms place number indicating correct description, letter signifying in which dance the step is used, number indicating correct rhythm and letter signifying mood in which danced:

| | Description | Dance in Which Used | Rhythm | Mood |
|---|---|---|---|---|
| Schottische | | | | |
| Polka | | | | |
| Waltz | | | | |
| Skip | | | | |
| Step Hop | | | | |
| Sliding | | | | |

Descriptions: *

1. Step close step.
2. Step hop step.
3. Hop step close step.
4. Step hop step close.
5. Step step close.
6. Step close step hop.
7. Hop step step.
8. Step hop step hop.
9. Step close step close.

Dance in which used:

a. Swedish Clap Dance.
b. Coming through the Rye.
c. Barn Dance for Four.
d. Pop Goes the Weasel.
e. Girl You Left Behind You.
f. Grapevine Twist.

Rhythm:

1. s l s l
2. l s L L
3. s s L
4. s l l L
5. L L
6. L L L
7. L s L L
8. L L L L

Mood:

a. Gay
b. Sad
c. Stately
d. Slow
e. Definitely even
f. Smooth

* Extra definitions and descriptions have been added to test student's discrimination.

IV. Diagram a quadrille using a ☐ to indicate the man,   O   to indicate lady.

V. Using above marks for man and lady, describe through diagram the dance called "Grapevine Twist."

VI. Give words to "Girl You Left Behind You."

VII. Describe the waltz, showing how to teach it on a square.

VIII. Describe briefly the following dances (write in outline form):
    Pop Goes the Weasel

    Barn Dance for Four

Gathering Peascods

Virginia Reel

# CHAPTER XVI

### FOLK DANCE SKILLS FROM A RHYTHMIC APPROACH

Certain dance skills are frequently found in folk dancing and may be isolated and taught from a rhythmic approach, either in folk dancing class or previously in a course in rhythms. Such skills include the schottische, polka, two step, waltz and mazurka. A brief analysis of these will be found on page 47. In Chapter V the schottische was analyzed in detail.

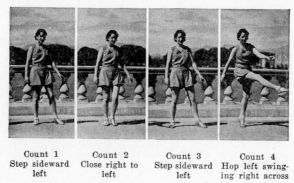

| Count 1 | Count 2 | Count 3 | Count 4 |
| Step sideward left | Close right to left | Step sideward left | Hop left swinging right across |

FIG. 41. THE SCHOTTISCHE

The other skills mentioned above may be similarly analyzed as follows:

The *Polka* is similar to the Schottische in that it is made up of a step, close, step, hop, but its uneven rhythm gives it a very different spirit from the schottische. The schottische is moderately slow and smooth, always done in even rhythm while the polka is gay, vivacious, fast, and uneven. A simple way to learn the polka is to combine a gallop and a skip; that is, do a step-close-step-hop in rhythm L s L s. Repeat and continue and soon you will catch the spirit of the polka.

Typical polka music is 2/4 with one polka pattern done to one measure of music. Since 2/4 music has only two quarter notes to a measure while 4/4 music has four quarter notes, it is evident that the polka takes only one-half the amount of time that the schottische takes. That is, to polka music we are doing

2/4 | step close step hop |

while in the schottische we did

$$4/4 \quad | \text{ step } \quad \text{ close } \quad \text{ step } \quad \text{ hop } |$$

In polka music the two quarter notes are divided (in order to make an uneven polka rhythm) into

step    close    step    hop    or    step    close    step    hop

Find some vivacious 2/4 music and do the polka until your feet catch its spirit.   The music suggested for skipping or galloping will do.   The "Hatter," "The Swedish Clap Dance" and other similar folk dance music will make good polkas.*   Be sure that the "step" before the "close" comes on the accent of the measure so that the hop comes at the very end of the measure.

|  "a"  |   1   |  "and"  |   2   |
| Hop   | Step  |  Close  | Step  |

Fig. 42.   The Polka

Technically, the polka begins with the hop, being "hop-step-close-step," see Figure 42, however, after one gets started and repeats the polka it really matters little whether one thinks of it as beginning or ending with the hop.   For the sake of accuracy, however, let us say that the polka is hop, step, close, step,

s    l    l    L    s    l    l    L

and remember that the hop may come at the beginning of the polka but that it is always done at the end of the measure of music; therefore, in doing a polka to music, we must not wait and begin on the accented beat of the measure.   We must anticipate the accent and start with a hop at the end of the preceding measure of music.

* See page 180.

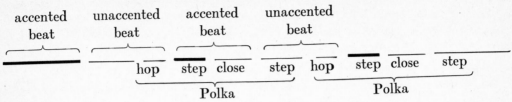

After one knows the Polka, it is very easy to learn the *Two-step*, for the latter is also vivacious. Do the polka; then continue, but leave out the hop and you have the two-step which is step, close, step in uneven rhythm.

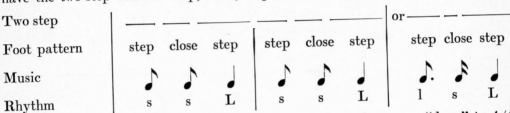

In modern social dancing the two-step is sometimes done as a "drag" to 4/4 music. In this case it has the same rhythm as above, but it is done at a slower rate of speed.

The two-step may also be done to 4/4 time by doing two to a measure of music, for example:

In like manner the Polka might be done to 4/4 music by doing two Polkas to one measure of music.

Or, similarly, the Schottische could be done to 2/4 music by doing one Schottische to two measures of music.

The waltz, when done correctly, is one of the most pleasurable dance forms. Because few people know the true waltz, many dancers are dissatisfied if the orchestra plays more than one or two waltzes during the evening.   The common mistake made is in doing a two-step to waltz music.

Waltz music is written in 3/4 time, therefore having three quarter notes to a measure.   The correct waltz is a step, step, close, in even rhythm.   Synchronized with music, it is

Instead of waltzing, many people two-step, some fitting the two-step to the music by making the parts even.

The two-step danced in an even rhythm is not so dissatisfying as when done in uneven rhythm for the latter does not fit the waltz music at all, being danced either

or in poorer rhythm it might even be done as below:

The old-fashioned waltz was very often taught on a square. Those who learn to waltz this way will find real enjoyment in it.   Mark on the floor a square measuring about 2 feet in length and width or merely imagine it, and stand in the back right-hand corner.   Your right foot is now near the outside of the square.

1. Step forward into the front right corner with the right foot.
2. Step diagonally forward into the left front corner with the left foot.

3. Bring the right foot over to the left and transfer the weight to the right foot.

This will take one measure of waltz music; that is, three beats (see Diagram A).

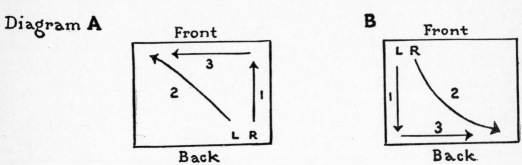

Diagram A

Front

Back

B

Front

Back

You now repeat moving backward, remembering on count one to start always with the outside foot, which is now the left.

1. Step back with left foot into left rear corner.
2. Step with right foot over to right rear corner.
3. Bring left foot over to right, transferring the weight.

These three counts will take one measure of waltz music, the whole pattern of six counts taking two measures. You are now in your original position ready to repeat. (See Diagram B.)

Try to waltz with a smooth evenness. A common mistake is that of moving

| 1 | 2 | 3 | 1 | 2 | 3 |
| Step forward left | Step sideward right | Close left to right | Step backward right | Step sideward left | Close right to left |

FIG. 43. THE WALTZ

the foot too quickly on the third count. If you are doing this, try dragging the third step a bit, so that you close just on count three and not before. Remember on count one you step either directly forward or back with the outside foot, on count two you step to the side with the inside foot, and on three you close. The weight is transferred from one foot to the other on every count.

After you have mastered this preliminary exercise, practice it to music, using a slow waltz. Later, facing a partner, try waltzing, one person stepping forward right, while the other steps backward left on the first count.

When this becomes easy you may try moving always forward on count one; first right, then left, while your partner continues moving backward on count one; first left, then right. Later try turning as you waltz.

In waltzing, the knees must never be stiff, but must bend slightly, especially on count one. A very smooth, even flowing movement is a requisite of the true waltz.

All 3/4 music is not waltz time. Waltz music is a 3/4 time which has a definite even beat with a smoothness in melody and accompaniment. Other 3/4 music may be either a Minuet or a Mazurka. The characteristic quality of a *Minuet* is a certain choppiness, or repetition of eighth notes, which calls for pointing of toes, and very delicate artificial movements, while in a *Mazurka* we have a vigorous, intense mood, and an additional accent on count two as well as on count one of each measure. This additional accent on count two can be made by preceding the note which occurs on count two by a note of shorter time value, for as was said before, in an uneven rhythm the accent tends to fall on the longer of two units. In a measure of 3/4 music this may be accomplished by one of two methods; either by holding the note of count two over the third count, or by splitting count one so that count two will be preceded by a short unit. For example:

Combining counts two and three, we have

or splitting count one we have

Examples of mazurka music written in this manner may be found in Scharwenka's "Polish Dance" or Chopin's "Mazurka," Op. 7 No. 1.

Try clapping the rhythms written above, and you will sense the mazurka spirit of a three-part underlying rhythm, with an accent on "one" and an added accent on "two." Clap the underlying rhythm with your left hand as you clap the Mazurka rhythm with your right hand.

The dance pattern for which mazurka music was originally written is done as a step, cut, hop.  Usually it is done sideward in this manner:

1. Step to the side with the right foot.
2. Bring the left foot into the place occupied by the right, at the same time lifting the right off the floor (this is called a cut step because one foot cuts the other off the floor as it takes its place).
3. Hop on the left, at the same time bending the right knee sideward, so that the right foot is raised to left knee.

1                    2                      3
Step sideward     Cut right dis-    Hop right bend-
    left           placing left          ing knee

FIG. 44.  THE MAZURKA

Repeat again starting right.  It will be evident that in doing the Mazurka one continues always in the same direction.  In order to change direction one can take three stamps in place which will bring the weight onto the right foot, leaving the left foot ready to begin the next mazurka.

The rhythm of the mazurka dance pattern is even, each part of the pattern coming on one of the three beats of the underlying rhythm of the music.  For example, with this mazurka rhythm the dance pattern is done, not following the rhythm of the notes, but following the underlying even beat.

| Mazurka Rhythm | s    L | s    L | l  s  L  L | l  s  L  L |
|---|---|---|---|---|
| Count Underlying beat | 1  2  3 | 1  2  3 | 1 & 2  3 | 1 & 2  3 |
| Step Pattern | St. cut hop | st. cut hop | st. cut hop | st. cut hop |

The *Polish Mazurka*, frequently called the Mazurka, is also particularly adapted to mazurka music both in spirit and rhythm.  The Polish step pattern consists of a leap-stamp-step, the leap being taken sideward, the stamp across in front and the final step backward in place.  The complete pattern is done in even rhythm with the accent on the stamp on count 2, at which time the weight is borne on both feet, and shifted to the forward foot just slightly before count 3.  Frequently the mistake is made of shifting the weight entirely on count 2 which results in a leap instead of a stamp and robs the step pattern of its characteristic strength.

| | | | | | | |
|---|---|---|---|---|---|---|
| Mazurka Rhythm | s L | | | s L | | |
| Underlying Beat | | | | | | |
| Step Pattern | Leap side | Stamp across | Step back | Leap side | Stamp across | Step back |
| | L | R | L | R | L | R |

It is difficult to find Mazurka music which is adaptable to the dance pattern. Many Mazurkas are written for instrumental music, and do not bring out a defi-

1              2              3
Leap sideward   Stamp left across   Step back right
right

FIG. 45. THE POLISH MAZURKA

nite Mazurka beat.  Scharwenka's "Polish Dance" lends itself to the dance form, but it must be played slowly until the step pattern has been mastered.  The folk dance music called Polka-Mazurka may be used.

A table summarizing the above discussion of simple dance patterns may be found on page 47, Chapter V.

For Dances in which these step-patterns are used, see list on page 180.  In addition see the following clogs and character dances:

| | | |
|---|---|---|
| Rig-a-Jig | Skip, gallop | Clog and Character Dances |
| Sleigh Bells | Skip, gallop | Clog and Character Dances |
| Captain Jinks | Skip, polka, two-step | Clog Dance Book |
| Lindy Lee | Skip | Clogs and Jigs |
| Arkansas Traveler | Two-step | Athletic Dances and Simple Clogs |
| Team Work | Schottische | Clog and Character Dances |
| Hurdy Gurdy | Schottische | Clog and Character Dances |
| Old Dutch | Schottische | Clog and Character Dances |

# PROGRAMS AND FESTIVALS

# CHAPTER XVII

## PLANNING THE PUBLIC PERFORMANCE

The problem of the public performance in dancing is one which deserves much thoughtful consideration, and if well organized, with sufficient time allowed for preparation, it should prove to be a great pleasure to the students and the spectators as well as to the instructor.

It is a deplorable situation when the public performance gets the main emphasis in dance work. It should always, without exception, be secondary to the personal and educational development of the individual. The American public is so accustomed to being entertained by football games, movies, jazz bands, and spectacular dance features that their sense of the artistic is apt to be dulled by the glaring sensational performances which the crowds flock to see and hear. Many of us have never known the joy of participation, but are constantly getting our thrills second-hand.

Especially in the field of dancing, the public, either the community, parents, or student body, is inclined to expect a program as a demonstration of the success of the work. If this program is forced upon the students before they are ready for it, if it cannot come as a natural development of their work, and be so organized as to avoid long tiring hours of practice, it will become a burden and will fail in recreational or educational value.

Ideally, a program should come at the time when the students have reached a point in their development where they are ready to express something through their dancing and to give back to the world some of the pleasure which they have experienced. It should be much the same as the musician who, having passed the stage where his music is practice or self-amusement, has entered the field of the artist, has begun to express his own personality in his music, and has begun to create through expression or composition.

Then and then only is he truly ready to meet the public—to have something worthwhile to give to them.

It should not be interpreted that dance students need be real artists before they can take part in a program. This would mean that only a select few would be allowed to participate, and that many communities would be deprived entirely of the privilege of the public performance. Rather, it is meant that the program must be so planned that something of real worth is offered, and that each participant sincerely and conscientiously perfects his own part so that it may contribute to the finish of the complete production.

The public performance should include, if possible, every girl who desires to participate. Dances may be planned for a large group of individuals of varying abilities. These illustrations are from the "Dance Orchestration" of Rubenstein's Romance in which each group represented a part of a large symphony and in their dance pattern each followed the rhythm of a certain instrument. The advanced students carried the more difficult parts, such as violins, cellos and cornets, while the beginners and intermediates added to the general effect by simple movements in the background. Every girl, no matter how small her part, may feel that she is contributing to the success of the whole.

Fig. 46. A Dance Orchestration

As much as possible the program should be organized and developed by the students, the instructor offering stimulation in the form of suggestions, constructive criticism, and wise guidance. The students should feel that it is their program, and that the individuals in the audience are their guests.

If the public performance is to come as a culmination of the class work in dancing, it should be planned and prepared as much as possible during class time. In this way every individual in the class will be able to participate, either in the dancing, the planning, or in the outside committees.

It has been found very successful, in the writer's experience, to call together a group of the more advanced students, either outside of class, or within the advanced class, for the purpose of discussing the possibilities of a dance program. If the general opinion of the group is that the work has developed to a point where a program would be a worthy undertaking, suggestions of a theme or general plan are made. Often the original suggestion must come from the instructor, but it should be made in such a way that the students feel they are formulating the plans. When a general idea has been agreed upon, a special committee for making more definite plans can be set to work. After about a week, the theme, general plan, and music should be in tentative form. It is then time to present the idea to the other dance groups.

All or part of the program should be planned to include a large group of participants. In the situation referred to here, the program has been given as a part of the class work, practices taking place within the class period and participation being required for completion of the term's work. The classes are assured that they will not be asked to do anything beyond their ability. In this way every girl is made to feel that she is an essential part of the whole, and the girl of marked self-consciousness or lack of ability will usually ask to be given an inconspicuous part, or duties on committees. (Depending upon the type of program, beginning classes may be excluded from this requirement if there is no opportunity of using them in a way which would add to the success of the production, or they may help with the practices and select the best from their group to participate.)

Ordinarily the theme is such that each group may be assigned several problems, and, through original work in class, may prepare their parts. Each group should have a chairman who works with the instructor and costume committee to check attendance of group at rehearsals, to check on costumes, and to act as leaders.

Complete general rehearsals should number about two or three. If each group has mastered its own problem, and the complete plan is clear to each student, this number of rehearsals is sufficient. About ten days before the program a mimeographed list of plans for organization may be given each person, which will help her understand her own part. (See sample, page 209.) At least five days before the production, it is well to require attendance at a complete rehearsal, at which time entrances and exits are explained. This gives the students an opportunity to see what their ultimate objective is, and what dances need more work. It also serves as a stimulus to polish up their parts before the time is too short.

Between this practice and the final dress rehearsal, individual and group practices may be scheduled according to need. Also, if it is an indoor program, the lights should be installed and tried out for color and shadows. (See paragraph on lights, page 218.) Each group should be checked by its chairman to see that all costumes are ready for the dress rehearsal.

On the night before the program there should be a complete dress rehearsal with lights and orchestra (if there is to be one). As much as possible everything should go just as it is expected to go on the final night. Except where absolutely necessary, this should not be used as a practice where details are repeated.

The instructor, with a notebook, pencil, flashlight, and a fellow critic, if desired, should sit in the place of the audience and watch for defects which need to be corrected. These defects may be corrected during or after the rehearsal, according to their nature. The individuals who are to direct activities behind scenes, to manage lights, turn pages for the musician or change victrola records, should all be on duty. The students, while not dancing or dressing, should be allowed to watch the rehearsal, as it is advisable not to have them in the audience on the final night. They should be cautioned against whispering behind the scenes, peeking through curtains or standing in wings, shouting in dressing room, wearing jewelry or watches, or dropping from the dance attitude before lights go out or curtains are drawn.

In order to begin the program with the audience in a receptive mood it is necessary to make the first impression as artistic as possible. This is especially true in the case of creative dancing. To be met at the door by a charming usher in evening frock or light dress, to be taken through a quiet lobby and seated in a room where soft light and introductory music lend a quietness to the atmosphere, will help to set the mood for the evening's performance.

On the night of the performance the instructor should, if possible, be seated in the audience. For the sake of future productions, it is well for her to see how the performance looks from the audience. In case of difficulties behind scenes, the student leaders will rise to the occasion and the strain of the evening will be lightened. Just before the program begins, the instructor should go to the dressing rooms to see that everyone is present and ready; to give a final word of encouragement, and to assure her students of her confidence in their success. Knowing that she is in the audience watching will give them an added incentive.

If costumes are furnished by the school, a definite arrangement should be made so that these are returned in condition to be put away for future use.

Opposite is a page of directions to students which was handed out in mimeographed form to each participant in a recital. Each dancer was also given a sheet showing order of dances with entrance and exit.

### Mimeographed Page of Directions for Students

This is the fifth annual Dance Recital to have been given by the Students of Creative Dancing at Oregon State College.  Each year we have had a pleased and appreciative audience and the interest in dancing has grown each year.  Let us make this year's recital better than the last.  This can easily be accomplished through the whole-hearted co-operation of each participiant.  Let us remember these things:

1. A perfect whole can result only if each part is perfect.
2. One person's tardiness or absence at a rehearsal will inconvenience many.
3. Jewelry and gum are taboo.
4. To keep the audience in a receptive mood means that no dancer must do anything to take the spectator out of the dance attitude.  Brushing one's hair out of eyes, fixing a shoulder strap, dropping from a final position before the lights go out, looking through the curtains or standing in the wings in sight of any audience, whispering or giggling behind scenes, and shouting in dressing room will detract from the finish of the production.  Let's avoid them all by having stubborn wisps of hair pinned down, shoulder straps fastened firmly together, and constant thoughtfulness of your movements.  Be in the wings during the dance just previous to the dance in which you are to participate.  Leave the wings promptly when through.

Everyone must be present at Dress Rehearsal Tuesday night dressed ready to dance at 7:15.  Plan to stay until 9:30.  Be sure you have a sheet telling order of dances with entrances and exits.  Know when you appear and how you get on and off.  All costumes must be completed by that time.  Report to the chairman of your group so that she will know you are present and correctly dressed.

I wish that each of you would plan to see all other dances.  The best time will be at dress rehearsal on Tuesday, March 3.  We will try to arrange seats for you at south end of room, near entrance to dressing-room, if you wish to watch the program Wednesday night after your dance is over.  Please do not go up to the balcony.  Opening doors from stairway allows noise and light to disturb audience.  And finally, remember this:

### The Way To Do Things *

*"If there is that in your nature which demands the best and will take nothing less, and you do not demoralize this standard by the habit of deterioration in everything you do, you will achieve distinction in some line if you have the persistence and determination to follow your ideal.*

*But if you are satisfied with the cheap and shoddy, the botched and slovenly, if you are not particular about quality in your work, or in your environment, or in your personal habits, then you must expect to take second place, to fall back into the rear of the procession.*

*People who have accomplished work worth while have had a high sense of the way to do things.  They have not been content with mediocrity.  They have not confined themselves to the beaten track: they have never been satisfied to do things just as others do them, but always a little better.  They always pushed things that came into their hands a little higher up, a little farther on.  It is this little higher up, this little farther on, that counts in the quality of life's work.  It is the constant effort to be first class in everything one attempts that conquers the heights of excellence."*

Please save us much trouble by keeping your costume until the first meeting of your class next week.  At that time bring it, neatly folded, underbody laundered, and check in to chairman of your group.  Will you also bring in writing your comments and criticisms of the dance program, answering such questions as: Do you think an annual recital is worth while?  What comments did your friends make?  What do you suggest for improvement?

Remember, I am depending on you to do your part with the best of your ability.

Signed ————————————————————

* Charles L. Wagner, Wagner Productions, N. Y. C.  Used with permission of author.

Themes for programs and festivals are varied and may be very detailed as in "Life of Dance," * or only a thread of thought for the purpose of connecting the dances. It is not necessary to have a theme, for a program of diversified numbers is very desirable. However, with a group of limited training, or in a community which has not been educated thoroughly in the trends of modern creative dance, a theme will prove most satisfying.

There are a number of excellent books and pamphlets suggesting themes and music for festivals.† One may go to these for ideas or they may be built about some well known folk-tale or may be historical in character.

The "Life of Dance" is an excellent Dance Drama which was planned by the dance students at the University of Wisconsin under the direction of Margaret H'Doubler. The music was written by one of the students in the group.

When this Dance Drama was presented at Oregon State College all classes participated. Each class was assigned a portion, and worked out, in class and through committees, the dances which they used interpreting their part of the theme.

The beginning class worked on Savage Rhythm and a picked group presented that. The intermediate classes were assigned the Pastoral, Bourgeoisie, Semi-barbaric, Machine Age and Jazz. The taller girls in the advanced class were the Potentialities, the smaller ones did the Ritual and the Carnival, while individuals were picked according to build, ability and personality to do Cosmos, Dance, Church, Angeli, Spirit of Court, Spirit of Ballet.

All practices took place in class time, except solo work, and the whole was put together in two rehearsals.

The "Life of Dance" took about twenty-five minutes. The second half of the program was made up of original dances by advanced and intermediate students. These were assigned as definite problems, or chosen from the original dances presented in class.

In the case of an out-of-door dance festival it is still more important to use many students. A natural setting is so massive ordinarily that small groups are not as effective as large ones. Many lovely effects may be gained through the dancing of a large group of girls even though the dances are simple. Beginners in dancing or folk dancing can easily be used here if each is assigned a problem which is within her ability. As was said before, a theme which will tie the dances together into one unit will lend to the effect and will make the dances more thoroughly appreciated by the audience.

For a large mixed audience a theme based upon a well-known story or fairy tale will hold a strong appeal for the children as well as the adults. Music may be arranged or if a competent musician is available it may be composed. Rip Van Winkle and Sleeping Beauty have both been used with success in out-of-door fes-

* See page 135.　　　　　　　　　　　　　　　† See pages 177 and 213.

The angry god-mother casts her curse as the infant princess is carried from the Christening

The princess celebrates her eighteenth birthday

The princess examines the spinning wheel

Following the peasants and their greetings, the witch brings to the princess a spinning wheeel

FIG. 47. SLEEPING BEAUTY

tivals.　Each was planned to include over one hundred girls.　Sleeping Beauty *
adapts well to both Creative and Folk Dancing while Rip Van Winkle was
planned to include Tap Dancing and Tumbling as well.　The plans for Rip Van
Winkle were made and the festival organized by students.　Dame Van Winkle,
Rip, and the Dog were the only characters chosen.　Youngsters from the Satur-
day classes were the village children who loved Rip and his dog.　The Folk Dancing classes were the villagers, with the group of "old men" from the class in Tap
dancing.　The dwarfs in the mountains were members of tumbling and tap dancing
classes.

For tap dancing a low stage (9 feet by 15 feet) made of boards laid across
and nailed to several 4 x 4's, was located at the very back of the outdoor setting.
The stage was pushed back under the trees and the overhanging branches tied up
by ropes.　This left the fore part of the grassy space for folk dancing and tumbling.

A general outline of "Rip Van Winkle" follows:

### Rip Van Winkle
#### (Story from Washington Irving)

Scene I

Market day in a small village (an English Province) at the foot of the
Kaatskill Mountains.　Rip enters with dog and children; children dance
"Chimes of Dunkirk."

Dog dances.　(Original clog on "all fours" to "Where Oh Where has
My Little Dog Gone.")

Dame Van Winkle enters and scolds Rip.　Children exit in fear.

Dame Van Winkle and Rip dance (Dutch Couple—Frost).　As villagers
enter, Dame Van Winkle, still scolding, exits with Rip, holding him by
ear.

Villagers enter with Norwegian Mountain March.　Repeat.　Form groups
of six's and dance—"Gathering Peascods."　In same groups, dance
"Reap the Flax"—Exit in long line.

Scene II

Same day in the Kaatskill Mountains.

Eight tap dancers dressed as dwarfs enter and play with tenpins and
ball (Bowling). Music used, "Dance of the Sprites," from Wisconsin
Blue Print.

Rip enters with dwarf carrying large keg; tenpinners and Rip drink.

Tumblers dressed as dwarfs enter and do "Seven Jumps."　Tumblers en-

---

* See Fig. 47, page 211.　A description of the dances is contained in "Dance Studies Analyzed,"
see page 133.　The music was composed by Eunice Steel, see "Music for Dance Dramas," page 135.

tertain Rip with stunts and pyramids; then join hands and do "Rig-a-jig-jig" (Frost)—Rip exits with them at end of dance.

The other dwarfs find Rip's gun—one shoulders it, the other seven fall in line and dance Military Tap. (See Chapter XIII.)—Exit.

SCENE III

Twenty years later in the same village—now an American settlement.

Rip enters from east side; children from west. Children stare at Rip and make fun of his long beard. A few villagers stroll through and stare at Rip.

Folk dancers enter in fours with barn dance (Dancing on the Green—Elsom and Trilling).

Folk dancers sit on either side of stage.

Old men with long beards enter during folk dance; they greet Rip as an old crony. Rip and old men do tap dance—Simple buck and wing (see Chapter XIII) done to "There was an Old Man."

The villagers group in eights and dance—"Girl I Left Behind Me" (see page 182), "Quadrille with Grapevine Twist" (Dances of our Pioneers —Ryan), "Pop Goes the Weasel" (see page 185).

Maypole dancers enter and circle pole as other villagers sit down in groups at sides and watch maypole dancers wind and unwind with (1) Grand Right and Left, (2) Spider Web, (3) Basket Weave, in each color. As maypole dancers finish and tie ribbon to pole the other villagers form large circle about maypole and skip right. Maypole dancers form inside circle and skip left. All exit in long spiral line.

Other suggestions for Programs, Pageants, and Festivals may be found in the following books: *

*Creative Dancing*                                          *Publisher*

1. The Dance and Its Place in Education, H'Doubler. Harcourt Brace and Co.
2. Dance Studies Analyzed, Thompson and Jewell. Address Oregon State College, Corvallis, Ore., Dept. of Physical Education.

*Pageants and Festivals*

1. Pageants with a Purpose Series—Sections of Physical ⎫
                                    Education Handbook  |
2. The Conflict                —Colby                 |
3. Mother Goose May Day        —Turner and Wills      |
4. The Festival Book           —Lincoln               ⎬ A. S. Barnes and Co.
5. The Technique of Pageantry  —Taft                  |
6. Folk Festivals for Schools and—Shambaugh           |
   Playgrounds                                        ⎭

* See also pages 133-135, and 177-179.

# CHAPTER XVIII

## ORGANIZATION OF STUDENT COMMITTEES

Some weeks before a program is to be prepared, committees and chairmen with the following duties may be chosen:

1. General student dance manager.—To call committee meetings, to check on work of committees, to act as assistant to director.

2. General business manager.—To plan budget, advise committees on possible expenses, to handle the money, to pay bills, and to write report of expense of production, including stage setting, lights, costumes, music, tickets, programs, etc.

3. Chairman and committees on:

   a. Program.—To select theme of program and adapt it to dance needs.

   b. Music.—To select appropriate music for dances, to see that music and orchestrations are ready, to schedule practices of orchestra.

   c. Rehearsals.—To plan rehearsals, post dates of rehearsals, and check on attendance, through group chairmen.

   d. Costumes.—To plan costumes, buy material and make costumes; to check out costumes, keeping list of people who have them, and to check in costumes and put them away for future use.

   e. Publicity.—To write articles for school and town paper and neighboring papers and to distribute posters. (All newspaper articles should be checked by instructor before they are published.)

   f. Posters.—Art students to design and make posters for advertising. (A wood block is a convenient way to make large number of posters. Lettering must be clear.)

   g. Program Cover.—Art student to design program cover. (A wood block is here usable. If pen and ink drawing is used, time must be allowed for sending away to have cut made. This usually takes 5 to 8 days.) Contest may be held in connection with choice of program cover.

   h. Programs.—Literary student to write material and explanations on program. To see that programs get to press, are proof read, and ready for performance.

   i. Tickets.—To have tickets printed, to distribute for sale and to sell at the door and to supervise checking in money to business manager.

   j. Invitations.—To make out list of persons whom instructor and students desire to invite as guests, and to write and mail these invitations. (Such a list might include school authorities, members of physical education department, head of music department, persons who have contributed as in lighting, etc., and persons out of the city who might be interested, as state supervisor of physical education, physical education instructors in neighboring schools, etc.)  A person who prints should assist.

   k. Stage setting and lights.—To arrange stage.  If indoors this includes curtains, lights, piano or victrola, etc.  If out-of-doors, it may mean superintending building of stage, erecting dressing rooms, moving piano, getting small trees to fill in background and sides.  This committee should include several persons who will be stationed on duty behind scenes during the program.  They will be assigned such duties as: (1) standing at breaks in curtain to close opening after dancer has passed through, (2) acting as messenger to dressing room to announce each dance in time for participants to go to next entrance, (3) giving signals to those operating the lights and to the accompanist when each group of dancers is ready.  The use of a soft gong as a signal will give a pleasant warning to the participants and will also act as a quieting influence upon the audience.

   l. Seating.—To plan a seating chart, to supervise arrangement of seats, to select and instruct ushers.

The budget depends entirely upon the type of performance, whether it is desired to merely clear expenses or to make money for equipment or some organization.  In either case it should be carefully planned so that expenses will not exceed available funds.  There are certain expenses which are definite.  These should be ascertained before costumes are bought.

1. Cost of lights—Flood lights may have to be rented and installed.  In many schools one is required to hire a school electrician to install these.
2. Rent—For use of building.
3. Janitorial service—Install seats, cleaning, etc.
4. Programs—Printing and paper.  Choice of paper should be made according to budget.  When budget is small, clever programs may be inexpensively made by mimeograph.
5. Tickets—Cost of printing.
6. Cards and stamps—Invitations.
7. Music—Cost of sheet music, orchestrations, and musicians.
8. Materials for stage setting—Renting curtains, moving piano, building stage or dressing rooms, etc.
9. Costumes—Costumes kept in good condition from year to year may be reused, saving much expense.

Music may be available, but usually some of it has to be purchased.  Per-

# Costumes for Creative Dancing

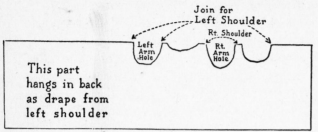

Join for
Left Shoulder

Rt. Shoulder

Left Arm Hole

Rt. Arm Hole

This part hangs in back as drape from left shoulder

Length of Material

**I - Short Costume with back drape**

Length of Material

NECK

Seam

Piecing

Fold

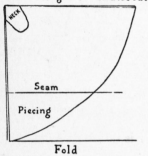

**II - Long Circular Costume**

Fold Length of Material

Fitted by Inverted Tucks

May also be worn as short slip under thin Costume

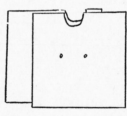

**III - Short Fitted Tunic**

Fold

NECK

Length of Material

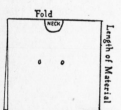

**IV - Short Costume with even drape on each side**

**V - Short Costume with uneven drape on each side**

haps it may be borrowed. If an orchestra is to accompany dancing, orchestrations of music will have to be bought, borrowed, or written by music student. If bought it should be ordered at least three weeks in advance as often it has to be ordered from New York. If a victrola is to be used, records may have to be purchased. (It has been found satisfactory in indoor programs, and in out-of-door if sounding board is erected, to use a victrola which contains amplifying tubes, as the Orthophonic.) Use of a victrola for a few numbers is an aid to rehearsals as well as in allowing rest periods for the orchestra or accompanist during the program.

## VI - Long Sleeved Costume with Circular Skirt

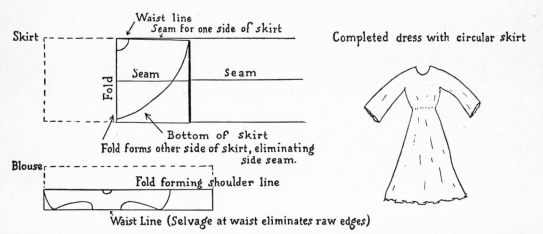

This costume has been found very effective for group work when made of unbleached cheesecloth which may be purchased by the bolt at 2½¢ a yard. The material should be dyed before cutting and the material to be used for skirts may be seamed in long lengths before skirts are cut. Construction after cutting consists only in seaming one side of skirt, and the under arm and waist seams. The wrist, neck and skirt bottom are left unhemmed. A small hole should be cut for neck and the material stretched over the head. Sleeves and skirt must be cut for length while being worn.

Costumes should be kept simple and inexpensive. For creative dancing, tunics * may be used, either long or short, made of soft material which drapes easily. The colors may be planned according to the mood of the dance. Materials which have been found usable are:

Rayon—39¢ a yard †—For short tunics or underbodies. Needs no slip. Has good sheen.

Celanese—59¢ a yard—Needs slip as very thin. Needs to be hemmed or hemstitched at neck and arms.

Georgette—$1.98 a yard—Needs slip usually. Needs to be hemmed or hemstitched at neck and arms.

Crepe de chine—$1.98 a yard—Does not need slip.

Baronette Satin—45¢-80¢ a yard—For short tunics, long circular costumes

* See diagram of dance costumes, page 216.
† The price mentioned here may vary slightly in various communities.

or slips.  Must be hemmed or hemstitched.  Gives beautiful effect under lights.

Cotton voile—50¢ a yard—Clings too much.

Cheese cloth—2½¢ to 11¢ a yard—For large groups excellent effects may be obtained.  The 2½¢ cheese cloth is an unbleached gauze.  If dyed and made to fit well is very effective at a distance.

Folk Dance costumes * may be made of almost any grade of material, depending upon the number of times they are to be used, as well as the budget.  Possible materials are:

Cheese cloth—2½¢-11¢—Especially good for blouses or full sleeves.

Paper cambric—13¢—Used for men's suits or women's skirts and jackets.

Satine—25¢-39¢—Used for men's suits or women's skirts and jackets.

Baronette Satin—45¢-80¢—Used for men's suits or women's skirts and jackets.

Rayon—39¢—Used for men's suits or women's skirts and jackets.

Cotton Challis—19¢—Cretonne—10¢ and up—Can find attractive figured materials for women's dresses.

Dimity—15¢—Women's dresses.

The lighting in an out-of-door program is comparatively simple, the important point being to have the dancer out of the shadows, and the sun out of the audience's eyes.  In an indoor program lights are extremely important and usually take careful planning to eliminate shadows, to get the right colors, and to cut off parts of room from view.

Often, as is our case, the winter program is given in the gymnasium.  If the building contains a dance studio, it is invariably too small to accommodate an audience, while the stage in a theatre or auditorium is frequently too small for dancing.  Long cotton flannel, or dyed unbleached muslin (dark grey or black is best), may be used as a back drape and at the front of wings.  Cotton flannel—unless it has been fireproofed—catches the light and gives a soft effect.

To eliminate shadows on floor and bodies, lights must be planned to compensate for each other.  That is, the voltage used from above must equal that used from the front and sides.  This may be determined by experimentation.  The type of gelatine paper used over the lights is also important, the thinner sheets being more advisable, as heavy gelatine paper keeps out too much light and results in a dull effect.

Thin, blue, gelatine paper has been found to be excellent for bringing out a good color on the skin.  It may be used on all side and ceiling lights while a flooded spot from the front (this should come from above), with operator to change color of gelatine slides, may be used to get a variety of color effects on costumes.  With use of flooded spot the following colors have been found most usable:

1. Straw—on scenes where variety of colors are used.  This gives the natural color but softens it.

* For design see Folk Dance Costume Book, and other references, pages 177-179.

2. Amber—used much as straw but gives yellow tinge.

3. Blue—takes color out of light shades resulting in white effect.  Good with black and white combinations.

4. Lavender—excellent on red.  Gives very sparkling, stimulating effect.

Usually unless a particular effect is desired we avoid using green or red lights on costumes and dancers.

1. Green—gives ugly tinge to skin.  It may be used with red grease paint to give effect of dark skin as in negro clogs, or to get a weird greenish effect on dances such as "Moods of the River," "Whirlwind."

2. Red—is not good on skin and changes blues and greens to browns or ugly dull shades.

Below is a chart showing a possible plan for the arrangement and lighting of gymnasium for the dance program.  This plan has been used successfully in writer's experience.

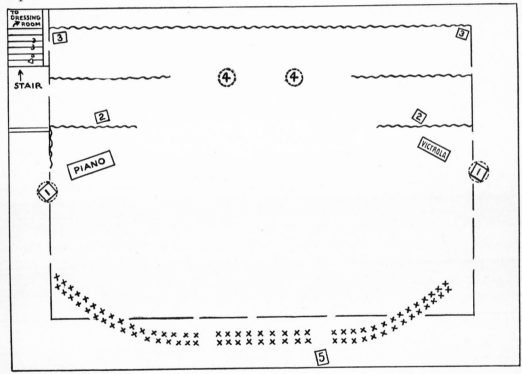

| ～～～～ Curtain | ① | Blue flood light from edge of balcony. |
| ——  —— Edge of Balcony | ② | Blue light from 10-foot ladder. |
| ✕✕✕✕✕✕✕ Chairs for audience on main floor ✕✕✕✕✕✕✕  (also seated in the balcony). | ③ | Light thrown to give color to curtain. |
| ▭▭ Small curtain or  dark blanket. | ④ | Blue light from ceiling. |
|  | ⑤ | Flooded Spot light from back of balcony. |

Until a satisfactory scheme of lighting has been developed a certain amount of experimentation will be necessary. If possible the stage setting should be arranged several days in advance and one evening devoted to lights. At that time, it should not be necessary for the dancers to be present, as members of the committee on stage setting and lights may wear or carry costumes of the colors to be used and in this way decisions as to proper lighting may be made. These decisions can be checked later at the dress rehearsal.

If the dance program is to be an educational experience, as many individuals as possible should be used in its organization, and each one's duties should be carefully analyzed to avoid any overlapping. In this way each one may know surely, and will assume more completely, her own responsibility; and by working many, rather than overworking a few, it will be possible to produce a program which will be not a burden and a source of drudgery, but in the true spirit of the dance, a real recreational and creative experience.

# INDEX

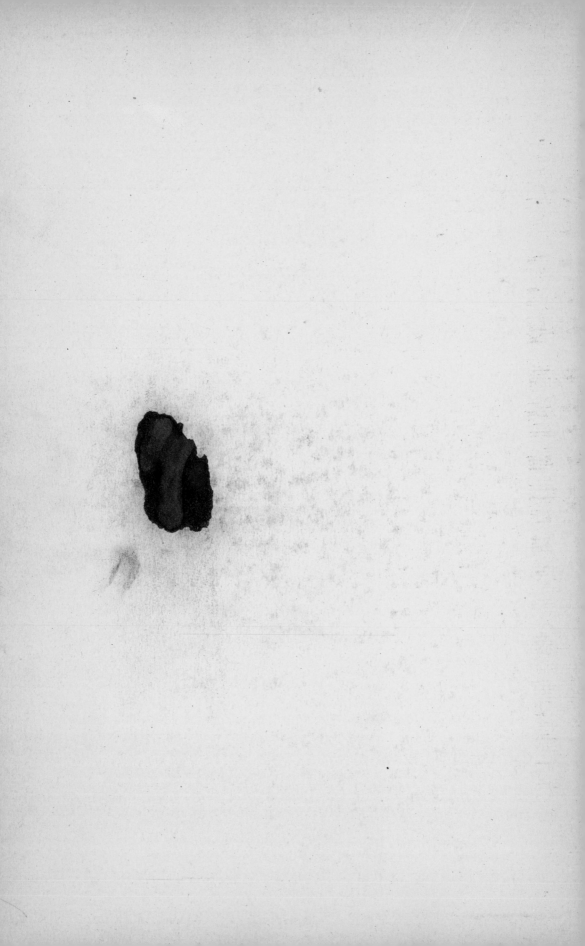